"If there is a foremost fundamental source that should integrate and reconcile the diverse models of reading and research, it is arguably sacred Scripture. Mark Reasoner has managed to weave together the distinctive paradigms of inspiration and interpretation in the Protestant, Catholic, and Orthodox traditions. This book will undoubtedly enrich critical scholarship, seminary instruction, and spiritual formation in ways that shed hardened stereotypes of the past and suggest fresh perspectives for analysis and meditation in the future."

— JOHN CHRYSSAVGIS
theological advisor to Ecumenical Patriarch Bartholomew

"This book applies the time-honored tradition of 'models' to diverse ways Christians approach the Bible. Using insights from Catholic, Protestant, and Orthodox perspectives, as well as the church fathers and the history of interpretation, Reasoner presents a veritable feast of judicious insights, exposing the strengths and limitations of each model. I highly recommend this resource to scholars, pastors, seminarians, and students alike. As with the Scriptures themselves, all can be nourished at this table!"

— RONALD D. WITHERUP, PSS
superior general of the Society of the Priests of Saint Sulpice

"In *Five Models of Scripture* Mark Reasoner provides readers with an important and timely book on scriptural interpretation by offering five models for reading and interpreting the Bible. Alongside a wealth of information about scriptural interpretation—its complex history, its nuances, its contemporary implications and significance—he offers practical advice to those in ministry and those studying Scripture in an academic environment. Yet this book is more than a reservoir of information. It is also an invitation to see Scripture as an abundant communal feast that sustains and delights."

— LISA M. BOWENS
Princeton Theological Seminary

"Mark Reasoner's *Five Models of Scripture* is the mature reflection of a man educated in America's evangelical Protestant commitment to Scripture who converted to a Roman Catholic hermeneutic in which the church's tradition guides the interpretation of Scripture. Mark's wonderful book confirms a long-held conviction of mine: had Catholicism always been this committed to Scripture there would never have been a Reformation. Every chapter in this book flows from years of personal Bible reading and the insights gained from classroom teaching."

— SCOT McKNIGHT
Northern Seminary

"This is an ecumenically sensitive presentation of five different models for reading the Bible. Reasoner's familiarity with a wide range of approaches within the Christian tradition is matched by his deeply respectful approach to positions other than his own. He had my full attention from the first to the last page. This is a work that engages the Christian Bible at the level at which it was written: for instruction regarding how to be a disciple of Jesus Christ."

— GARY A. ANDERSON
University of Notre Dame

FIVE MODELS
of SCRIPTURE

Mark Reasoner

WILLIAM B. EERDMANS PUBLISHING COMPANY
GRAND RAPIDS, MICHIGAN

Wm. B. Eerdmans Publishing Co.
4035 Park East Court SE, Grand Rapids, Michigan 49546
www.eerdmans.com

27 26 25 24 23 22 21   1 2 3 4 5 6 7

ISBN 978-0-8028-7682-9

Library of Congress Cataloging-in-Publication Data

Names: Reasoner, Mark, author.
Title: Five models of scripture / Mark Reasoner.
Description: Grand Rapids, Michigan : William B. Eerdmans Publishing Company, [2021] | Includes bibliographical references and index. | Summary: "A succinct guide to different models for engaging with Scripture, illustrated by examples from the history of interpretation"—Provided by publisher.
Identifiers: LCCN 2021005481 | ISBN 9780802876829 (paperback)
Subjects: LCSH: Bible—Hermeneutics. | Bible—Criticism, interpretation, etc.
Classification: LCC BS476 .R4254 2021 | DDC 220.6—dc23
LC record available at https://lccn.loc.gov/2021005481

CONTENTS

CONTENTS

PART FOUR: SCRIPTURE IN REAL LIFE

ACKNOWLEDGMENTS

As reading Scripture is a communal activity, so this book has drawn nourishment from many others. First, overflowing thanks go to my parents, Rollin and Esther Reasoner, who instilled in me a deep attachment to Scripture. Then I wish to thank teachers at all levels of my schooling who encouraged me to engage and learn from Scripture. And I thank my colleagues and students at the two schools at which I have taught: Bethel University (St. Paul, MN) and Marian University (Indianapolis, IN).

Joe Anderson helped me bring this manuscript to completion, and I thank him for his counsel. At Marian University, the library staff under the able direction of Jessica Trinoskey has been helpful. Librarians Caitlin Balgeman, Lynné Colbert, and Edward Mandity helped me gain access to many materials beyond the walls of the school library, and I am very thankful for all they did to that end.

I express sincere thanks to the following people who read and commented on one or more chapters of this book in draft form: Charles Bobertz, Timothy Brookins, John Chryssavgis, Matthew Levering, John T. Noble, Mary O'Brien, James Prothro, Charles Puskas, William Rettig, and Brooks Schramm. Their comments have been helpful, yet of course I alone am responsible for the shortcomings of the book before you. Project editor Jennifer Hoffman, copyeditor Ryan Davis, and proofreader Tim Baker contributed significantly to the clarity and organization of this volume. For others whom I have consulted on specific matters in this book, or whom in my fallibility I have neglected to list, I am equally thankful. Finally, I express joyful thanks to my wife and our five children for all the ways they bring grace to life.

ABBREVIATIONS

AB	Anchor Bible
Barn.	Barnabas
BT	*Black Theology: An International Journal*
CCC	*Catechism of the Catholic Church* (New York: Doubleday, 1994).
CR	Corpus Reformatorum
CurTM	*Currents in Theology and Mission*
D	Deuteronomistic source (of the Pentateuch)
E	Elohist source (of the Pentateuch)
EB	The Earth Bible
Ep.	*Epistle*
ET	English translation
FC	Fathers of the Church
Ign. *Eph.*	Ignatius, *To the Ephesians*
Inst.	Calvin, *Institutes of the Christian Religion*
J	Yahwist source (of the Pentateuch)
JTS	*Journal of Theological Studies*
LCC	Library of Christian Classics
LW	*Luther's Works* (series of English translations, Concordia and Fortress)
LXX	Septuagint
MT	Masoretic Text
NABRE	New American Bible, Revised Edition
NPNF[2]	*Nicene and Post-Nicene Fathers*, Series 2
OSHTh	Oxford Studies in Historical Theology
P	Priestly source (of the Pentateuch)
PG	Patrologia Graeca
PL	Patrologia Latina
ST	Thomas Aquinas, *Summa Theologiae*
WA	*Weimar Ausgabe* (complete edition of Luther's works)
WA TR	*Weimar Ausgabe Tischreden* (complete edition of Luther's "table talk")
WSA	The Works of Saint Augustine: A Translation for the 21st Century

INTRODUCTION

*During my university and seminary years, I concentrated on philosophy
and philosophical theology, and my interest in the Bible remained compar-
atively minimal. Moreover, the manner in which the Bible was presented
to me during the years of my intellectual formation did little to pique my
curiosity about the scriptural world.*

—ROBERT BARRON[1]

It is not uncommon to hear seminarians say—and I have heard it from both
Protestant and Catholic sides—that one's love for Scripture fades while studying it in seminary. As a seminarian once remarked to me, "Scripture courses
should be everyone's favorite, but they're not." Though he was still in the middle of his seminary training, he seemed already aware that in his education a
break had occurred in what potentially could have been a fruitful engagement
with Scripture. His comment matches Robert Barron's autobiographical comment in the epigraph above.

I offer this book as a guide to those preparing as best they know for Christian ministry—whether Orthodox, Catholic, or Protestant—with the goal to
clarify the models of Scripture that they encounter in their seminary formation
and in their ministries. The hope beyond this goal is that those who read this
book will grow in their appreciation of the variety of models of Scripture and
grow toward Christian unity as they understand how other Christians read
and proclaim Scripture in ways different from their own.

But before the overview for the book continues, perhaps you need to know
something about me. I benefited from a wonderful education at an evangelical
Protestant seminary, earning the standard pastoral degree (MDiv) and an MA
in New Testament there. Decades later, after studying the New Testament in
graduate school, teaching at an evangelical Protestant university, and then
being received into the Roman Catholic Church, I now teach Scripture to undergraduates in a Roman Catholic university. Most of my students—Catholics,

1. Robert Barron, "Bridging a False Divide."

Protestants, and others who are not Christians—take my classes simply to fulfill general education requirements, but I do have some college seminarians in my classes, and over the years I have kept in contact with friends and former students in Orthodox, Catholic, and Protestant seminaries. I often think about why Scripture is boring for some people, and I like to try different ways to make it come alive for students.

Outline of This Book

As this book's title indicates, it is primarily about models of Scripture. These are ways that Scripture is pictured. Each model represents what the essence of Scripture is envisioned to be by a particular approach to it.

Part One: How God Speaks in Scripture

Before we can get to the models, we have to consider the contours of what we mean by Scripture. The first part of this book, "How God Speaks in Scripture," therefore discusses in the first chapter why Christians have different books in their Old Testaments and how this affects the character of their Scriptures. The next chapter covers the topic of inspiration and explores the major differences in how Christians view the inspiration of Scripture.

Part Two: The Five Models of Scripture

The next part of the book presents the five models of Scripture that characterize how Christians read their Bibles. I am not the first to attempt this. John Goldingay's two books *Models for Scripture* and *Models for Interpretation of Scripture* offer witnessing tradition, authoritative canon, inspired word, and experienced revelation as primary ways to view Scripture. The latter book offers exegetical insight specific to each of his models introduced in the prior volume. I think there is room for another set of models that are more directly tied to how students, pastors, and their parishioners experience Scripture, especially one that takes account of all branches in the Christian family.

The first model we will discuss is the model of viewing the Scriptures as documents. In this model, the books of the Bible are often read as primarily written for other peoples in other cultures. A variety of approaches, such as historical criticism, redaction criticism, form criticism, and feminist criticism, would make ready use of the documents model of Scripture. The documents model is perhaps the model most conducive to the objectification and externalization of the Scriptures. In the twentieth century, much of William F. Albright's work was oriented toward this view of Scripture. Albright's archaeological work was done primarily to lend credence or credibility to the Old Testament as a set of documents from the past. F. F. Bruce's book *The New Testament Documents: Are They Reliable?* is an example of this model. In this model, attention quickly turns to the historical accuracy of the biblical texts. Today this model is behind some introductions to various parts of the Bible, such as Bart Ehrman's best-selling *The New Testament: A Historical Introduction to the Early Christian Writing.* Ehrman's agenda is different from Bruce's, but they both approach Scripture as a set of documents to be analyzed for historicity. When the approach of historical criticism is used on the text of Scripture, this model is often driving the approach.

The second model we will discuss is that of stories. This model views the essence of Scripture as narratives. The narratives are located sometimes at the surface of the text, as for example the narrative of the Israelites' exodus from Egypt in Exodus 12–14. At other times, the narrative might be identified below the surface of the text. Richard Hays's *The Faith of Jesus Christ: The Narrative Substructure of Galatians 3:1–4:11* is an example of this narrative model.

The third model we will discuss is the model of prayers. "Prayers" is the Hebrew name of the book of Psalms and serves as a useful designation of all the ways in which Scripture, even in those genres that are not explicitly prayers, functions as the text of liturgy and thesaurus for communion with God.

The fourth model we will discuss is that of laws. This model reads the Scriptures as a guidebook. This interpretive move can be illustrated by how in some discourse the term "Torah," defined in its limited sense as the books of Moses that contain a significant amount of law, can be used to describe all of the Tanak as Torah. This is different from the tendency to read all of Scripture through a metanarrative of law versus gospel, a metanarrative to be considered in the third part of the book. The book titled *The Year of Living Biblically* primarily views the Bible as a set of laws, though it is written by a secular Jew. This model's exponents include Christians from all sorts of communities.

The fifth model we will discuss is that of oracles. This model uses the term "oracles" as it is used in the prophetic books of the Bible. The term can be used either for prophecy that represents God's word for a specific situation or for prophecy in its more common connotation, as a divine prediction of the future.

Within this second part, I will be emphasizing the thesis of this book: the church benefits from reading Scripture with a plurality of models. These different models call readers and proclaimers to use more than one approach to Scripture.

Part Three: Developments in Scripture Reading

In "Developments in Scripture Reading" I describe the literal and spiritual senses that Christians have found in the text of Scripture in the past two millennia. Then I explain the reason and purpose behind the way that some Christians regard the canon as their exclusive authority—the *sola Scriptura* principle. The last chapter in this section deals with the metanarratives that Christians use to make sense of the sixty-plus books that make up our Scriptures. Recognizing these metanarratives helps us understand why other Christians read the Bible differently than we do.

Part Four: Scripture in Real Life

The fourth and final part of the book, "Scripture in Real Life," contains two chapters that deal with how we encounter the Bible in daily life. The first chapter deals with how the Bible is employed in worship settings of Protestant, Catholic, and Orthodox believers. In the second chapter of this section and last chapter of the book, I address the challenge of staying in a positive relationship with Scripture while studying it in school or using it regularly in ministry.

CHURCH AND SCRIPTURE

When Desiderius Erasmus and Martin Luther argued the question of the bound or free will in 1524–1525, their debate initially focused on what Scripture taught regarding the question. That phase of the debate segued into a clear disagreement on the nature of the church. Erasmus wrote that there are plenty of ambiguous matters in Scripture; about these it is fine to be skeptical or uncertain. But what is necessary for the Christian life is clear. The ambiguous matters of Scripture should not be contested, since they are not necessary for salvation, but it is best to believe what the church teaches about such matters.

Luther answered that God's word is clear, and believers should be certain of what it says. If there are ambiguous matters, these are only due to questions of language that can be solved through study. Those who claim they cannot understand something in Scripture or are uncertain about it are probably hampered by their own spiritual blindness. God provides the Holy Spirit to individual believers, argued Luther, and the Spirit will clarify Scripture's meaning for them.² At the place where Erasmus appealed to the church, Luther appealed to the Spirit's illumination of the reader.

Fourteen years later, Bishop Sadoleto wrote to the leaders of Geneva, challenging them to return to the Catholic Church because this church was the only guarantor of the gospel. Calvin replied that the true church was composed of those who followed the Holy Spirit's leading to subject their wills to Scripture. So once again a debate related to Scripture turned on a definition of the church. Each side sought a principle inherent in its own position that would counter the other. For the Catholic side, its canonization of Scripture or its authoritative teaching on it was the reason that Christendom should follow Catholic teaching on Scripture. For the Protestant side, it was Scripture itself or the Spirit's witness through Scripture that functioned to counter Sadoleto's call to return to the Catholic fold.³

Thus began Western civilization's malaise over reading texts. This malaise brought skepticism into the mainstream of Western thought and birthed the hermeneutical impasse of Christianity. Christians could no longer agree on what Scripture means. The Spirit is supposed to lead believers into truth, and this includes guiding them into Scripture's true meaning. Catholics would continue to say that the Spirit leads the Catholic Church as a whole, while Protestants said that the Spirit leads individual believers. Anglican author Ephraim Radner argues that since Christians cannot agree on what Scripture means or on how the Holy Spirit illumines us in regard to Scripture's truth, one can say that the Spirit has left the church because of our disunity. Radner finds this prefigured in the Old Testament as well, when the Spirit departed from a divided Israelite nation, a figurative reading that was already invoked in earlier centuries.⁴

Though I focus on Scripture in the following chapters, there are places where the ecclesiastical question—the question of the identification of the church—inevitably arises. As Nikos Nissiotis notes near the beginning of an

2. This survey of the exchange between Erasmus and Luther is indebted to the summary provided by Radner, "Absence of the Comforter," 358–59.

3. Radner, "Absence of the Comforter," 360–61.

4. Radner, "Absence of the Comforter," 357–79, citing Congar, "Schism of Israel," 160, 182–83, who describes how John of Santa Maria, Joachim of Fiore, Gregory IX, Bonaventure, Humbert of Romans, and Nicholas of Clemanges treated the division of East from West in 1054 with the division of Israel under Jeroboam I. On the Protestant schism of the sixteenth century, Radner notes how the same figurative reading was applied by Robert Bellarmine, *De gemitu columbae* II, 4, and Jean Hamon, *Commentaire sur les Lamentations de Jérémie* (Paris: Chez Le Clere, 1790), 3.

article on the interpretation of Scripture, "The big question is in how far and in what way our present situation and our vision of the future of our Church depend absolutely or relatively on the past of the Church and in how far we are tied to this past when we try to 'renew' the life of the Church."[5]

I do my best to respect readers' diverse ecclesiastical affiliations. It would have been easier to write this book simply for Catholic seminarians. But Scripture is too sumptuous a feast to limit a book like this to one branch of the family. Another Catholic has published a book with contributions by Catholic and Protestant authors, so there is precedent for my attempt in this volume.[6] In addition, since people's interest in Scripture and Scripture literacy is waning so dramatically in Western civilization, we need to learn from each other and work together to let Scripture speak into our lives.

Yes, I actually regard the Catholic hermeneutic, in which the Catholic Church's teaching office provides the boundaries and referees on the field of exegesis, as preferable to the hermeneutic popularized by the Anabaptists during the Reformation, in which the individual believer marks the boundaries and functions as both player and referee. I also regard the Catholic hermeneutic with its millennia of tradition and conversations across time and cultures as preferable to approaches that have selected a single individual or limited body of believers as the arbiters of exegesis. And so there will be places where I point out the ecclesiastical stakes in a given approach to Scripture. It is better to name the elephant in the room than to proceed as if the church question does not matter in exegesis.

The pictures of Scripture that the church fathers give us of a mansion with many rooms or a sumptuous feast must always be kept in mind.[7] The value of these pictures is their depiction of Scripture as an accessible and ever-surprising resource. Too often I encounter people who think that with one university-level class in Old Testament and another in New Testament, they have finished with Scripture. Actually Scripture is a vast landscape with plenty of terrain still to explore. There is over a lifetime of Scripture reading awaiting each one of us.

Beneath the cognitive skill of understanding how people read Scripture and the relational skill of conversing about Scripture with those who read it

---

5. Nissiotis, "Unity of Scripture and Tradition," 183.

6. Ratzinger, *Schriftauslegung im Widerstreit*.

7. For the metaphor of Scripture as a mansion with many rooms, see Origen, *Philocalia* 2.3 (Lewis, 32). For Scripture as food, see Origen, *Philocalia* 12.2; 15.9–10 (Lewis, 56, 69–70). For Scripture as a feast or banquet, see Gregory the Great, *Moralia in Job* 1.21.29 (Bliss and Marriott, 47).

differently, I have a goal related to readers' affections. It is my goal in this book to help readers grow in their love for Scripture in ways that will help them plant this love in those to whom they minister.

The thesis of this book, as noted, is that Christians benefit from picturing Scripture with a plurality of models. If individual readers and the church as a whole will employ more than one model when reading Scripture, they will draw more nourishment from it than would be possible by using only one model. Also, Christians are able to hear and respond to other Christians' readings of Scripture in meaningful, productive ways when they first understand the model (or models) that their conversation partner is using. We will grow in understanding and unity as we learn about the primary canons, models, and stories that other believers use when encountering and speaking the words of Scripture. And we will gain new insights into the world of the text as we explore the models of Scripture. So let us take and read together.

part one

HOW GOD SPEAKS
in SCRIPTURE

1

CANONS

It seemed good to me also, having been urged thereto by true brethren, and having learned from the beginning, to set before you the books included in the Canon, and handed down, and accredited as Divine, to the end that any one who has fallen into error may condemn those who have led him astray; and that he who has continued stedfast in purity may again rejoice, having these things brought to his remembrance.

—ATHANASIUS[1]

In our extended family we Christians operate with explicitly different Old Testament canons, so our study best begins here. In our day-to-day use of the New Testament, we may be operating with functionally different canons as well, but that is an idea we will consider in the metanarratives chapter below. The goal for this chapter is to leave you with a clearer idea of how we came to have different Old Testament canons and how the difference matters in the way we live out our faith.

CONTENTS OF OUR OLD TESTAMENT CANONS

Most people are aware that there are more books in the Catholic and Orthodox Old Testaments than in a Protestant Old Testament, but fewer people know why. The books that are found in the more expansive canons are called "deuterocanonical," which means "secondarily added to the canon." At times the word "deuterocanonical" can carry the connotation of a lower level of inspiration. The term "apocrypha," which according to its etymology means "hidden things," has a little more negative connotation than the term "deuterocanonical." Protestants often use "apocrypha" for the "extra" books in a Catholic Old Testament.

---

1. Athanasius, "Letter XXXIX," 551–52.

The following chart shows the contents of the Old Testament in the categories and order maintained by the Jewish, Protestant, and Catholic/Orthodox communities.[2]

COMPARISON OF THE HEBREW BIBLE, THE PROTESTANT OLD TESTAMENT, AND THE CATHOLIC/ORTHODOX OLD TESTAMENT

Hebrew Bible	Protestant Old Testament	Catholic/Orthodox Old Testament
Torah	*Pentateuch*	*Pentateuch*
Genesis	Genesis	Genesis
Exodus	Exodus	Exodus
Leviticus	Leviticus	Leviticus
Numbers	Numbers	Numbers
Deuteronomy	Deuteronomy	Deuteronomy
Former Prophets	*Historical Books*	*Historical Books*
Joshua	Joshua	Joshua
Judges	Judges	Judges
1–2 Samuel	Ruth	Ruth
1–2 Kings	1–2 Samuel	1–2 Samuel
	1–2 Kings	1–2 Kings
Latter Prophets	1–2 Chronicles	1–2 Chronicles
Isaiah	Ezra	Ezra (Greek/Russian
Jeremiah	Nehemiah	Orthodox also include
Ezekiel	Esther	1 Esdras and Russian Or-
The Twelve: Hosea, Joel,		thodox includes 2 Esdras)
Amos, Obadiah,	*Poetry/Wisdom*	Nehemiah
Jonah, Micah, Na-	Job	Tobit
hum, Habakkuk,	Psalms	Judith
Zephaniah, Haggai,	Proverbs	Esther (with additions)
Zechariah, Malachi	Ecclesiastes (Qoheleth)	1–2 Maccabees (Greek and
	Song of Solomon	Russian Orthodox also
Writings		include 3 Maccabees)
Psalms	*Prophets*	
Proverbs	Isaiah	*Poetry/Wisdom*
Job	Jeremiah	Job

2. This chart is adapted from the tables in Collins, *Short Introduction*, 4–5.

Hebrew Bible	Protestant Old Testament	Catholic/Orthodox Old Testament
Song of Songs	Lamentations	Psalms (Greek and Russian Orthodox include Psalm 151 and Prayer of Manasseh)
Ruth	Ezekiel	
Lamentations	Daniel	
Qoheleth (Ecclesiastes)	The Minor Prophets:	Proverbs
Esther	Hosea, Joel, Amos,	Ecclesiastes (Qoheleth)
Daniel	Obadiah, Jonah,	Song of Solomon
Ezra-Nehemiah	Micah, Nahum, Ha-	Wisdom of Solomon
1–2 Chronicles	bakkuk, Zephaniah,	Ecclesiasticus (Wisdom of Sirach)
	Haggai, Zechariah,	*Prophets*
	Malachi	Isaiah
		Jeremiah
		Lamentations
		Baruch (includes Letter of Jeremiah)
		Ezekiel
		Daniel (with additions)
		The Minor Prophets: Hosea, Joel, Amos, Obadiah, Jonah, Micah, Nahum, Habakkuk, Zephaniah, Haggai, Zechariah, Malachi

The headings for the left column in the table above are different than those of the middle and right columns, beginning with the name of the collections. Judaism calls its Scripture the Hebrew Bible. Another term used for the Hebrew Bible is Tanak, sometimes spelled TaNaK to show that the term is an acronym, based on the terms *Torah* (Law), *Neviim* (Prophets), and *Ketuvim* (Writings). The terms "Hebrew Bible" and "Tanak" designate more than simply the books included in the canon; they also denote how the books are categorized and grouped together, and how they are traditionally read. "Hebrew Bible" is not interchangeable with "Old Testament," for the canonical organization of these collections is very different, and the reading traditions behind each of them is very different. By concluding with 1–2 Chronicles, which contain a narrative of David's preparation for the temple and end with Cyrus's call to rebuild the temple, the Hebrew Bible, which Jews read, is temple-oriented.

By concluding with Malachi, which refers to a "messenger of the LORD" and the "LORD coming to his temple," the Old Testament, which Christians read, is messiah-oriented.

BACK STORY OF THE DEUTEROCANONICAL OLD TESTAMENT BOOKS

When the Hebrew Bible was translated into Greek, some other books besides the thirty-nine books of the Tanak (Law, Prophets, Writings) began to circulate as additional parts of this Greek version of the Jewish Scriptures. These books were 1 Esdras, Tobit, Judith, Additions to Esther, Wisdom of Solomon, Ecclesiasticus or Wisdom of Ben Sira (Sirach), Baruch, Letter of Jeremiah (often published as the sixth chapter of Baruch), Prayer of Manasseh, 1 Maccabees, 2 Maccabees, and poetic and narrative additions to the book of Daniel—Prayer of Azariah, Song of Three Young Men, Susanna, and Bel and the Dragon. This is like what happens to translated works today. Often the translator will add a preface to the work, and the publisher might add one or more documents to provide a cultural or historical context for those reading the volume in translation. Most of the deuterocanonical additions contribute toward making sense of Jewish life outside the land and Jewish life under the rule of foreign powers.

The Greek version of the Old Testament, called the Septuagint, was produced with some or all of the books just listed. Since its manuscripts do not consistently include all these extra books and since Philo of Alexandria never quotes any of these extra books, it is inaccurate to speak of an "Alexandrian canon," as if there were a fixed set of books different from the Palestinian canon of thirty-nine books, that Alexandrian Jews accepted as their Scripture.[3] It is possible that the technological change of binding separate books into one codex—as distinct from keeping each biblical book, or accepted groups of books like the twelve prophets (Hosea to Malachi), separate in single, dedicated scrolls—may have led to the impression that all books within a given codex had canonical status.[4]

The Old Testament text that was translated into Greek was then translated into the Old Latin version, with the deuterocanonical books integrated among the Palestinian canon of thirty-nine books. Those church fathers like Origen and Jerome who knew some Hebrew, as well as Melito

---

3. Metzger, *Introduction to the Apocrypha*, 176–77.
4. Metzger, *Introduction to the Apocrypha*, 177–78.

of Sardis, had at least learned what the rabbis considered canonical, and always held the deuterocanonical books such as Tobit and 1–2 Maccabees to be outside the canon, though they admitted that readers found them spiritually beneficial.[5]

Another book, known as 2 Esdras, was later included in Old Latin versions of the Old Testament, but it and 1 Esdras are not included in the Catholic Old Testament canon. Greek fathers of the fourth century, such as Amphilochius, Athanasius, Cyril of Jerusalem, Epiphanius, Eusebius, and Gregory of Nazianzus, distinguished between Old Testament books within (e.g., Genesis) and outside (e.g., Tobit) the Hebrew canon, even while quoting Old Testament books from outside the Hebrew canon as Scripture.[6] This ambivalence continued in Orthodox usage for centuries to follow.

When producing his Latin Bible for the church, Jerome indicated in his prefaces to the deuterocanonical books that they were not to be regarded as authoritative for doctrine in the way that the thirty-nine books of the Palestinian canon were. His distinction was noted and echoed by such medieval scholars as Gregory the Great, Walafrid Strabo, Hugh of St. Victor, Hugh of St. Cher, and Nicholas of Lyra. But most medieval scholars probably did not observe this distinction. The status of these deuterocanonical books became more contested when the practices of praying for the dead and giving alms as a way of working out one's salvation came under scrutiny during the sixteenth century.[7] "Deuterocanonical" in the rest of this chapter refers to books that are within the forty-six-book Old Testament canon, though accorded a secondary value beneath books in the Hebrew canon.

The following survey of the varying canonical collections follows the summary by Bruce Metzger.[8] In the Vulgate editions copied and printed from the fifth through the sixteenth centuries, the deuterocanonical books were interspersed among the thirty-nine fully accepted books of the Old Testament. The first Bibles to group the deuterocanonical books together were the 1527–1529 Swiss-German Bible produced in Zürich, which presents the deuterocanonical books in its fifth volume and begins with the notice that the books in that volume were not considered part of the Bible by people long ago and not in the Hebrew canon; the 1526 Dutch Bible published in Antwerp

5. Metzger, *Introduction to the Apocrypha*, 178.
6. Metzger, "Introduction to the Apocrypha," xv.
7. Metzger, "Introduction to the Apocrypha," xii, xv–xvi.
8. Metzger, *Introduction to the Apocrypha*, 182–88.

by J. van Liesvelt; and the Luther Bible of 1534, which groups the deutero-canonical books together in a section after Malachi. Luther did not include 1 and 2 Esdras in the group, explaining that they didn't offer anything that could not be found in *Aesop's Fables* or even in more inconsequential books. He called this section "Apocrypha," labeling it as a group of books not at the level of Scripture, but holding good and useful content. "Apocrypha" and its adjective "apocryphal" therefore refer to books that are outside the canon, regarded as of lesser value than what Catholic and Orthodox readers ascribe to the deuterocanonical books.

Bibles published later in the sixteenth century followed suit. The 1535 Coverdale Bible placed Baruch immediately after Jeremiah but grouped most of the other deuterocanonical books together after Malachi. The 1560 Geneva Bible, the Bible used by John Bunyan, Shakespeare, and the Pilgrims, and the first English Bible to offer a text divided into verses, published the deuterocanonical books in a section called the "Apocrypha," introducing them as books that were commonly considered not to be read or preached from in church services and containing no grounding for doctrine. This Bible did place the Prayer of Manasseh directly after 2 Chronicles but labeled the prayer as part of the Apocrypha.

The 1611 King James Bible followed the pattern of most of the sixteenth-century Protestant Bibles, publishing the deuterocanonical books as "Apocrypha" in a section immediately following the Old Testament. In the marginal cross-references of Old and New Testaments in this 1611 edition, there are 113 references to deuterocanonical books, thus illustrating how its editors recognized the many connections between the books they accepted as fully canonical and books they called apocryphal. In later printings of the King James Bible in following years, all these cross-references to the Apocrypha were omitted.

Official Pronouncements on the Canon of Scripture

The canonical history of the Christian Scriptures is checkered with councils or synods that met, discussed, and ruled on which books to consider canonical Scripture. Near the beginning of most chronological surveys comes the Council of Jamnia, which occurred after the fall of Jerusalem. Rabbis at this council debated whether the books of Qoheleth (Ecclesiastes) and Song of Songs "defile the hands." They decided to keep these books within the Hebrew canon of Scripture.

Athanasius's Easter Letter of 367 CE lists all thirty-nine books of our Old Testament except Esther and includes Baruch and the Letter of Jeremiah as the canonical Old Testament. He presents Esther, Wisdom of Solomon, Sirach, Tobit, Judith, the Teaching of the Apostles, and the Shepherd of Hermas as books that church fathers recommend believers read in order to become more godly. Athanasius's description of the New Testament canon matches the twenty-seven books of our New Testament.[9] This New Testament canon was confirmed in the West at the Council of Hippo in 393. That council, as well as the councils in Carthage in 397 and 419, also confirmed that the deuterocanonical books of the Old Testament were canonical Scripture.[10]

The sixteenth-century Roman Catholic Council of Trent, in response to Protestant criticism of its use of the deuterocanonical books, pronounced an anathema on all who would not regard all books of the Latin Vulgate Bible as holy and included in the canon. At the same time, the council ruled in 1546 that the Prayer of Manasseh and 1 and 2 Esdras (usually so named in Protestant editions of the Apocrypha; Catholics often refer to them as 3 and 4 Esdras) were outside the canon of Scripture.[11]

Non-Catholic rulings on the Old Testament canon have been varied. In article 6 of the 1561 Belgic Confession, a document produced for Protestant communities in Holland and Flanders and still a benchmark for Reformed denominations around the world, the Old and New Testaments are treated as separate from the Apocrypha, "which the Church may read and take instruction from, so far as they agree with the canonical books; but they are far from having such power and efficacy as that we may from their testimony confirm any point of faith or of the Christian religion; much less to detract from the authority of the other sacred books." The Church of England's Thirty-Nine Articles, formulated in 1562, is unclear about the status of the Apocrypha. Its article 6 enumerates the thirty-nine books of the Old Testament and then explains that there are other books that Christians can read for moral examples and godly instruction, listing the deuterocanonical books there. Yet in article 35 of the Church of England's *Books of Homilies* they are described as containing good doctrine. These two books have around eighty quotations or

---

9. Athanasius, "Letter XXXIX," 552.
10. Metzger, "Introduction to the Apocrypha," xv.
11. Metzger, "Introduction to the Apocrypha," xvii.

references to the Apocrypha, drawing from every book in it except for 1 and 2 Esdras and 2 Maccabees.[12]

The Westminster Confession of 1647, a statement that remains a benchmark for Reformed churches today, declares that the deuterocanonical books cannot at all be considered Scripture and are not to be regarded as closer to Scripture or more helpful than any other noncanonical writings.[13]

The Orthodox record with regard to the canon for the first sixteen centuries is difficult to categorize. Because the Septuagint was used as the Scripture for a long period of time, some Orthodox theologians—Theophylact of Bulgaria, Andrew of Crete, Theodore the Studite, and Germanus—employ the deuterocanonical texts interchangeably with the protocanonical texts. Some deuterocanonical texts are cited authoritatively in proceedings of the ecumenical council of Nicaea II in 787 and the Council of Constantinople organized by Basil in 869. But revered Eastern theologians such as Athanasius, Nicephorus, and John of Damascus all explicitly hold to the Palestinian canon of Old Testament books. In 1672 the Synod of Jerusalem explicitly named Judith, Wisdom of Solomon, 1–4 Maccabees, Bel and the Dragon, and Sirach as fully in the canon of Scripture. There is still some variety in the Russian and Greek Orthodox Churches today regarding the Old Testament canon. The Russian Orthodox Church published the deuterocanonical books as fully canonical in the Slavonic Bible of 1581, but later Russian Orthodox synodal rulings align their Old Testament canon with a Protestant, thirty-nine-book Old Testament.[14]

CANON AND CHURCH

In the introduction to this book, we saw that interpretation is related to ecclesiology; that is, how one gets meaning from the Scriptures is related to the church in which one worships. An analogous connection occurs regarding canon. How one talks about and decides the limits of the Old Testament canon is also related to how one views the church. A good entry point is to consider the difference in attitude that the early church doctors Jerome and Augustine display in their understanding of church and canon.

Jerome does not consider the Septuagint (abbreviated LXX) to be inspired, since its most basic identity is that it is a translation and because there is no

---

12. Metzger, *Introduction to the Apocrypha*, 189–91; quotation from 190.
13. Metzger, *Introduction to the Apocrypha*, 192.
14. Metzger, *Introduction to the Apocrypha*, 192–95.

single version that comes down to us directly from the texts translated. This accounts for his uneasiness about claiming that the extra books that are in the LXX are Scripture in the same sense as the books that are in the Hebrew canon of Scripture. For example, he is not ready to say that Judith is Scripture in the same sense as Judges. In contrast, Augustine is more ready to look to what the churches are doing with the books. If most catholic churches are using certain books, then Augustine considers them to be canonically secure. He especially values the collections used in churches founded by an apostle or in cities that received a letter of the Pauline or Catholic letter collections. The basic difference in their approaches is that Jerome considers the authors of the texts while Augustine considers how the text is used by the church.[15]

Hugh of St. Victor quotes Jerome's skeptical comments about certain of the LXX books and so favors the thirty-nine-book Hebrew canon for the Christian Old Testament. But Hugh expands the New Testament canon, so that the last section of its gospels, apostles, and fathers organizational scheme includes Jerome and other church fathers. Thus while Augustine had looked to practices within the church as indicative of how the canon should be formed, Hugh looks to the writings of the church fathers as a valid extension of the inspired writings, both as prescriptive for the Old Testament canon and as constituting inspired Scripture that is analogous to the Writings section of the Hebrew Bible.[16]

Thomas Aquinas understands the canon to be determined not on the criterion of which writings are earliest, which sometimes is invoked by Jerome, nor on the criterion of church usage, Augustine's criterion. Instead, he locates the decisive criterion in official decrees from the Catholic Church, including its councils and synods. He recognizes the Holy Spirit as active and guiding the Catholic Church in its discernment of Scripture. For Thomas, therefore, the Old Testament canon of the Vulgate, which reflects the LXX, and the standard twenty-seven-book canon of the New Testament should be regarded as the Christian Scriptures.[17]

---

15. Patton, "Canon and Tradition," 80–82.

16. Patton, "Canon and Tradition," 82–84, citing Hugh of St. Victor, *Didascalion* 4.2, who quotes Jerome from the end sections of *Praefatio in Salamonem* and *In libros Samuel et Malachim*.

17. Patton, "Canon and Tradition," 85–89, citing *ST* II-II.1.9; III.25.3, ad. 4. Patton notes that Thomas's reliance on official church teaching for determining canon and authoritative exegesis gave him "more flexibility" in interpreting Scripture, since the final say lay for him with the church, not with the interpreter (89).

Nicholas of Lyra prefers the Hebrew canon's Old Testament. He cites Jerome to support this, but his decision is also informed by his debates with Jewish scholars of his day and his respect for the Hebrew text. For Nicholas, what is closer to the event is best, so those books composed earliest, including the thirty-nine-book Hebrew canon, are inspired in a way that later books—the books added in the translation of the LXX—are not. His relative lack of regard for official church pronouncements may be related to his order's conflicts with the contemporary pope, John XXII, over the virtue of poverty.[18]

WHAT PRACTICAL DIFFERENCE DOES THE OLD TESTAMENT CANON MAKE FOR CHRISTIANS?

I've made the historical survey above of lists and approaches to the canon, especially the Old Testament canon, to show you the differences of opinion on exactly how to handle the books received from the LXX into the Old Testament. What difference does it make for nonacademic Christians whether they have thirty-nine or forty-six books in their Old Testaments?

A significant difference is that, with the inclusion of the deuterocanonical books, the character of the Old Testament becomes more oriented toward wisdom literature. Sirach and Wisdom of Solomon significantly add to the length of the wisdom literature category within the Old Testament. In addition, Tobit includes elements of wisdom literature. The wisdom orientation found in these books includes the vision of enjoying the fruits of one's labor in this life.[19] Partially because the Catholic Old Testament has the books of Sirach, Wisdom of Solomon, and Tobit, the Catholic spirituality is more earth-affirming than some Protestant spiritualities.

The deuterocanonical books include material that seems fictional in character. For example, near the beginning of Judith, we read repeated descriptions of Nebuchadnezzar as king of the Assyrians (1:7, 11), even saying that he lived in Nineveh, the Assyrian capital (1:1). Those familiar with other biblical books or with secular history associate Nebuchadnezzar with the Babylonians, whose capital was Babylon. So the very beginning of this book signals that it is a fictional story. Similarly, the book of Tobit, with its account of how the

18. Patton, "Canon and Tradition," 89–93, citing the preface to Lyra's *Postilla litteralis super totam Bibliam.*

19. Examples of how wisdom literature considers wealth and other comforts to be legitimate rewards for God's people in this life are Job 42:11–12; Prov 8:20–21; Sir 44:10–11; Wis 7:11; 8:5–7, 18; Tob 4:21. It is true that Wisdom of Solomon broaches the immortality of the soul as a means of explaining how some righteous can die young and how the wicked can prosper (2:22–3:10), but still Wisdom includes the idea of rewards in this life (7:7–12).

fish that jumped out of the river would have swallowed Tobias (6:2–3), how seven of Sarah's husbands died on their respective wedding nights (6:13–14), and how her father was digging Tobias's grave while Tobias and Sarah spent their wedding night together (8:9–12), seems to indicate that the work is fictional. These narratives condition the reader not to expect that the genre of every narrative in the Bible is the reportage that moderns expect of historical narrative. Catholic readers, given their familiarity with the fantastic, fictive elements in the deuterocanonical books, may be more prone to identify more nonhistorical elements in other narratives, such as the narrative of Jonah and the great fish or various episodes within the book of Daniel.

The deuterocanonical books do not include prophetic books.[20] Even the book of Baruch is filling in the gaps of the narratives related to Jeremiah and Judah's exile in Babylon, rather than providing prophetic announcements. Thus, the Protestant Old Testament, especially in the way it ends with Malachi, has a more emphatically prophetic "personality" than either the Catholic Old Testament or the Hebrew Tanak, which orders its thirty-nine books so as to conclude the collection with 2 Chronicles. This may partially account for how Protestants display greater interest in the contemporary fulfillment of prophecy than do Catholics, though this phenomenon is also due to the idea, accepted in some strands of American evangelicalism, of a rapture of believers from the earth.

Because the heroes and heroines of 1–2 Maccabees are those Jews who resisted the Seleucid authorities in power, those branches of the Christian family who accept these books as canonical and authoritative may be more prone to encourage civil disobedience than those who do not accept any Maccabean literature as canonical. Anabaptists of the sixteenth century treated these books as Scripture and found in them great encouragement and guidance for the martyrdoms they were experiencing.[21] In the Catholic branch of our family, the Mass for martyrs St. Charles Lwanga and companions includes a reading from 2 Maccabees 7, as does the Sunday Mass in year C for the thirty-second Sunday in ordinary time. Weekday Masses draw from 1–2 Maccabees all through the thirty-third week in year 1 of the lectionary.

LITERARY AND THEOLOGICAL FUNCTIONS OF THE DEUTEROCANONICAL BOOKS

The deuterocanonical books add to the impact of the thirty-nine-book Palestinian canon of the Old Testament in distinct ways. We have already observed

---

20. Metzger, "Introduction to the Apocrypha," xiv.
21. Johns, "Reading the Maccabean Literature."

how the deuterocanonical books as a whole are especially oriented toward Jews living outside the promised land—that is, diaspora Jews. Within the Old Testament, Tobit—like Esther and Baruch—provides examples of how diaspora Jews can follow God. In effect, these books are saying, "You can follow the God of Israel and be a confirmed child of Abraham even if you live outside the promised land." But in addition to that general contribution, a number of specific contributions help us understand why Jews came to value these books that were added to the Palestinian canon.

Filling Gaps

The books 1–2 Maccabees fill in a gap in the historical timeline for readers of the canon. By describing the battles of the Maccabees against the Seleucid forces that ruled the land in the second century BCE, these books provide pictures of life in the land during the intertestamental period, including background for the origin of the Hanukkah festival.

The Additions to Esther similarly fill in narrative gaps to provide more detail in the drama of the Jewish queen in the Persian Empire. These additions help the reader follow the narrative more easily.

Providence

Second Maccabees develops the idea of providence to show how God can protect the temple and superintend even the details of his people's lives. This more comprehensive idea of God's providence is also seen in how people are punished for their sins. Andronicus is executed in the same place where he killed Onias (4:38). Jason receives no funeral and is not buried with his ancestors, since he had not buried many (5:10). Details of what Antiochus suffered before he died are narrated to remind the reader of how Antiochus had abused others (9:5–6).[22]

Life beyond Sheol

Second Maccabees also develops the idea of the resurrection, as does Wisdom of Solomon. After death, the righteous receive eternal life, while the wicked receive divine punishment (2 Macc. 7:36). In the resurrection, people's bodies will be restored (7:11, 23; 14:26). Life in the resurrection means that one can

---

22. Metzger, *Introduction to the Apocrypha*, 146–47.

rejoin and share life with other family members who have been raised in the resurrection (7:6, 9, 14, 29).[23]

This picture of life beyond the grave is related to the riddle in wisdom literature of how God's justice works out in this life. The book of Job, some wisdom psalms, Proverbs, and Ecclesiastes all ponder the phenomena of evil people who die in peace or good people who are in difficult straits. This is a puzzle for these books, because they do not articulate the idea of a judgment after death. Wisdom of Solomon weighs in on these questions by presenting God as judging people after they die (3:1–11). It thus provides a way to explain the apparent comfort of the wicked or the injustice that the righteous receive. In the next life, God will set all things right. Second Maccabees 12:38–46 also looks to a resurrection after death, in which those who have died in sin can be restored to right relationship with God.

Intersection of Spiritual and Physical Worlds

Second Maccabees vividly portrays the interaction between the unseen, spiritual world and life on earth. Thus angels take care of people (10:29; 13:2), God can work supernaturally on behalf of God's people (3:25; 5:2; 13:2), and prayer and sacrifice are ideally offered for those who have died so that their punishment for sin will be ended (12:43–46).[24] Of course, this interaction can be seen in Daniel, but it gets special emphasis in deuterocanonical texts like 2 Maccabees, as well as in Tobit.[25]

Creation ex Nihilo

The doctrine of creation *ex nihilo* is due more to theological logic than to decisive exegesis of Genesis 1. But 2 Maccabees 7:28 supports the idea of creation out of nothing with a clarity not found elsewhere in the canon.[26]

Almsgiving, Paragon of Righteousness

Tobit emphasizes the value of almsgiving more than any other book of the Bible, a value that is echoed in the New Testament (Acts 9:36; 10:4; Gal 2:10).

---

23. Metzger, *Introduction to the Apocrypha*, 147.
24. Metzger, *Introduction to the Apocrypha*, 146–47.
25. Dan 3:24–25; 8:15–17; 9:20–23; 10:10–14; Tob 3:16–17; 12:11–22.
26. Metzger, *Introduction to the Apocrypha*, 147.

Tobit reflects a move in the Hebrew language that came to regard the word for righteousness, *tsedaqah*, as equivalent to almsgiving.

Theology of Marriage

Tobit also provides a theology of marriage and portraits of how a married person relates to parents and in-laws (4:19–5:1; 11:16–19; 14:8–13). Especially significant is Tobias's prayer on his wedding night, a marvelous example of trust in God and of a theological understanding of marital intimacy (8:4–9).

Encouragement through Suffering

The deuterocanonical books contain much that can encourage readers. While buried in long-term depression, John Bunyan (1628–1688) heard, apparently in church, a text from Sirach 2:10 that described how no one has been disappointed who has trusted in God. After hearing this, he read through his entire Bible to see if anyone trusting God had been disappointed. In recounting this story, Bruce Metzger asks if Bunyan would have been able to come out of his depression to write *Pilgrim's Progress* if he had not encountered that text from Sirach.[27]

Mixed Marriages and Gentile Converts

Deuteronomy presents Ammon and Moab as being far outside Israel; children resulting from a marriage with someone from either of these two nations are proscribed from membership in Israel to the tenth generation (23:3). The book of Ruth critically responds to this proscription by presenting Ruth as someone from Moab who turns out to be the grandmother of King David (4:17, 22). Ruth's marriage to the Jew Boaz is treated as entirely legitimate, an instance of the levirate law assisting a vulnerable widow (3:9–4:6; Lev. 25:25; Deut. 25:5–6). The deuterocanonical book of Judith completes this response to Deuteronomy 23:3 by presenting someone from Ammon—Achior—as a proselyte who is fully accepted in Israel (14:10).

27. Metzger, *Introduction to the Apocrypha*, 199–200.

Supplying Missing Prayers

The Hebrew text of Esther is famous for its lack of the word "God" or the name of the God of Israel as well as any explicit reference to prayer.[28] The Additions to Esther that are included, via the Septuagint, in the deuterocanonical version address these perceived lacunae by including prayers of Mordecai and Esther that directly address God (Esther C).

Manasseh, the evil king of Judah, is described near the end of Chronicles as repenting. After he prays, God restores him to his kingdom in Judah (2 Chron. 33:13). An actual prayer is provided and included in the Old Testament canon of the Orthodox Church but not in the Roman Catholic or Protestant canons.

The Palestinian canon describes the exile of Judah as coming to an end. Though Daniel prays to God for the exile to end, there is no account of other Judean exiles praying. This lacuna is filled by Baruch 2:11–3:8.

The Hebrew text of Daniel describes Daniel's three friends being thrown into the fiery furnace, where an angel appears with them. The Septuagint adds a prayer that they pray (Dan 3:26–90). This prayer is used in the Liturgy of the Hours.

Contributions to English Literature

Chaucer's *Canterbury Tales* is indebted in places to the deuterocanonical books. He mentions Holofernes and Judith in "The Monkes Tale" in lines 3757–64. In "The Tale of Melibeus" he mentions "Jesus son of Sirach" (author of Sirach) in lines 2185, 2235, and elsewhere, and he mentions Judas Maccabaeus in lines 2848–49. Shakespeare's plays contain over eighty allusions to eleven of the deuterocanonical books. Most come from Sirach. Shylock describes Portia as a judge like Daniel in *The Merchant of Venice*. This is noteworthy since the shorter form of Daniel as found in the Palestinian canon does not portray him as a judge, while in the deuterocanonical episode regarding Susanna, Daniel is clearly portrayed as a judge. The famous lines "The quality of mercy is not

---

28. Although the name of God does not occur in the Hebrew text, four acrostics, two using the first letter and two using the last letter of four consecutive words, spell the proper name of the God of Israel, the Tetragrammaton: Esther 1:20 (initial letters spell the name backward); 5:4 (initial letters spell the name forward); 5:13 (final letters spell the name backward); 7:7 (final letters spell the name forward). E. Bullinger, *Companion Bible*, appendix 60, depending on the Massorah.

strain'd, / It droppeth as the gentle rain from heaven" seem to be almost a quotation of Sirach 35:20.[29]

THE SCRIPTURAL CANON IN THE CLASSROOM

A significant issue to be aware of in the classroom is that Paul, to whom seven to thirteen of the New Testament's letters are credited, was using the LXX for his Bible. This means that he was reading Wisdom of Solomon, Sirach, Tobit, and the other deuterocanonical books as part of his Bible. When tracing the allusions and echoes of Scripture in his letters, therefore, it is best to widen one's horizon beyond the thirty-nine-book Old Testament and consider the full forty-six-book Old Testament as the scriptural canon with which Paul was working.

Romans and the Wisdom of Solomon

One difference that a familiarity with the full Old Testament makes is that it allows one to be more appreciative of scriptural allusions in the New Testament that might not be caught by those reading only with protocanonical books of the Old Testament. Thus, Paul's interactions with the book of Sirach and the Wisdom of Solomon in his letter to the Romans are lost on many readers of that letter. Bruce Metzger, who as a Protestant had no compelling reason to find connections between the deuterocanonical Old Testament books and the New Testament, lists the following parallels between Romans and the Wisdom of Solomon.[30]

PARALLELS BETWEEN ROMANS AND THE WISDOM OF SOLOMON

Romans	Wisdom of Solomon
1:20: God's existence and power can be understood by looking at the natural world; people who do not acknowledge God are without excuse.	13:5: The beauty and awesome characteristics of the natural world point to a creator.
1:21: Humans did not honor or offer thanks to God and instead became vain in their thoughts.	13:8: People are without excuse for not acknowledging God the creator.

---

29. Metzger, *Introduction to the Apocrypha*, 207, 209–10. On Shakespeare, Metzger seems to rely especially on the second of the two books he cites: Carter, *Shakespeare and Holy Scripture*, and R. Noble, *Shakespeare's Biblical Knowledge*.

30. Metzger, *Introduction to the Apocrypha*, 158–61.

Romans	Wisdom of Solomon
1:22–23: While considering themselves to be wise, humans became foolish, worshiping images of humans, birds, other animals, or reptiles.	*12:24; 13:1:* All those who did not acknowledge God became foolish, worshiping as divine some animals that were despised.
1:26, 29–31: God handed people over to shameful desires, and they became filled with all kinds of evil.	*14:24–27:* People engage in sexual sin, and other sins as well, all brought on by their choice to worship idols.
9:20: The human person has no right to question God, just as the clay that is formed cannot question the potter.	*12:12:* No one can hold God accountable, spurn God's judgment, or indict God for destroying peoples.
9:21: A potter has the right to make from the same lump of clay a piece of art and a vessel for everyday use.	*15:7:* A potter can make out of the same lump of clay vessels for clean and unclean uses.
9:22–23: God patiently waited for his creatures who are destined for destruction in order to show how awesome he is to those creatures whom he prepared ahead of time for his glory.	*12:20:* God, who carefully and after a long wait punished those who opposed Israel, giving Israel's enemies significant opportunity to repent, has rigorously judged his own children.

Metzger is right to note parallels, and he is aware of how the New Testament authors can use the same vocabulary as the deuterocanonical writers but with different meanings.[31] But Metzger does not mention the exegetical impact that an awareness of the parallels provides. This usually comes at places where we can see the New Testament tracking with an Old Testament text but then at a critical point taking a new direction. For example, though Paul follows the Wisdom of Solomon in describing humanity as idolatrous and in sin, he does not follow Wisdom's last three chapters in its stark contrast between most of humanity and the Jewish people, which it celebrates as always protected by God (Wis 19:22). By contrast, after indicting humanity of sins characteristic of the gentiles, Paul ambushes his own people, indicting them for hypocrisy and sin (Rom 2:1–11). In general, Paul in Romans is not as positive as the Wisdom of Solomon regarding God's constant blessing on the people of Israel (Rom 8:36; 9:1–3; 11:25), though he does insist on Israel's salvation (11:26–29).

---

31. Metzger, *Introduction to the Apocrypha*, 163.

And Paul in Romans is more insistent on how God's grace extends to all of humanity, unlike Wisdom's way of limiting divine grace to those worthy of it (Wis 2:1; 3:10; 10:1). Paul's distinction-blind and worldwide description of the recipients of God's grace is based on his deep appreciation for the gift that God has given humanity in Christ.[32]

Other Pauline Parallels with the Wisdom of Solomon

In addition to noting parallels between Romans and the Wisdom of Solomon, Metzger notes other Pauline parallels with the deuterocanonical book.[33]

OTHER PAULINE PARALLELS WITH THE WISDOM OF SOLOMON

2 Cor 5:1–9: If the earthbound tent in which we live perishes, we will have a dwelling from God that lasts forever in heaven. While we are in our earthbound tent, we worry.	*Wis 9:10–19:* The body that will perish can burden our spirit and the earthbound tent weighs down the worried mind.
Eph 6:13–17: Put on God's armor: the chest guard of righteousness, shoes representing the message of peace, the shield of faithfulness, the helmet of deliverance, and the Spirit's sword, which is God's word.	*Wis 5:17–20:* God will put armor on his creation so they can withstand God's enemies: righteousness as a chest guard, justice for a helmet, holiness as an impregnable shield, and anger for a sword.

Romans and Sirach

Romans commentator J. D. G. Dunn is aware of the intertextuality between Paul's Letter to the Romans and Sirach, frequently offering references from Sirach in his exegesis of Romans. For example, in his exegesis of Romans 4:23–24, Dunn notes that Paul departs from the standard inclusion of Abraham's law observance within his faith, seen in Sirach 44. A knowledge of Sirach's depiction of Abraham's piety thus helps us appreciate the unique portrait of Abraham that Paul introduces.[34]

---

32. Linebaugh, *God, Grace, and Righteousness*, 168–69.
33. Metzger, *Introduction to the Apocrypha*, 161–63.
34. Dunn, *Romans 1–8*, 239.

Hebrews and Deuterocanonical Books

Metzger notes how the author of Hebrews seems familiar with several deuterocanonical books of the Old Testament.[35]

PARALLELS BETWEEN HEBREWS AND DEUTEROCANONICAL BOOKS

Hebrews	Deuterocanonical books
Heb 1:1–3: multiple . . . radiance	*Wis 7:22–26:* multiple . . . radiance
Heb 11: Exemplars of faith	*Sir 44:* Godly ancestors of renown
Heb 11:35: Some of the faithful were tortured, not accepting escape, since they knew they would rise to an improved life.	*2 Macc 6:19:* Eleazar was tortured. *2 Macc 7:9, 11, 14, 23, 29, 36:* The martyrs were certain they would be raised to life after their deaths on earth.

The Epistle in the Deuterocanonical Books and the New Testament

Metzger identifies written communication from one person or group of people to another as actually occurring in different genres, the epistle and the letter. He notes how the epistle is addressed to a public audience and is written to be a lasting declaration, while letters are temporary. The genre of the epistle became popular in the literary culture of Alexandria, Egypt, around the fourth century BCE. It emerges in deuterocanonical writings in the Epistle of Jeremiah (aka Baruch 6), other sections of the book of Baruch, and at the opening of 2 Maccabees. Metzger thinks that Paul's letters, while personal and addressed to specific situations, have been influenced by the genre of the epistle and thus are a sort of hybrid between the private and temporary letter and the public and defined epistle. While not claiming that Paul, Peter, and others, such as the author of Hebrews, were consciously trying to model their writing according to the epistles in the deuterocanonical canon, Metzger thinks that the correspondence that has come down to us in the New Testament has been influenced by the genre of the epistle.[36]

---

35. Metzger, *Introduction to the Apocrypha*, 163–64.
36. Metzger, *Introduction to the Apocrypha*, 153–54.

The Scriptural Canon in Ministry

The Christian Scriptures are a significant part of God's revelation to humanity, and we will be considering their status as inspired revelation in the next chapter. But our Scriptures also provide us with a common discourse that serves to help us communicate with each other and with God when we meet for worship. Certain canon-related questions arise in these settings that can threaten the unifying potential of Scripture, so we must consider them here.

"Old Testament" in Christian Discourse

In the course of your ministry, you will encounter people who will want you to call the thirty-nine to forty-six books that begin our Bibles something other than the Old Testament. Some will want you to call this section the Hebrew Bible. Others will want you to call it the First Testament, to avoid any negative connotation that the word "old" carries, and perhaps also to remove or weaken the connection between Old and New Testaments traditionally held in Christian theology. Motivation for calling the Old Testament by another name can also come from historical study that presents the term as likely originating with Marcion.[37] But as Jon Levenson notes, Christians read the Old Testament alongside the New Testament, always assuming that the Old Testament's revelation is completed in the New Testament.[38] To acknowledge that we are reading the first main section of the Bible as dependent on the New Testament, it is best simply to call this collection by its traditional name, the Old Testament, while affirming against Marcion the enduring value of the texts we group together from Genesis through Malachi.

Differing Chapters and Verses in the Psalms

A significant area in which canonical issues figure in ministry is how people's Bible chapters may be divided and numbered differently. One place where this is most noticeable is in the book of Psalms.

---

37. Kinzig, "Καινὴ διαθήκη," 537–44, argues that it was Marcion and his followers who not only saw different deities in Judaism and Christianity but also emphasized the difference between the Christians' original Scriptures shared with the Jews, which the Marcionites probably called the "Old Testament," and the canon that Marcion attempted to establish, his ten-book "New Testament."

38. Levenson, *Hebrew Bible*, 9.

In Acts 13:33, when Paul introduces his quotation of "You are my son; today I have begotten you," some manuscripts (D [fifth century], 1175 [tenth century], and possibly Origen [third century]) quote Paul as saying this is from the first psalm rather than the second. This might indicate that there was also some fluidity in the numbering of the beginning psalms in the early centuries CE.

The translators of the Septuagint numbered the Psalms differently (in 250–150 BCE) than the Masoretes did when they standardized their Hebrew text of the Psalms (in 800–1000 CE). Jerome's Vulgate (ca. 400 CE) follows the Septuagint's psalm enumeration. The first big change happens at Psalm 9, composed of twenty-one verses in the Hebrew text, but in the Greek and Latin translations this psalm has absorbed the psalm that follows it, so that Psalm 9 is thirty-nine verses in length. Since Psalm 10 in the Hebrew text has been absorbed by Psalm 9 in the Septuagint and Vulgate, their Psalm 10 is a translation of Psalm 11 in the Hebrew text. The chart below shows how the numeration systems of these texts diverge and then converge to end at the hundred fiftieth psalm.

Most English translations of the Bible in use today follow the numeration of the Hebrew text. Translations that are especially attentive to the Vulgate use its numeration. This means that the longest chapter in the Psalter, which we usually call Psalm 119, is numbered as Psalm 118 in the Douay-Rheims and Ronald Knox translations.

NUMERATION SYSTEMS OF THE PSALMS

Masoretic Text and most English translations	Septuagint and Vulgate
1–8	1–8
9–10	9
11–113	10–112
114–115	113
116:1–9	114
116:10–19	115
117–146	116–145
147:1–11	146
147:12–20	147
148–150	148–150

Variation in versification within a psalm is usually due to whether or not the superscription is numbered among the verses of the psalm. For example, at the beginning of the Miserere, or Psalm 51, the Hebrew text numbers the heading as verse 1: "For the leader. A psalm of David." Then it numbers verse 2 for the next part of the superscription: "when Nathan the prophet came to him after he had gone in to Bathsheba." This results in a twenty-one-verse format for the psalm, which is what we find in the NABRE. But if editors decide not to count the superscription among the verses, we would then have the same psalm in a nineteen-verse format, such as we see in the KJV or the NIV.

The chapter or verse divisions should never be a battle in which to invest your energies. Spend your energy on making sure that whoever is following along with Scripture readings can find and read the text in the Bible they have, regardless of how it divides up chapters and verses.

The End of Malachi

The Hebrew and Greek texts of Malachi contain a twenty-four-verse final chapter, numbered as chapter 3. The Latin text contains a six-verse final chapter, numbered as chapter 4. The content of these conclusions remains the same; it is simply that the Vulgate has divided the twenty-four verses of the final chapter of this minor prophet into an eighteen-verse third chapter and a six-verse fourth chapter. Translations diverge differently here than they do regarding the versification of the Psalter. For the ending of Malachi, the Jerusalem Bible and the NABRE have a twenty-four-verse concluding third chapter. The Spanish translation La Palabra also concludes Malachi in this way. The Douay-Rheims, KJV, NIV, and NRSV have an eighteen-verse chaper 3 and a six-verse chapter 4. The Spanish translation Reina-Valera 1995 also concludes Malachi with this fourth chapter.

In general, your Scripture-oriented goals in ministry should revolve around getting people to read and meditate on Scripture. Don't talk too much about differences in chapter and verse divisions, or even about differences in the Old Testament canon. Instead, find ways to draw people to Scripture and motivate them to meditate on it. Bible studies, scripturally related anecdotes when making announcements, and Scripture in the homily and in your personal interactions with congregational members are all ways of helping your flock graze in the green pastures of God's Word.

Comfort for Those Grieving the Dead

A significant job that pastors perform is comforting, counseling, and providing liturgical closure for those whose loved ones have died. Make full use of your canon in pastoring at this time in people's lives. Second Maccabees 12:38–46 narrates how Judas Maccabeus, because of his firm belief in the resurrection of the dead, sent money for offerings at the temple for deceased soldiers. The last four verses of this paragraph can be used in Catholic Masses for the deceased. It is a text that can offer encouragement to any Christian whose family member or friend dies prematurely or when they were not ready to die. For those whose faith traditions discourage the use of 2 Maccabees, texts from Psalms, the Gospel of John, or the book of Revelation can be used to provide special comfort for those who have recently lost a loved one.[39]

CONCLUSION

The last example about comfort for the grieving points to what the canons of Scripture are in the end: approved sets of divinely given resources that speak into our lives. Wherever we find ourselves in the Christian family, it is in our own and our parishioners' best interests to read extensively within the canons set for us in order that we may absorb and pass on God's truth to others.

---

39. Pss 16:11; 23:1–6; 116:15; John 6:54–58; 11:25–26; 14:1–3; 16:33; Rev 21:1–4; 22:1–5.

2

INSPIRATION

If any one ponders over the prophetic sayings with all the attention and reverence they deserve, it is certain that in the very act of reading and diligently studying them his mind and feelings will be touched by a divine breath and he will recognize that the words he is reading are not the utterances of man but the language of God; and so he will perceive from his own experience that these books have been composed not by human art or mortal eloquence but, if I may so speak, in a style that is divine.

—ORIGEN[1]

Because Jews and Christians encounter the transcendent while reading their Scriptures and because their respective Scriptures describe God's word as coming directly from God (Ps 119; 2 Tim 3:15–16), Jews and Christians identify their Scriptures as being inspired by God.

Although in some circles the phrase "word of God" might make Christians first think of the words on the pages of our Bible, this is due to the influence of a development of Lutheran theology that happened after Luther. For Christian theologians, Catholic, Protestant, and Orthodox, the Word of God is first and foremost not the books of Scripture but the Son, whom John 1:1–3 describes as being in the beginning with God. It is secondly the message of God, when it is proclaimed in the power of the Holy Spirit to others (1 Cor 1:18–24; 1 Thess 2:13). Only in a third sense is it the written words on the pages of our Bibles.[2]

But Western Christianity does divide over whether to regard the word of God as a means of grace. The Catholic Church emphasizes the seven sacraments as means of grace.[3] They are given priority over the word of God in popular consciousness. A Catholic late to Mass is more concerned to arrive

1. Origen, *On First Principles* 4.1.6 (Butterworth, 346–47).
2. Jenson, *Systematic Theology*, 2:270–73.
3. The Catholic Church defines sacraments as "perceptible signs (words and actions)

in time to receive Jesus in the Eucharist than to hear Scripture readings or the homily, for example. Lutheran and Reformed communities understand the word of God, as defined in the second sense above, to be a means of grace and even more significant than the sacraments as traditionally understood. This explains why the Reformed theologian Louis Berkhof treats the word of God in his *Systematic Theology* in the section "The Means of Grace," under the larger heading "The Doctrine of the Church and of the Means of Grace."[4]

Besides the sacramental significance with which Protestants hold the proclaimed word of God, they also prioritize it in their construction of systematic theology, according it an epistemic priority not found among Catholic or Orthodox theologians. The Protestant evangelical theologian Wayne Grudem, who considers himself—like Berkhof—Reformed in his theological perspective, shows the priority given to Scripture by beginning his *Systematic Theology* with "The Doctrine of the Word of God." This is part 1 of his *Systematic Theology*, occurring before "The Doctrine of God." In contrast, Robert Jenson, a Lutheran theologian fully conversant with the Catholic tradition, treats the doctrine of Scripture rather late, as chapter 29 of the thirty-five chapters in his *Systematic Theology*. His chapter is titled "The Word and the Icons" and comes in his section "The Church."

The Catholic tradition's definition of seven sacraments, which do not include the sermon, thus typically results in less emphasis on Scripture and its exposition in public worship as compared with Protestant churches, in which the sermon—traditionally understood as the exegesis and proclamation of Scripture—takes center stage. This also means, as can be seen in the above comparison of where theologians treat the doctrine of Scripture, that Scripture is not viewed as the sole foundation of one's theology in Catholic and Orthodox traditions. But in Protestant circles, Scripture is very significant and is the starting point for constructing a theology. This also means that the doctrine of the inspiration of Scripture receives less "air time" in Catholic and Orthodox churches than it does among Protestants. But it is still a significant doctrine, since the Catholic and Orthodox churches consider Scripture as authoritative alongside and interpreted by tradition. This chapter examines dimensions of inspiration throughout the branches of our Christian family and then proceeds to examine the implications of God's inspiration of Scripture.

---

accessible to our human nature. By the action of Christ and the power of the Holy Spirit they make present efficaciously the grace that they signify" (*CCC* §1084).

4. Berkhof, *Systematic Theology*, 610, 616.

DIMENSIONS OF INSPIRATION

The multifaceted concept of inspiration includes God, Scripture's human authors, others who preserved, edited, selected, and arranged the books of Scripture, and readers over the centuries who have heard, repeated, prayed, and read the words of Scripture. As an entry into appreciating and understanding the concept, this section considers the agency, duration, and level of Scripture's inspiration.

Agency: How Did God Inspire Scripture's Authors?

Is it God alone who is responsible for the words the human authors wrote, or did God allow the human authors of Scripture to use their abilities and their own spiritual insight when they were writing? Most readers who recognize the different genres of Scripture and the cultural embeddedness of Scripture's discourse grant that God allowed the human authors the freedom to compose as they saw fit. The church fathers sometimes describe Scripture's inspiration with metaphors of the flutist (God) playing the flute (human author) or the scribe (God) holding the pen (human author). But these metaphors participate in the model of dictation to a degree that does not seem to match the human fingerprints and variety of content that is found in Scripture. The dual authorship is therefore best understood by the analogy of the incarnation.[5] Just as Christ came embodied as a human, so God's word comes embodied in human discourse, with its inherent limitations.

The human agency involved in inspiration explains why a specific scriptural text seems to favor Israel while another favors Judah. It would explain why one inspired author can be more favorable to the Roman Empire than a contemporary author who was also inspired to compose Scripture. Very few Christians consider that all of the Bible is inspired in a dictation mode. The Vatican II constitution known as *Dei Verbum* strongly affirms inspiration but does not describe a specific form of agency; that is, it does not say exactly how God inspired human authors.[6] Here is how that constitution addresses the question of agency in scriptural inspiration: "In composing the sacred Books, God chose and employed certain men, who, while engaged in this task, made full use of their faculties and powers, so that, with God himself acting in them

---

5. Farkasfalvy, *Theology of the Christian Bible*, 54. Incarnation as an analogy for divine inspiration of Scripture is clearly taught in *Dei Verbum* §13.

6. Witherup, *Scripture*, 49.

and through them, they as true authors committed to writing everything and only those things that he wanted written."[7]

It is worthwhile considering how our understanding of the human authors of Scripture influence our view of inspiration. The authors came from a variety of cultures, and their cultural heritage shows within Scripture. This can include narrative features that span cultures, such as the ancient sailors' practice of sending out birds when nearing land, or features unique to a single culture, such as the Israelite idea that all Amalekites and Canaanites should be annihilated (Gen 8:6–12; Exod 17:8–16; Josh 6:15–21). And so we must admit that the Bible has limitations that come with the cultures in which it was written. As Peter Enns says, "A thoroughly encultured Bible, like a thoroughly encultured Jesus, is exactly what God has given the church and should therefore be embraced as is and engaged honestly and without apology."[8] The cultural packaging that God allowed to come with the biblical authors' messages can be viewed as part of God's "accommodation" to us.[9] God accommodated the message to the writing abilities of the Bible's authors, the text-recording technologies of the times in which the Bible was written, and the cultures in which the Bible's authors lived. So the human authors of Scripture wrote from within specific cultural settings that differed geographically and in time from one another.

Since Scripture's human authors wrote from specific cultural settings at different times, and since each author was not the same as another author, their works within the canon differ from one another. Job's friends state that our actions have consequences and therefore that Job's actions must somehow be the cause of his suffering. Though this perspective is integral to the message of Deuteronomy, it is rejected by the implied author of Job, who offers another explanation for Job's sufferings.[10] Enns also points out that Chronicles offers some differences from the Deuteronomistic History as found in 1 Samuel to 2 Kings. Chronicles downplays or ignores David's sins, portrays the twelve tribes as more united than we see in the Deuteronomistic History, highlights Solomon's initiative in building the temple, and presents God as directly punishing sinners and not those sinners' children or grandchildren.[11] To these I would add that 2 Chronicles 33:12–13 describes Manasseh as repenting and returning from Babylonian exile to Judah, while a reading of 2 Kings 21:16–18

7. *Dei Verbum* §11 (Béchard, *Scripture Documents*, 24).
8. Enns, *Inspiration and Incarnation*, x.
9. Bloesch, "Sword of the Spirit," 15.
10. Enns, *Inspiration and Incarnation*, 80–82.
11. Enns, *Inspiration and Incarnation*, 84.

would indicate that he died unrepentant in Judah, without a conversion experience in Babylon. There are also inflated numbers in Chronicles: David pays the owner fifty silver shekels for the temple site and the oxen in 2 Samuel 24:24, while in 1 Chronicles 21:25 he pays six hundred gold shekels for the site. These differences are no doubt due to the situation in which the Chronicler was writing and his purpose in writing. Chronicles is written after the Deuteronomistic History and with the purpose of providing a big-picture view of all that God accomplished for Israel through the house of David and how God will continue to bless his people if they worship properly at the temple in Jerusalem.[12]

There is variety within the legal material of the Old Testament. According to Exodus 21:2, 4, 7, only male Hebrew slaves were to be freed after six years of service. But according to Deuteronomy 15:12, the Israelites were to release all Hebrew slaves after six years of labor, whether male or female.[13] Exodus 12:8–9 says to roast, not boil, the Passover lamb. The Hebrew text of Deuteronomy 16:7 explicitly directs the Israelites to boil the Passover lamb.[14] According to Deuteronomy 23:3, people from Moab or Ammon are not to be admitted into the congregation of Israel. Children of intermarriages between Israelites and either of these nations are not to be admitted into Israel for ten generations. But Boaz of Bethlehem marries Ruth, a Moabite, and their grandson is Jesse, the father of David.[15] And in the book of Judith, the model convert is Achior, an Ammonite, who is circumcised and fully accepted within Israel (5:5; 6:10–21; 14:10). Enns is right to point out that differences of this sort are not new discoveries. People have been discussing and explaining them in various ways for two millennia. If we treat these differences as problems that threaten the Scripture's status as the word of God, we are imposing a modern construct on Scripture that Scripture itself rejects.[16]

A reader's understanding of the identities of the Bible's human authors can affect how one views inspiration. Those readers who consider each book of the Bible to have been written by a single, named author may more readily attribute inspiration to each author. On the other hand, those who are open to hypotheses about multiple people working to compose a book of the Bible have first to think about the processes by which our Scriptures came into existence. For those who consider all of Scripture to be inspired by God, one has to ask if God was inspiring the copyists and editors who gave the Bible its current

12. Collins, *Short Introduction*, 290–91.
13. Enns, *Inspiration and Incarnation*, 90.
14. Enns, *Inspiration and Incarnation*, 91–92.
15. Enns, *Inspiration and Incarnation*, 96.
16. Enns, *Inspiration and Incarnation*, 107–8.

shape. It is entirely possible to view the whole process of composition and collection into the canon as inspired. Books whose authorship is contested, such as Malachi and Ephesians, should continue to be acknowledged as inspired, even if we do not know the author. As readers, students, and proclaimers of Scripture, we regard Malachi or Ephesians as equally able to convey God's word to us as books whose human authors are readily acknowledged, such as Jeremiah or Romans.

Orthodox theologian Theodore Stylianopoulos notes that those traditions that see Scripture as independent of the church, such as we see in articles of the Chicago Statement on Biblical Inerrancy, argue that the actual authors of the biblical books are those to whom the books are traditionally ascribed. But Orthodox theologians, according to Stylianopoulos, who see inspiration as enveloping the whole process of composition, editing, copying, and placing in a canon, are not as concerned about proving the identities of the human authors. He notes how Orthodox liturgy uses some postbiblical texts whose authors' identities are uncertain, and reminds readers that the early church debated the authorship of Hebrews and Revelation. Since from an Orthodox perspective "the ultimate criterion of truth is the life of the Church," it does not matter whether we can prove that the authors traditionally associated with the books of the Bible actually wrote those books.[17]

So what does the variety arising from the plurality of human authors show us about Scripture? It shows us that the unity that the rabbis and church fathers have seen in the Hebrew Bible and Christian canon is at a deeper level than at the surface. Christians can affirm that as God did with the incarnation of the Son, so God does with Scripture. God accommodates the divine message to humanity by communicating through human authors on levels that humanity can understand.[18] This means that there will of necessity be differences. For as soon as two or more people are given the freedom to write as they are inspired to write, there will be differences.

Duration: Does Inspiration Happen at One Moment or throughout a Process?

With regard to the time of inspiration, did the inspiration happen only when the words of Scripture's books were first written, or did the inspiration include the processes of editing, copying, grouping together with other texts, and canonizing that led to the books' places in a Bible today? If inspiration includes

17. Stylianopoulos, *New Testament*, 1:42.
18. Enns, *Inspiration and Incarnation*, 108–9.

these other processes, then we might say that inspiration includes not only the human authors of Scripture but also its editors, copyists, and compilers.

For those who accept the idea that multiple sources are behind the Pentateuch, such as J, E, D, and P, the composition process spans centuries, and inspiration must therefore have occurred along this whole process. Some might balk at accepting the idea of divine inspiration across a span of time, but this is qualitatively no different than saying that God inspired Moses sometime before 1000 BCE to write his five books and that God was inspiring other writers for the next millennium until the final books of the New Testament were written. If God can inspire different writers each to write their book(s) of the Bible, God can inspire multiple writers behind a single book, just as God inspired the authors of the Psalms.

Consider also how Proverbs 25 begins with the statement that it contains additional proverbs of Solomon copied by Hezekiah's scribes. This opens a window onto the process by which our canonical book of Proverbs was formed. The process of inspiration thus includes the work of Hezekiah's scribes, centuries after Solomon lived, since what these later scribes passed on affects the meaning of the whole book.

Level: In What Content and Scale Is Scripture Inspired?

We may approach the level of inspiration first through the lens of content. Is everything that Scripture says inspired? Or is Scripture inspired especially in regard to what leads us to God? The Catholic Church has been working out how best to speak of Scripture's inspiration for centuries, in ways appropriate to contemporary circumstances in the Christian family.

The Council of Trent responds to Protestant developments, and so begins its section on Scripture with an insistence that the gospel Christ proclaimed, described as "the source of all saving truth and rule of conduct," is "contained in the written books and unwritten traditions that have come down to us, having been received by the apostles from the mouth of Christ himself." Thus there is an emphasis that the inspiration of Scripture is not sufficient as a guide to all truth but is complemented by the traditions that have come down to us.[19]

Trent also emphasized the significance of reading Scripture with the church, instead of trying to interpret it on one's own in ways that depart from what the

---

19. Trent Session IV, 1st Decree (Béchard, *Scripture Documents*, 3); cf. Grudem, *Systematic Theology*, 127–35 on "The Sufficiency of Scripture."

church, including the church fathers, has taught.[20] Trent also commanded, in continuity with centuries of tradition, that the Scriptures be taught to those in religious orders and to all who attend Mass.[21]

In Vatican I, the constitution known as *Dei Filius* summarizes changes in Christian emphases and practice since the sixteenth century in ways that show how Scripture was first invested with more authority than traditionally done and then divested of much of its authority.

> No one is ignorant that the heresies proscribed by the Fathers of Trent, having rejected the divine Magisterium of the Church and allowing religious questions to be settled by the judgment of each individual, gradually dissolved into many sects, all disagreeing and contending with one another, until at length not a few people have lost all faith in Christ. And even the holy Bible, which previously they had declared the sole source and judge of Christian doctrine, has begun to be held no longer as divine but to be numbered among the fictions of mythology. Then there arose and spread far and wide throughout the world that doctrine of rationalism or naturalism, which in its complete opposition to the Christian religion as a supernatural institution strives with utmost zeal to shut out Christ, our one Lord and Savior, from the minds of people and from the moral life of nations and thereby to establish the reign of what they call pure reason or nature.[22]

The constitution known as *Dei Verbum* from Vatican II describes the content of the inspiration of Scripture in relation to the purpose that Scripture also describes. The following quotation picks up from the last sentence quoted in the agency section above from *Dei Verbum* §11.

> Therefore, since everything asserted by the inspired authors or sacred writers should be regarded as asserted by the Holy Spirit, it follows that we must acknowledge the Books of Scripture as teaching firmly, faithfully, and without error the truth that God wished to be recorded in the sacred writings for the sake of our salvation. As it is written: "All scripture is inspired by God

20. Trent Session IV, 2nd Decree (Béchard, *Scripture Documents*, 4–5).

21. Trent Session V, 2nd Decree (Béchard, *Scripture Documents*, 6–9), though the word "Scripture" is not used when the decree enjoins that priests "feed" their congregants what must be believed for salvation and which virtues must be cultivated and which vices must be shunned.

22. *Dei Filius*, introduction (Béchard, *Scripture Documents*, 15).

and is useful for teaching, for refutation, for correction, and for training in righteousness, so that the one who belongs to God may be competent, equipped for every good work" (2 Tim 3:16–17).[23]

We see here that *Dei Verbum* is saying that the whole of Scripture teaches the saving truth. This does not mean that there are no errors whatsoever in such details as chronology, geography, or historiography. But it does mean that, taken as a whole, Scripture teaches us the truth without error so that we may fully participate in the salvation God has prepared.

Evangelical theologian Donald Bloesch similarly views Scripture as a certain word of God about how God provides salvation in Christ. He does not think that Scripture's own witness regarding its character and function means that it is authoritative in all areas of human knowledge: "We must not infer from this that Scripture gives exact knowledge of mathematics or biology or any other science. Neither does it present a history of Israel or a biography of Jesus that accords with the standards of historical science. What we do have in Scripture is a faithful account of God's redemptive works, an incisive portrayal of the divine plan of salvation."[24]

We may approach the question of the level of inspiration also in terms of its scale. Is Scripture inspired such that what any verse says is God's final word on a topic? Or is it rather that Scripture as a whole is inspired, so that any verse we read needs to be read alongside the rest of Scripture? The Catholic position is that the whole of the scriptural witness must be taken into account when interpreting a specific text within it: "Since Sacred Scripture must also be read and interpreted in the light of the same Spirit by whom it was written, in order to determine correctly the meaning of the sacred texts, *no less serious attention must be devoted to the content and unity of the whole of Scripture*, taking into account the entire living tradition of the Church and the analogy of faith."[25] This means that a single verse cannot be trumpeted as proof for a given understanding of God's predestination of individuals, nor even that a single verse can be considered all one needs to know for salvation. Each sentence of Scripture must be read in light of the canon as a whole.

The scale of inspiration as the whole canon can be seen in the way that Luke-Acts views Jesus as fulfilling the Old Testament Scriptures, and the preaching about Jesus as worthy of being recorded in written form. Luke-Acts

---

23. *Dei Verbum* §11 (Béchard, *Scripture Documents*, 24).
24. Bloesch, "Sword of the Spirit," 14.
25. *Dei Verbum* §12 (Béchard, *Scripture Documents*, 25, my emphasis).

thus provides a precedent for understanding the end result of the inspiration of Scripture to be our canon of Old and New Testaments.[26]

In popular discourse among all sorts of Christians, of course, there are plenty of cases where a believer latches onto a single verse and views it as all one needs to know about a given topic. This sort of interpretive strategy can be exacerbated when the Christian regards a certain part of Scripture as more significant than all other texts of Scripture—for example, when Luther described Romans as containing the purest gospel, or when the Anabaptists (whom Luther detested) viewed the Sermon on the Mount as the essence of their faith. All of us need to keep reading the Old and New Testaments on an annual basis, letting God speak to us through our whole canon.

In contrast with the Catholic Church and Protestants such as Luther and Calvin, the Orthodox tradition is not comfortable equating Scripture with divine revelation. For the Orthodox theologians of the Eastern church, Scripture is the *record* of divine revelation, written by humans in human terms. Eastern fathers whom Orthodox Christians especially follow emphasize the limitations of Scripture. Thus, Origen called Scripture the "baby talk" that God employs to communicate with us, and Chrysostom called Scripture God's "condescension"; his term is *synkatabasis*. The practical result of this approach to Scripture is that its inspiration, and divine revelation itself, is viewed as an ongoing, dynamic process in which the human subject participates.[27]

While the Orthodox emphasis on Scripture as God's condescension to humanity overlaps conceptually with Calvin's idea that God accommodates his message in Scripture to humanity's limitations, Calvin does consider Scripture itself as inspired, unlike the Orthodox treatment of Scripture as the record of divine revelation. Also, Calvin would not say that inspiration is a dynamic process that includes the human subject.

In a way that is analogous to *Dei Verbum* §11, Orthodox writers emphasize that what Scripture says about salvation is what is inspired and an integral part of God's revelation to us. They do not regard every single verse of the Bible as inspired, nor do they think that Scripture can completely communicate the mystery of God to us. Since God is a mystery, God cannot be described completely by Scripture, nor should Scripture be considered perfect in all respects as God is.[28]

---

26. Farkasfalvy, *Theology of the Christian Bible*, 159–64.

27. Stylianopoulos, *New Testament*, 1:37.

28. Stylianopoulos, *New Testament*, 1:39–40.

RESULTS OF INSPIRATION

The inspiration that Christians recognize in Scripture has direct results in the ways Scripture functions and in the ways Christians respond to it. This last main section of the chapter details the specific results of Scripture's inspiration so that you can more deeply understand how your branch of the Christian family understands and reads Scripture.

Infallibility versus Sufficiency

In the quotation from *Dei Verbum* §12 above, the Catholic Church teaches that Scripture is to be read in the context of the whole canon and with "the entire living tradition" (this includes the magisterium and the second century's rule of faith) and the "analogy of faith" (approaching the text as believers and not as critics). The Orthodox Church similarly values tradition when reading the Bible. The Orthodox in fact do not divide Scripture from tradition; in Orthodox thought, Scripture is an integral part of the tradition. John Breck favorably quotes Sergius Bulgakov's definition of tradition as the "living memory of the Church" in the context of describing how early traditions shaped how and what the New Testament authors wrote.[29]

At this point it is also worth noting that when considering tradition, one has to ascertain how a given branch of the Christian family uses the term. While some Protestants use the term as equivalent to the Christ-event, Orthodox and Catholics tend to use the term to refer to the rulings and church councils that have occurred from the first century up to today.[30]

Despite holding to the inspiration of Scripture, we Catholics do not attribute infallibility to Scripture itself. This is because we recognize that it must be interpreted faithfully and does not on its own contain all that one needs for its proper interpretation. Infallibility is instead attributed to the magisterium of the Catholic Church, which depends on tradition when interpreting Scripture.

The Orthodox analogue to the Catholic idea of infallibility is sufficiency or *autarkeia*, the term used by Athanasius. (This word is used in 2 Cor 9:8 and 1 Tim 6:6, though not in regard to Scripture.) For Athanasius and the Orthodox today, Scripture's sufficiency means that a fullness of truth can be found in

29. Breck, *Scripture in Tradition*, 9.
30. Nissiotis, "Unity of Scripture and Tradition," 184–85.

Scripture. This is very different from the Protestant use of "sufficiency" when speaking of Scripture.[31]

For Protestants, Scripture is sufficient in the sense that everything one needs for the proper interpretation of the Bible is found within it. We will consider the Protestant idea of Scripture's sufficiency in chapter 9 below, and for now note that it is connected in some sectors of Protestantism to Scripture's reliability by the idea of inerrancy. Inerrancy is a Protestant affirmation that, as a result of its inspiration, Scripture does not contain anything contrary to fact.

Most Protestant statements that define Scripture's inerrancy qualify the term. For example, in the Chicago Statement on Biblical Inerrancy, article 9 states, "We affirm that inspiration, though not conferring omniscience, guaranteed true and trustworthy utterance on all matters of which the Biblical authors were moved to speak and write. We deny that the finitude or fallenness of these writers, by necessity or otherwise, introduced distortion or falsehood into God's Word." But in article 13 of the same statement we read, "We deny that it is proper to evaluate Scripture according to standards of truth and error that are alien to its usage or purpose. We further deny that inerrancy is negated by Biblical phenomena such as a lack of modern technical precision, irregularities of grammar or spelling, observational descriptions of nature, the reporting of falsehoods, the use of hyperbole and round numbers, the topical arrangement of material, variant selections of material in parallel accounts, or the use of free citations."

The first sentence of the quotation from article 13 is a preemptive thrust against expectations that the Bible conforms to the standards of modern science. The second sentence is fascinating, for it allows for plenty of loopholes in one's understanding of inerrancy. For example, to say that the doctrine of Scripture's inerrancy is not to be discarded because of "variant selections of material in parallel accounts" allows those who understand it according to this statement to discount real differences in the Gospels' parallel accounts. The quotation above comes close to Calvin's paradoxical description of Scripture as inerrant because it comes from God yet full of human fingerprints that could include errors because of God's accommodation of the message by sending it through human authors.[32]

---

31. Stylianopoulos, *New Testament*, 1:41.

32. Sparks, *God's Word in Human Words*, 256, citing Calvin, *Commentary on the Book of Psalms*, 5:184.

In the end, it is best to realize—as we consider in the *sola Scriptura* chapter below—that all written texts need interpretation. No written text speaks authoritatively on its own. This means that if one is to speak of the inerrancy of Scripture, one needs to speak of the inerrancy of a given interpretation of Scripture.

Inspiration and Authority

Claims of the Bible's inspiration are often not-so-veiled attempts at asserting the Bible's authority and utility. If the Bible is divinely inspired, then such inspiration is in effect a basis for calling others to listen to its message. And as we see in 2 Timothy 3:16, the divine inspiration of Scripture is a strong foundation for asserting the Bible's usefulness in teaching others. The difficulty, of course, is that considering Scripture to be inspired in no way means that two people with such a belief can agree on what a given paragraph of Scripture means. All written texts that serve as the basis for a people's behavior need someone, such as a single authority, or an institution, like the Catholic Church, to interpret and so guide in the reading of the document.

Protestant theologians typically describe the Bible's supernatural origins when identifying its authority. For example, Bloesch writes, "The authority of the Bible is derivative: it is anchored not in itself but in its divine Author and divine centre, Jesus Christ. It is a signpost that points to Jesus Christ, and at the same time it is a vessel that carries the truth of Jesus Christ. Luther described it as the 'carriage of the Spirit.' He also referred to Scripture as the 'swaddling clothes' in which the Christ-child is laid." Bloesch posits, first of all, the divine author as the origin of Scripture's authority. He goes on to assert that Christ and the salvation Christ brings constitute the most significant revelation brought to us in Scripture. Additionally, in his positive use of the "carriage of the Spirit" metaphor, he seems to be asserting that Scripture is authoritative because it teaches us and can provide keys toward the Holy Spirit's indwelling.[33] Most Christians of the last two millennia would not disagree with what Bloesch has written. However, many would say that his picture is incomplete. He has neglected to mention the church. It was the church that selected and canonized Scripture. And as we will see in the *sola Scriptura* chapter, the church is necessary for guiding our reading of Scripture.

Catholic and Orthodox theologians are more likely to include the church in their discussion of the origin of Scripture's authority. They emphasize that it is

---

33. Bloesch, "Sword of the Spirit," 16.

the church that has recognized Scripture as inspired and therefore invested it with authority. This leads to a more tradition-conscious way of reading Scripture. If one views Scripture as simply falling out of heaven, there is more of a tendency to use one interpretation of it as the only legitimate interpretation, which all people must heed. If one by contrast views Scripture as the church's book, one will not accept only one interpretation as legitimate until one has considered how the tradition has handled the passage.

Both Catholic and Orthodox churches view Scripture as the creation of the church. In their consciousness, Scripture was composed by, collected by, and canonized by the church. Protestants by contrast, as we saw in reference to Wayne Grudem's *Systematic Theology* at the beginning of this chapter, are more prone to treat God's word as its own category, closer to the doctrine of God and not inside the doctrine of the church.

Still, Scripture does not offer a running commentary as we read it. If you are a Protestant operating in a *sola Scriptura* approach, it is wise to consider who it is in your circle who is regarded as the authoritative interpreter of Scripture.

Inspiration and the Imprint of Scripture's Creation Accounts

Because Christians in all branches of Christianity consider Scripture as somehow inspired or a record of inspired teaching, Scripture's creation accounts elicit significant attention. These accounts, whether in Genesis, Job, Psalms, or Proverbs, have deeply imprinted themselves on readers' consciousness.[34] This impression is helpful in the way it exalts God as the beneficent creator and identifies humans as divine image-bearers who are given freedom to follow God and serve as stewards of the natural world.

The similarities of the creation story in Genesis 1 and the flood narrative in Genesis 6–9 with other ancient Near Eastern stories lead many to regard some narratives in the Old Testament as myth. Everyone reading the word "myth" in discussions of Scripture needs to understand that "myth" in these contexts does not in the first place mean something that is by definition untrue. Academic students of religion do not define "myth" when used in their discipline's discourse as though the term necessarily describes something that did not happen or that is not true. In 1931 J. R. R. Tolkien and Hugo Dyson went on a walk with C. S. Lewis, who considered himself an atheist. They explained to him how various cultures' myths find their highest expression in the central

---

34. Creation accounts in the Old Testament are found in Gen 1:1–2:4a (P); 2:4b–3:24 (J); Job 38:4–41:34; Ps 104; Prov 8:22–31.

narratives of the Bible. The conversion of Lewis from atheism to theism can be linked to that long conversation, when he realized that Scripture's main narratives are the most foundational and most true myths of any culture. Evangelical author Peter Enns defines myth as *"an ancient, premodern, prescientific way of addressing questions of ultimate origins and meaning in the form of stories: Who are we? Where do we come from?"*[35] The Orthodox Jew Jon Levenson uses "myth" when he explains Scripture. Here is his working definition: "I . . . use the term myth to describe the cast of mind that views certain symbols in terms of an act of unlimited scope and import that occurred, in Brevard Childs' words, in 'a timeless age of the past.'"[36]

Myths are stories by which we live. Do not damn your professor for using the word "myth" when talking about Scripture's creation accounts. Your professor is not denying the inspiration of Scripture by means of this term. Myths are stories by which we live, and when you begin comparing the Bible's creation and flood accounts with those from the ancient Near East, you will begin to understand why Jews and Christians have always considered Scripture's creation and flood accounts to be God's inspired word for us.

CONCLUSION

Because Western Christians regard Scripture itself as inspired, and Eastern Orthodox as the record of God's inspired revelation, we all come to Scripture as we come to no other text. This text makes demands of us. It is not simply a record of God's word to our spiritual ancestors. It is God's word to us and needs to be interpreted in light of tradition and the church's teaching.

Scripture itself gives examples of the docility and sensitivity we are called to cultivate in relation to it. Psalm 119 bubbles over with desire for following God's word. The repeated synonyms for "law," such as "testimonies," "statutes," and "ordinances," as well as the abecedarian form in which the psalm is written, all point to the written Scripture as the object of the psalmist's admiration and desire. Frequent expressions of conformity to God's word encourage readers to follow the psalmist's example.[37] Isaiah 66:1-2 is another text that models docility before God's word: "Here is what the LORD says, 'My throne is heaven and my footstool is earth. What house for me could you construct, and what is my resting place? My hand made all these,' says the LORD, 'and therefore

---

35. Enns, *Inspiration and Incarnation*, 39.
36. Levenson, *Sinai and Zion*, 102-3, citing Childs, *Myth and Reality*, 20.
37. Ps 119:4-5, 10, 15, 35-36, 67, 88, 101-2, 128, 167.

all these are mine. But to this person I pay regard, the one who is contrite and humble in heart, trembling at my word.'" In the following context, Isaiah predicts God's vindication for people with this attitude (Isa 66:5).

In the New Testament letter of 1 Timothy, Timothy is commanded to study and teach Scripture in ways that result in "love coming from a pure heart, clean conscience and genuine faith" (1:5) and to be consistent in the public reading of Scripture (4:13). Most of the New Testament books' quotations and allusions to the Old Testament are evidence of extensive immersion in Scripture.

Therefore, beyond the theoretical question of what doctrinal formulation one will accept regarding the inspiration of Scripture, the significant question is how carefully we attend to Scripture and how pliable we are to the divine guidance we receive from it. It is not enough to be able to parrot a definition of inspiration that satisfies professors or church authorities. What matters is how we consume and conform our lives to Scripture.

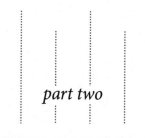

part two

FIVE MODELS
of SCRIPTURE

DOCUMENTS

And [John] the Presbyter used to say this, "Mark became Peter's interpreter and wrote accurately all that he remembered, not, indeed, in order, of the things said or done by the Lord."

—EUSEBIUS[1]

Evangelical commentator Robert Gundry employed both the documents model and the stories model when he wrote his commentary on Matthew's Gospel. He treated the gospel as a record of events in Jesus's life, imprinted by the memories of eyewitnesses and early believers, and in this way was using the documents model. But he also understood Matthew to be writing a narrative according to the expectations awakened by Matthew's reading of the Old Testament, and so was also employing the stories model. With the stories model activated, Gundry presents narratives within Matthew such as the visit of the magi or Herod's slaughter of the innocents in an attempt to kill Jesus as not necessarily the record of what happened, but as possible additions to the story to emphasize favorite themes in Matthew.[2] Evangelicals who held exclusively to a documents model for the Gospels denounced Gundry's commentary soon after it appeared. Because the Evangelical Theological Society viewed Gundry's commentary as presenting the Gospel of Matthew as not inerrant, it asked him either to change his position on Matthew or withdraw his membership from their organization. He chose the latter option.[3]

In contrast to this drama, Catholic commentator Joseph Fitzmyer noted that the Catholic position on the early chapters of the gospel is not to consider

1. Eusebius, *Ecclesiastical History* 3.39.15 (Lake, 297).

2. Gundry, *Matthew*, 26–41, 627–40; e.g., "unhistorical embellishment" in historical novels is similar to Matthew's technique (631); Matthew's literary art is analogous to the rabbis' creative works of "midrash and haggadah" (637).

3. Keylock, "Evangelical Scholars Remove Robert Gundry."

them as historically accurate. Fitzmyer is also motivated by literary considerations to note that Luke and Acts, as historical documents, are different
from what we expect of historical documents today: "Since Luke's is a form of
historical writing laced with a concern for religious guarantee, proclamation,
and didactic, it may well fit into categories of ancient literary writing but fail
to live up to the standards of modern historiography." He goes on to write,

> Biblical inspiration does not make history out of what was not such or in-
> tended to be such. The guarantee that is implied in biblical inspiration con-
> cerns truth, but the truth that is involved is often not literal but analogous
> and differs with the literary form being used: poetic truth, rhetorical truth,
> parabolic truth, epistolary truth, even "gospel truth"—apart from historical
> truth itself. Nor is every affirmation in the past tense, even in a narrative,
> necessarily meant to be "historical." The extent to which it is metaphorical
> or symbolic would still have to be assessed [and excluded] before one comes
> down on the side of historical truth.[4]

I retell the story of Gundry's commentary and compare its reception with
Fitzmyer's discussion of the historical value of some parts of the early chapters
of the Gospels to help you understand the difficulties that arise when people
consider a narrative in the Bible while differing on whether such a narrative
represents a document from the time the narrated events occurred or not.
Gundry and Fitzmyer, an evangelical Protestant and a Catholic, both seem
open to employing both documents and stories models when reading the Gospels. Gundry's peers in the Evangelical Theological Society, as they reviewed
his commentary in the early 1980s, held to a rigidly defined documents model.
The moral of the story for us is always to clarify what our expectations are
when we read the text and, when disagreements arise, to discuss the models
with which the differing parties are reading Scripture.

DEFINITION AND CHARACTERISTICS OF THE DOCUMENTS MODEL

This model reads the Bible as a compilation of direct imprints from the past,
providing direct evidence for events and ideas contained in the discourse or for
the life situation of the author (or authors) and the first audience of the text.

---

4. Fitzmyer, *Gospel According to Luke I–IX*, 15 (first quotation), 17–18 (block quotation).
The latter quotation is followed by a reference to the Pontifical Biblical Commission's *Instruction on the Historical Truth of the Gospels*.

You know that someone is using the documents model . . .

. . . when they seek to identify and argue that a specific human authored a book of the Bible. Those focused on reading Exodus–Deuteronomy as documents produced during Israel's exodus and wilderness experience will argue for Moses as the author of these books. Similarly, those focused primarily on reading the Gospels as straightforward records of Jesus's ministry on earth sometimes focus on proving the traditionally named authors of the canonical gospels.

. . . when they emphasize that eyewitness testimony is behind a given book of the Bible. The statement of Papias (ca. 60–130 CE), preserved in Eusebius,[5] that Mark wrote his gospel from Peter's teaching is good evidence for understanding Mark not to have been an eyewitness himself but a disciple and secretary of Peter, who was an eyewitness. Richard Bauckham seeks to confirm Papias's testimony regarding the Gospel of Mark by noting how the gospel shows a number of features that fit with eyewitness testimony. The Gospel of Mark refers to Peter more frequently than the other gospels. It uses what appears to be Peter's eyewitness testimony at the beginning and ending.[6] It also uses "internal focalization" to present the narrative as though we experience it through Peter's psychological and spatial vantage points.[7]

. . . when they seek to discover and prove the date(s) when a given book of the Bible was written and/or edited. Early dates for Old Testament books such as Deuteronomy and New Testament books such as Luke often amount to attempts to draw readers out of the stories or oracles models and into the documents model. But even an argument for a late date of a book depends on a mindset that the book is a document best representing a later cultural and historical moment rather than an earlier one.[8]

. . . when they seek to discover and prove what sources were used in the composition of a biblical book. Whether one encounters Julius Wellhausen's Documentary Hypothesis in relation to the Pentateuch or B. H. Streeter's

---

5. Eusebius, *Ecclesiastical History* 3.39.15.
6. Bauckham, *Jesus and the Eyewitnesses*, 124–27.
7. Bauckham, *Jesus and the Eyewitnesses*, 163.
8. Pervo, *Dating Acts*.

work on the Synoptic Gospels, most source-critical works, whether their results are viewed as conservative or liberal, are locked into a documents model of the biblical books.[9]

. . . when they seek to harmonize Scripture's differing accounts of the same event. Singular commitment to the documents model and a specific view of Scripture's inspiration led Harold Lindsell to say that when all four gospels' accounts of Jesus's trial are read, it is best to understand that Peter denied Jesus six times. This was what he needed to say in order to harmonize the accounts. Lindsell adopted the reconstruction that Peter was given two warnings regarding how he would deny Jesus three times. In the fulfillment of these warnings, Peter did deny Jesus, for a total of six times. Lindsell concludes that the witness of the four gospel authors "agrees with a completeness and precision that never marked the word of four witnesses in a courtroom."[10] In general, people who do not read Scripture on multiple levels seek to harmonize accounts that seem in tension with one another, as Lindsell does by saying that Peter actually denied Jesus six times, or they come to view the Bible as unreliable. This is because they can only read biblical narratives as documents. But if one follows the patristic and medieval traditions of reading the Bible on both literal and spiritual levels, one is more apt to say that in certain places Scripture is best read not on the literal level but on a spiritual level. Augustine, who was bothered by what he considered the poor literary quality of the Old Testament, began to take steps toward following Christ and entering the church when he heard Ambrose insisting that certain texts be read spiritually and not on a literal level.[11]

. . . when they present a book of the Bible as evidence for what a community believed or how a community lived. Christian scholars sometimes employ the documents model for this goal when studying the Old Testament. They may have an academic, historical interest in ancient Israel. Often there is a deeper agenda, such as to show that worship practices of the Israelites were somehow inferior to Christianity. In the New Testament, this sign of the documents model is especially evident in approaches that view the canonical gospels as written within or addressed to specific communities.[12]

9. Wellhausen, *Die Composition des Hexateuchs*; Streeter, *Four Gospels*.
10. Lindsell, *Battle for the Bible*, 174–76, quotation from 176.
11. Augustine, *Confessions* 6.4.6 (Boulding, 140).
12. For example, this approach to the Gospel of Matthew is on full display in Sim, *Gospel of Matthew*; Vledder and van Aarde, "Social Stratification." And on the Gospel of John this

Specific Applications of the Documents Model

The two main ways of applying this model, not necessarily mutually exclusive, are to read the biblical books as faith-corroborating time capsules or as artifacts of authors' and first audiences' faith and life situations.

Faith-Corroborating Time Capsules

Those who begin with the Bible in their explanation of the Christian faith can tend to view it as a repository of ancient documents. The discourse in the Bible is then treated as primary evidence for the antiquity of the Bible and the correspondence between its record and historical events.

In this time-capsules application of the documents model, differences in the biblical narratives among themselves or differences between a biblical narrative and what is known of life in the ancient Near East or Mediterranean world are considered to be challenges to the Bible's authenticity and reliability and deserving of tension-resolving explanations. Readers who consider the Bible to be a collection of documents that record what happened in the past are apt to treat Genesis 1–3 as an account that matches how our world came to be. Thus, they accept that the earth was prepared in seven days—whether each of these days was twenty-four hours or many years long. They tend to view the origins of the human race as starting with Adam and Eve, who really lived in a garden, where a serpent spoke to Eve. The documents readers do not immediately think of reading the Bible alongside extrabiblical writings that are similar in genre in order to understand the Bible better. For example, the documents approach does not immediately prompt one to read the Gilgamesh epic or the Enuma Elish in order to understand any of the Old Testament's creation accounts (Gen 1:1–2:4a; 2:4b–3:24; Job 38–41; Ps 104; Prov 8:22–31).

In the descriptions of the selection of the site for the Jerusalem temple provided by Deuteronomistic writers (2 Sam 24) and the Chronicler (1 Chr 21), there are significant differences in the cost of the land and sacrificial oxen that David bought when choosing the temple site. The Deuteronomistic writers say that it cost David fifty silver shekels, while the Chronicler tells us that David paid six hundred gold shekels for the site (2 Sam 24:24; 1 Chr 21:25). The more invested a reader is in reading Scripture as a set of documents, the more difficulty she will have with it. The one who can read Scripture only as documents will try to harmonize the two texts. Someone with more sensitivity to

---

approach is operative in R. E. Brown, *Community of the Beloved Disciple*; Byrne, "Faith of the Beloved Disciple."

the genres of Scripture might read 2 Samuel 24 as a document containing the actual amount that David paid for the threshing floor, while reading 1 Chronicles 21 as a theologically informed retelling of the story.

When Christians try to relate Old Testament prophets to the New Testament, the time-capsules application of the documents approach can predispose readers to regard Old Testament prophecies as discourse with only single referents. Thus, Isaiah 7:14 is read only as a prediction of the birth of Jesus, since Matthew 1:23 is read as a document stating that Jesus's birth fulfills this prophecy. Explanations for how Isaiah 7:14 makes perfect sense as a prophecy first fulfilled in the lifetime of King Ahaz might be ignored by someone locked into the time-capsules application of the documents model.

The "documents as time capsules" approach can lead to a regard for the Gospels as transcripts of what Jesus actually said. But how could all four gospels be transcripts when Jesus's discourse is presented differently? Bruce answers the question by suggesting that part of the difference in discourse is that Jesus was speaking to rural folk in Galilee in the Synoptic Gospels and to the religious authorities in Jerusalem and to his own disciples in John. He harmonizes the difference in narrated time—one year of ministry in the Synoptic Gospels and three years in John—by saying that the Synoptic Gospels' narratives of Jesus's ministry occur in the time period occurring between John 5 and John 7.[13] It is characteristic of the documents model that little attention is paid to influences on the text that are secondary to the recorded discourse and events, such as the author's literary or theological agenda and the author's audience.

Artifacts of Authors' and First Audiences' Faith and Life Situations

The view that the Scriptures are essentially documents is not limited to the conservative side, however. Jewish scholar Benjamin Sommer sets up a dichotomy between those who read the Bible as Scripture and those who read it as a collection of artifacts from an ancient time period. The latter only acknowledge people living millennia ago to be the audience of the writings in the Bible. But those who read the Bible as Scripture claim that it was written for themselves and others reading it today. After all, the Old Testament emphasizes the descendants of Abraham, Isaac, and Jacob, and these descendants are alive today.[14] Another scholar who approaches the Bible as a collection of artifacts is the historian Bart Ehrman. The value of the New Testament books,

13. Bruce, *New Testament Documents*, 53, 55.
14. Sommer, *Revelation and Authority*, 11–12.

as Ehrman views them, is not first of all in reliably guiding the reader to understand what happened in the life and ministry of Jesus, but rather in leading the reader to appreciate the process by which some expressions of Christian belief and practice won out over other expressions amid the diversity of early Christian belief and practice. Ehrman's is the approach of a historian who views the New Testament as evidence for the struggle to assert a dominant interpretation of the life and significance of Jesus.[15]

Ehrman writes his New Testament textbook as a historian. He admits that some historians can affirm that the miraculous events recorded in Scripture happened, but states that when historians affirm the miraculous, they are speaking as believers, not as historians. Ehrman articulates his basic principles for explaining the miraculous in Scripture: the philosophical question of whether a miracle can happen is different from the historical question of whether a miracle can be demonstrated to have happened; in the ancient world, people expected the divine realm to interact with the human realm, and thus more readily called certain events "miracles"; we define miracles now as occurrences that are inconsistent with how our world usually functions, according to Enlightenment-based science, and therefore miracles are events that are least likely to have happened. This leads Ehrman to conclude that "since historians can establish only what probably happened in the past, they cannot show that miracles happened, since this would involve a contradiction—that the most improbable event is the most probable." And the implication of this orientation for Ehrman is that he is "not able to affirm or deny the miracles that [Jesus] is reported to have done."[16]

Ehrman's approach is understandable in light of his decision to view the New Testament as a collection of documents from the past, no different in historical value from the Elephantine papyri found in Egypt. The problem with his approach is that the people who preserved, collected, and canonized the New Testament writings, as well as many students who use his textbook today, regard the New Testament as more than the "artifacts" sort of historical documents. For them it was and is a record of how the transcendent God entered into our world as a human, and a guide to how to worship God and live as a result of this entrance of the transcendent into human experience. To treat the New Testament only as a set of documents, and read them only through the lens of Enlightenment-based science, is similar to how a historian of medicine, living five or more centuries from now, might read my or your medical records. We and our primary care providers do not read our medical records in this

15. Ehrman, *New Testament*, 3–7.
16. Ehrman, *New Testament*, 244.

detached sort of way. And since Scripture still speaks to humanity today, it is inadequate to read it only as a collection of artifacts, in the detached way that this application of the documents model can generate.

But once one has learned of some of the historical questions behind Scripture, such as the lack of any evidence for camels in the land of Canaan during the time of Abraham, the lack of any sign of military conquest of Canaan in the Iron Age, or the fact that Quirinius was not governor of Syria when Jesus was born (cf. Luke 2:2), then it is difficult to read the Bible simply as a compilation of time capsules. Indeed, if we are to love God with all our minds, then for those of us who have studied the Bible academically, we must read it both as scriptural time capsules and as artifacts of others' faith. If we turn our minds off and seek to read it only as scriptural time capsules, we are not fully loving God with our minds (Deut 6:5).[17]

To prepare ourselves for reading the Bible responsibly, we must ask and respond to this question: Is the Bible unique among all other writings, or is it simply one artifact from ancient times on the level of inscriptions, records, and manuscripts that have survived from the cultures that produced the biblical texts?[18] I answer first that it is unique among all writings. The church recognizes the Bible's inspiration. And Scripture continues to speak to humanity, despite declining familiarity with it, in ways that no other writing does. At the same time, the Bible is a cultural artifact and can be fruitfully studied with methods used for other artifacts from the cultures contemporary with it. With Sommer, I advocate reading the Bible both as Scripture and as an artifact.[19] In the context of this chapter, I am saying that there are parts of the Bible that are best read as faith-corroborating time capsules. And there are other parts that must be read as artifacts of others' faith. Reading the Bible as a collection of artifacts that can be taken apart can provide insights we would not otherwise see, and can help us appreciate the unique contributions of Scripture. While I cannot replicate Sommer's ability to bridge the ages from the earliest sources in the Pentateuch through the medieval rabbis and on to modern Jewish theologians, I think something analogous can be done with the New Testament, and in this book I will demonstrate how both applications of the documents model, whether viewing the Scriptures as faith-corroborating time capsules or the artifacts of others' faith, can enrich our understanding of the New Testament as Scripture.

17. Sommer, *Revelation and Authority*, 12–13.
18. Sommer, *Revelation and Authority*, 14–15.
19. Sommer, *Revelation and Authority*, 24–26.

OLD TESTAMENT TEXTS OFTEN READ AS DOCUMENTS

Not all Old Testament accounts of the Israelites' occupation of the land of Canaan are corroborated by material evidence. For example, archaeology shows that the Canaanite cities of Heshbon and Dibon were not occupied during the time of the Late Bronze Age, when the Israelites' entry to the land of Canaan is supposed to have occurred. Also, the Israelite villages in the central highlands of Canaan that have been excavated show no signs of fortification, thus raising questions about the military conquest that the book of Joshua portrays.[20] Textual studies of Joshua lead scholars to believe that it was completed at or after Judah's exile to Babylon in 586 BCE.[21] It thus appears to be a composition written to inspire the people of Judah when they were exiled or returning from exile in Babylon.

This is therefore a case in which the documents model points beyond itself. Some of the narratives of conquest of the promised land need not be accepted as a day-to-day transcription of how the Israelites, after forty years in the wilderness, occupied Canaan. Some of the conquest accounts have been preserved as Scripture for what they teach about God's presence with his people, and how covenant-keeping leads to God's blessing. But though they are integrally part of God's word, they do not all have to function as the time-capsules application of the documents model would lead readers to expect. Divergence from what the material evidence indicates helps us better understand the agenda of these texts. We can now see and understand how some events, though not a straightforward record of what actually occurred, came to be added to the text.

A documents-oriented consideration of the sense in which the book of Joshua records the occupation of the promised land can help us with the moral challenge that the conquest narratives of Joshua raise. If the Israelites gradually emerged as a people in Canaan, rather than occupying it by battling under Joshua's leadership, then some of the "holy war" narratives, such as the fall of Jericho or the annihilation of the town of Ai, can be recognized as compositions that express how God is present and holy among his people. Since they likely did not happen, they provide less of an incentive to annihilate native populations than they provided Cotton Mather for his sermons and writings about killing American Indians, or the Dutch settlers who similarly used these sorts of texts to inspire and justify their conquest of South Africa.

20. Collins, *Short Introduction*, 116–17.
21. Collins, *Short Introduction*, 112.

NEW TESTAMENT TEXTS OFTEN READ AS DOCUMENTS

Those viewing the Bible as a collection of documents consider the Gospels to be eyewitness accounts of all that happened. They might be ready to concede that the author of Luke's Gospel was not an eyewitness, since he does not include himself among the eyewitnesses (1:2). But in general, they will read the Gospels as biographies written by eyewitnesses or compiled from eyewitnesses' records. The infancy narratives of Jesus in Matthew and Luke are often the places where those who read the Gospels as historical documents can sniff out authors who do not share this model of Scripture.

The New Testament scholar F. F. Bruce wrote a small book that has been through a number of editions, *The New Testament Documents: Are They Reliable?* This book begins with the assumption that the New Testament's books are documents whose status as "truly historical records" needs to be weighed.[22] As part of his agenda in proving that the New Testament documents are indeed reliable, Bruce dates the Gospels and Acts rather early: Mark to 64/65, Luke to just before 70, and Matthew just after 70. He also considers Acts to have been written soon after Luke.[23] The copious manuscript evidence for the New Testament's books is presented as evidence for their "authenticity" and "general integrity."[24]

Bauckham also finds confirmation of the eyewitness-based character of the Gospel of Mark in its "plural-to-singular narrative device." This is a pattern in which a plural subject is followed immediately by a singular subject, referring to Jesus. For example, in Mark 14:32 we read, "And *they* came to an area named Gethsemane, and *he* said to his disciples . . ." The synoptic parallels make the subjects of both clauses singular (Matt 26:36; Luke 22:39–40). This plural-to-singular tendency is much more predominant in Mark than in Matthew or Luke. In this example, Matthew and Luke make it clear that the disciples are with Jesus by adding phrases to that effect, but they do not switch subjects from plural to singular in midsentence as Mark does. One could argue that Mark has a clumsy style, which Matthew and Luke seek to improve. But taking into account the other distinctive features of Mark's narrative, Bauckham argues that Mark has intentionally structured his gospel to provide Peter's perspective to readers.[25]

---

22. Bruce, *New Testament Documents*, 1.
23. Bruce, *New Testament Documents*, 7.
24. Bruce, *New Testament Documents*, 15, citing Kenyon, *Bible and Archaeology*, 288–89.
25. Bauckham, *Jesus and the Eyewitnesses*, 179.

Bauckham interprets Papias's statement about the composition of Matthew to reflect the idea that Matthew was an eyewitness, since he aligns Peter and Matthew in Papias's statement. Just as Peter recounted his experiences of Jesus's life and teachings and these were recorded by Mark, so Matthew wrote down Jesus's teachings in Hebrew and these were translated by others into Greek.[26] In this way of construing the text, Matthew appears like Peter to have been an eyewitness, though Papias does not explicitly state that.

Bruce imagines Luke to have been a companion of Paul, which is a reasonable assumption based on the "we" passages in Acts. He thinks that Luke could have taught Paul the details of Jesus's life and teachings.[27] Bruce thinks that the Synoptic Gospels were written by forty to fifty years after the crucifixion, based mostly on eyewitness testimony, and that they were "transmitted along independent and trustworthy lines."[28] It is difficult to affirm the independent transmission of the Synoptic Gospels' material, however, for as Bruce himself acknowledges, Matthew and Luke contain a great amount of material that is found in Mark, and Matthew and Luke also share a significant amount of material not found in Mark, what is called the Q material (from the German word for source, *Quelle*).

Luke employs a historiographical term for eyewitnesses (*autoptai*) in his prologue and reserves his "witness" or "testimony" language to Jesus's contemporary followers and Paul.[29] And Bauckham notes how "we" is used as the subject in Johannine literature of the New Testament to connote authoritative testimony.[30] He correlates the "we" statements in the Gospel of John with the claim in John 21:24 to argue that the beloved disciple is the eyewitness author of the whole gospel.[31] Bauckham claims that the more explicitly interpreted narrative that is provided in John's Gospel does not detract from his claim that it is written by an eyewitness. This is because Greco-Roman historiography involved recounting history as though it had a plot, and included interpretation of the events. Bauckham thus claims that John, which is the only gospel that explicitly claims to have been written by an eyewitness, appropriately fits the expectations of

---

26. Bauckham, *Jesus and the Eyewitnesses*, 222–23.

27. Bruce, *New Testament Documents*, 39.

28. Bruce, *New Testament Documents*, 43.

29. Bauckham, *Jesus and the Eyewitnesses*, 389.

30. Bauckham, *Jesus and the Eyewitnesses*, 370–81, citing 3 John 9–12; 1 John 1:1–5; 4:11–16; John 1:14–16; 3:10–13.

31. Bauckham, *Jesus and the Eyewitnesses*, 390–409.

Greco-Roman history.[32] Bauckham's thesis finally is that in the testimony or witness that people have provided about Jesus, history and theology intersect.[33]

A time-capsules application of the documents model insists that all of Scripture represents "historical truth," to use Fitzmyer's phrase cited in the introduction to this chapter. Those readers who are locked into the documents model and cannot reconcile how certain gospel narratives are time-capsule descriptions might easily turn to the other application of the documents model—that of the artifacts of others' faith and life—such as we saw above in regard to Ehrman's New Testament textbook. It is probably better not to stay completely with one model, but always to balance the documents model with at least one or two other models. Since the Gospels were preserved for how they provided a life narrative for believers to follow, they must always be read with the stories model. And since the Gospels were read daily or weekly as believers gathered in worship, they must also be read with an appreciation for the prayers model of Scripture.

KEY ISSUES IN THE DOCUMENTS MODEL

The long section that follows on history and the historical-critical method might bore some readers, and you have my permission to skip this and move toward the end of this chapter, to the "Documents Model in the Classroom" or the "Documents Model in Ministry" headings, whichever fits your situation. But I include the key issues on history and the historical-critical method below so that students can understand how their teachers have come to treat the Bible as a dissection specimen to be cut open and coldly analyzed. This approach is the result of centuries of focused reading and investigation of Scripture from within the documents model. As one who thinks that no single model of Scripture should be employed when trying to give a complete account of the text, I do not think that every aspect of the development traced below has been helpful for our engagement with Scripture. But as the past must be recounted when any family is moving toward unity, we need to know what has happened with our use of the documents model so that we can understand where we are today.

32. Bauckham, *Jesus and the Eyewitnesses*, 410–11.
33. Bauckham, *Jesus and the Eyewitnesses*, 508.

What Is History?

It is especially among those who view Scripture's books as documents that one's idea of history comes into play. An early step in the specific option within this model of Scripture that reads Scripture as a documentary record of what happened in the lives of named characters in the text was the Septuagint translators' decision to group the books of Joshua through 2 Chronicles into a section called "History." Christian Bibles in our own day continue to designate this section of the Old Testament as "History" or "Historical Books." In contrast, Judaism places Joshua, Judges, and 1 Samuel to 2 Kings in the "Early Prophets" and places the other books in our English Bible's "History" section—Ruth, 1–2 Chronicles, Ezra, Nehemiah, and Esther—in the "Writings" section of the Hebrew Bible.

A fundamental question is whether the passage of human history has a plot or not. C. H. Dodd weighs in on this question when he writes that God rules over history, so that God's will and purpose are displayed in the unfolding of history's events. At the same time, Dodd denies that the Bible has any evidence for viewing the course of history as preplanned or fixed by God ahead of time.[34]

The approach to the Bible's books as though they are faith-corroborating time capsules, whether this occurs through attempts to correlate biblical narratives to archaeological finds or through the quest to prove the Gospels' early composition and claim that they were written by eyewitnesses, is used by some as the primary foundation for the reader's confidence in the value of the Bible. The difficulty with this approach is that it is rather easy to find aspects of biblical narrative that cannot, on a literal reading of the text, be historically accurate. If any piece of evidence contradicts the text's claims, such as archaeological results that do not match the biblical witness or tension between parallel accounts in the biblical text, it is not uncommon for some to decide that the Christian faith itself is unreliable and abandon the Christian faith. These results come from too rigid a grasp on the documents model.

The Bible's books are documents in the sense that they record what our ancestors in the faiths of Judaism and Christianity considered stories, laws, poetry, apocalyptic, and genealogies worth preserving and valuable for communicating God's immanence and transcendence in relation to humanity. They do include time capsules that can corroborate faith. Other parts are best

---

34. Dodd, *Bible Today*, 130.

regarded as artifacts of others' faith rather than a historical record. As documents, the Bible's books accurately represent key ideas that are central to Judaism and Christianity: the existence of God, God's creation of and sustenance of the physical world, the election of Israel, the incarnation of God's Son in the person of Jesus of Nazareth born of the Virgin Mary, and the crucifixion and resurrection of Jesus. But there are plenty of internal signals in some biblical books demonstrating that they cannot be read as though all their contents match in all details what happened.

Historical Criticism: The Documents Model as a Battleground

The documents model of Scripture has been the site of much reflection and many battles over the nature of history and the purpose behind the narratives in the Bible. The reflection and battles occurred as Western civilization experienced in the Enlightenment a reevaluation of history and God's involvement in it. This reevaluation led to a new way of reading Scripture within the documents model, historical criticism. In the following survey I point out some key moments in the move among academic readers of Scripture from the "time capsule for us" application of the documents model to the "artifacts of others' faith" application.

Up to the Enlightenment, scholars viewed history as a stage in which God is fully present. To live a human life on earth was to participate in a world where God was also active. But then, beginning with John Duns Scotus, human experience began to be understood as independent of God. Duns Scotus rejected the idea of final causality at work in our world. He understood humans to have the freedom that God has. Whereas formerly philosophers had understood God to know humanity in the very act of knowing himself, Duns Scotus claimed that God knows humanity objectively, in a manner independent from God's self-knowledge. These steps all led to a view of history in which people are free agents in a world in which God is not immanently active.[35] As this view of history spread into the fabric of Western civilization during the Enlightenment and modern period, exegesis of Scripture came to be viewed as a historical investigation of the Bible as a set of documents from the past, perhaps acknowledged as the documents of our ancestors in the faith. The central question of exegesis moved away from that of the church fathers and medieval

---

35. Levering, *Participatory Biblical Exegesis*, 18–20, citing Boulnois, *Être et representation*; Boulnois, "Reading Duns Scotus"; Ingham and Dreyer, *Philosophical Vision*, 97, 147, 149.

exegetes, "How is God—active in the unfolding history of humanity—teaching us how to live?" The question under the changed view of history became "How did the events narrated in the Bible actually happen?" or, in the nonnarrative texts, "How did the biblical authors' various religious views function in their respective cultural, historical, and social contexts?" Orthodox scholar Michael Legaspi summarizes this change by describing how Scripture, a text viewed as inspired and understood through the traditions of the community of faith, died, beginning in the sixteenth century, by the hands of those who considered themselves to be defending it. They killed it by trying to evaluate its narrative assertions and general relevance with the ever-sharpening tools of historical criticism and philology, which are more concerned with "objective" historical reconstruction than with learning what God's dealings with humanity are in history. Legaspi then describes how the academic Bible came to replace Scripture, beginning about two centuries later.[36]

Another step in the movement from trust in the Scripture's narratives and regard for its books as time capsules written for us to a more detached perspective on them as artifacts of others' faith occurred when it became possible for individuals to interpret the Bible for themselves. In the early sixteenth century, Desiderius Erasmus assumed that the Bible was the church's collection of writings, to be interpreted by the church fathers and contemporary church leaders. In contrast, Martin Luther taught that an individual could interpret the Bible for herself or himself, enabled by the Holy Spirit and any other spiritual gifts given to that individual.[37]

Resistance to the view of the New Testament's books as faith-corroborating time capsules came with the rise of historical criticism. A key moment in its rise was the publication of *On the Proof of the Spirit and Power* by Gotthold Ephraim Lessing (1729–1781). In trying to sort through the Bible's record of miracles and the question of whether miracles happened or not, Lessing said that there were truths of religion and truths of history. The former were considered to be innate truths that all would recognize as truth. The latter were described as statements that can be verified by historical research, though not forming the basis for religious faith. This distinction between two kinds of truth led to the expression "Lessing's ditch," a divide between what the rationalist Lessing thought were innate truths all would accept and the truths that

---

36. Legaspi, *Death of Scripture*, 10–12, 21–22, 129–69.
37. Legaspi, *Death of Scripture*, 16.

could be historically verified.[38] The practical result of Lessing's distinction was that a reader could interpret a narrative such as Jesus's raising of Lazarus from the dead as religiously true but not historically true.

As acceptance of what could be historically verified continued to wane, theologians tried out other foundations for Christian theology, such as a person's religious sensibility or the moral conviction of what one should do. The former foundation was attempted by Friedrich Schleiermacher (1768–1834) and the latter by nineteenth-century theologians following the ethical orientation of Immanuel Kant (1724–1804).[39]

Further impetus in the nineteenth century against viewing the biblical books as historical documents came with Ernst Troeltsch (1865–1923). He taught that historical truths were what could be shown to be probable, analogous to what we observe in our world, and embedded in what we know to be our world. Troeltsch's particular focus of the historical method resulted in increasing skepticism regarding what could be proven as historically true.[40]

A flag of surrender in regard to the time-capsule view of the Bible's documents was finally raised by New Testament scholar Martin Kähler (1835–1912). He concluded that since very little could be proven as historically true, we should stop trying to verify the historical claims made of Jesus in the Gospels and instead simply focus on the kerygmatic Christ—Christ as portrayed in the Gospels and proclaimed in Acts.[41] In the framework of this chapter, Kähler was advocating that the Bible should no longer be looked on as a collection of faith-corroborating time capsules, but only as a set of artifacts that displays others' faith.

The trajectory traced above paved the way for the claim of Reformed theologian Karl Barth (1886–1968) that history offered no basis for faith, that faith should rest rather on the proclaimed Jesus that is seen in the Gospels and other New Testament books.[42] New Testament scholar Rudolf Bultmann (1884–1976) followed Barth in jettisoning history as a path to understanding Christ. Bultmann wrote, "I do indeed think that we can know almost nothing concerning the life and personality of Jesus, since the early Christian sources show no interest in either, are moreover fragmentary and often legendary; and other sources about Jesus do not exist. . . . What has been written in the last hundred

---

38. Dunn, *Christianity in the Making*, 1:68, citing Lessing, *Lessing's Theological Writings*, 51–56.

39. Dunn, *Christianity in the Making*, 1:71.

40. Dunn, *Christianity in the Making*, 1:69–70.

41. Dunn, *Christianity in the Making*, 1:72.

42. Dunn, *Christianity in the Making*, 1:73–74.

and fifty years on the life of Jesus, his personality and the development of his inner life, is fantastic and romantic."[43]

Dunn clarifies the quotation above, explaining that Bultmann was primarily criticizing attempts to describe Jesus's personality and spiritual life. Bultmann directed attention to what he considered to be the main result of the historical records of Jesus and his ministry: the Gospels in themselves are not the main evidence for people's belief in Scripture; instead, they show those who study them how the early Christian communities worshiped and lived. This is definitely an "artifacts of others' faith" application of the documents model. In his use of form criticism (analysis of gospel paragraphs by focusing on specific discourse forms—e.g., miracle story, controversy story, or teaching summary), Bultmann offered the situation-in-life in which the actions and sayings of Jesus were repeated and valued. He did this while asserting that deeds and words were composed or revised on the basis of the needs of the community.[44] This assertion marginalized traditional views that the Gospels were transcripts of what Jesus had actually said. Thus, Bultmann was not treating the Gospels as time-capsule documents that directly reflect Jesus's words and actions; instead, he treated them as artifacts that reflect the sensibilities of the early church.

The Jesus that Bultmann offered to believers was a Jesus encountered in one's own attempts to understand one's existence. The quest for the historical Jesus begun in the nineteenth century was considered impossible to pursue, since Kähler had rejected the Gospels' historical value for the life of Jesus, and since Bultmann had emphasized their primary function to be recording the early church's discourse. That quest for the historical Jesus was also considered invalid because it sought support for faith from historical evidence, a quest that was caricatured as denying the very nature of faith. According to Bultmann, people had no ability and no necessity to know anything regarding Jesus's life on earth.[45]

Scholars returned to a historical consideration of Jesus's life on earth after Bultmann's student Ernst Käsemann asserted in 1953 that significant danger lay in separating the Jesus of history from the Christ of faith. He noted that this could give rise to docetism, the view that Jesus only seemed to be human but was not actually human. He observed also that the Gospels themselves showed how the early church took great interest in the historical life of Jesus on earth, and recommended that scholars return to study this life as history.

43. Dunn, *Christianity in the Making*, 1:75, citing Bultmann, *Jesus and the Word*, 8.
44. Dunn, *Christianity in the Making*, 1:76–77.
45. Dunn, *Christianity in the Making*, 1:77–79.

In response, Bultmann admitted that what Jesus preached is also part of the proclamation of the church. Bultmann thus revised his earlier approach, which treated Jesus's teachings under the heading of Judaism. In this second quest initiated by Käsemann, the Gospels were again brought under the spotlight of historical scrutiny, and people argued that they do serve as documents from which historical truth can be gleaned. Käsemann considered Jesus's self-presentation as above Torah and the person of Moses as a central idea that could be proven by historical research. Günther Bornkamm argued that Jesus's proclamation of the kingdom of God as the start of the new age was another historically verifiable datum. Joachim Jeremias added to this the description of Jesus addressing God in prayer as Abba. This quest empowered scholars to identify certain sayings of Jesus as actually spoken by Jesus. The tools that allowed scholars to do this were the criteria of authenticity, especially the criterion of dissimilarity: if a given account of Jesus's words or actions would likely not have arisen in Judaism or in the early church, then it must reflect what Jesus actually said or did.[46]

But the criterion of dissimilarity was found wanting, for it disallowed any continuity between Jesus and the Judaism of his day, a difficult assertion to make in the light of how embedded humanity is in cultures of origin. A third quest for the historical Jesus thus began in the mid-1980s. This quest reacted against the second quest's overdependence on the criterion of dissimilarity and asserted instead that the first consideration for historical research on Jesus of Nazareth is to understand him as a first-century Jew, at home among other Jews. This was a helpful corrective, for liberal New Testament scholars had painted first-century Judaism in a most negative light, in order to highlight the uniqueness of Jesus.[47]

In the late nineteenth century, concerned about the rise of historical criticism, Pope Leo XIII wrote an encyclical that called on Catholic biblical scholars to out-hustle the historical critics in order to demonstrate the truth of Scripture.

> Since the divine and infallible magisterium of the Church rests also on the authority of Holy Scripture, the first thing to be done is to vindicate the trustworthiness of the sacred records at least as human documents, from which can be clearly proved, as from primitive and authentic testimony, the divinity and the mission of Christ our Lord, the institution of

---

46. Dunn, *Christianity in the Making*, 1:79–82.
47. Dunn, *Christianity in the Making*, 1:82–86.

a hierarchical Church, and the primacy of Peter and his successors. It is most desirable, therefore, that there should be numerous members of the clergy well-prepared to enter upon a contest of this nature and to repulse hostile assaults, chiefly trusting in that armor of God recommended by the Apostle (cf. Eph 6:13–17), but also not unaccustomed to modern methods of attack.[48]

The last phrase of the quotation above includes the recommendation that Catholics involved in the study of Scripture know the methods of study, including the historical-critical method, in order to defend the integrity of Scripture and its witness to the Catholic faith.

It was an open question for many Scripture scholars in the mid to late nineteenth century regarding how they should approach Scripture in light of the apparently reasonable questions and assertions of the historical-critical method. Alfred Loisy left the Catholic Church since he thought the historical-critical method's findings had undermined the scriptural moorings of the magisterium. In contrast, Dominican scholar Marie-Joseph Lagrange found a productive way to use some aspects of the historical-critical method to enhance our understanding of Scripture while still respecting patristic interpretations.[49]

In 1902 Leo XIII founded a group called the Pontifical Biblical Commission to help the Catholic Church interpret the Bible in faithful and responsible ways. Leo XIII presented the purposes for the commission in his letter *Vigilantiae studiique*: to promote the study of Scripture among Catholics, to use scientific methods to answer academic attacks on Scripture, and to study and provide guidance on questions regarding Scripture. The group was originally composed exclusively of cardinals, but in 1971 Paul VI, with his *motu propio* called *Sedula curia*, reconstituted the commission so that it no longer was composed exclusively of cardinals but rather became composed of those who teach biblical studies, so that the group now serves as a consulting body to the Congregation for the Doctrine of the Faith.[50]

This group helps the Catholic Church interpret Scripture faithfully in light of challenges from within and without the church. Significant documents that the commission has issued within the last half century are *The Interpretation*

---

48. Leo XIII, *Providentissimus Deus* §35 (Béchard, *Scripture Documents*, 51–52).

49. Levering, *Participatory Biblical Exegesis*, 55–57.

50. See "The Pontifical Biblical Commission," http://www.vatican.va/roman_curia/con gregations/cfaith/pcb_documents/rc_con_cfaith_pro_14071997_pcbible_en.html.

of the Bible in the Church (1993); *The Jewish People and Their Sacred Scriptures in the Christian Bible* (2001); *The Bible and Morality: Biblical Roots of Christian Conduct* (2008); and *On the Inspiration and Truth of Sacred Scripture* (2014).

After Leo XIII, further impetus for the academic, scientific study of Scripture among Catholics came in the encyclical of Pius XII titled *Divino afflante Spiritu*. Pius XII wrote the encyclical in response to the popularity of an anonymously published booklet that sharply criticized the scientific study of the Bible, advocating instead for a mystical exegesis. The pope responded by stating that the scientific study of the Bible remains a legitimate and even necessary approach to Scripture. Fifty years later, John Paul II noted how Leo's encyclical *Providentissimus Deus* maintained the divine origin of Scripture, while Pius's *Divino afflante Spiritu* maintained the human side of its composition. In a way that parallels the incarnation, then, Scripture must be studied in light of both its divine and its human aspects.[51] What this means, practically speaking, can start to be seen in John Paul II's description of the human element in Scripture as seen in the different literary genres and other linguistic expressions within Scripture:

> *Divino afflante Spiritu* . . . particularly recommended that exegetes study the *literary genres* used in the sacred Books. . . . This recommendation starts from the concern to understand the meaning of the texts with all the accuracy and precision possible and, thus, in their historical, cultural context. A false idea of God and the Incarnation presses a certain number of Christians to take the opposite approach. They tend to believe that, since God is the absolute Being, each of his words has an absolute value, independent of all the conditions of human language. Thus, according to them, there is no room for studying these conditions in order to make distinctions that would relativize the significance of the words. However, that is where the illusion occurs and the mysteries of scriptural inspiration and Incarnation are really rejected, by clinging to a false notion of the Absolute. The God of the Bible is not an absolute Being who, crushing everything he touches, would suppress all differences and all nuances. On the contrary, he is God the Creator, who created the astonishing variety of beings "each according to its kind," as the Genesis account says repeatedly. . . . Far from destroying differences, God respects them and makes use of them (cf. 1 Cor 12:18, 24, 28). Although he expresses himself in human language, he does not give

---

51. John Paul II, "Address on *The Interpretation of the Bible in the Church*," §§6–9 (Béchard, *Scripture Documents*, 173–76). The parallel between Scripture and the incarnation was previously made in Pius XII, *Divino afflante Spiritu* §20, and again in *Dei Verbum* §13.

each expression a uniform value but uses its possible nuances with extreme flexibility and, likewise, accepts its limitations.[52]

This statement regarding the respect that must be paid to the literary genres and conventions used in Scripture means, for example, that once one sees how the seven-day creation account in Genesis 1:1–2:4 is mirroring and answering the Babylonian creation account on seven tablets, conforming to the genre of a Babylonian creation account while challenging its content, one does not need to hold that God created the earth in seven days. Or again, once one sees the humor and sociopolitical incongruities in the books of Esther and Jonah, one can readily read them as novellas designed to make specific points about Israel's place on earth, rather than historical accounts of actual experiences of characters named Esther and Jonah. As John Paul II says in the quote above, we need to grant that God's inspiration of the human authors of Scripture allowed these authors the freedom to use different modes of communication—literary genres—rather than assuming that every part of the Bible communicates truth in the same way. Jewish author Everett Fox notes the differences in genre within the single book of Exodus. Note how his recommendation for reading Exodus arises out of the variety that is in the book.

> The book emerges as a mix of historical recollection, mythical processing, and didactic retelling, what Buber and others have called a "saga." What is preserved in the book of Exodus, therefore, is a Teaching (Heb. *Tora*) based on a set of experiences, which became history for ancient Israel. Hence to understand better the workings of the book, we need to turn to its themes and its structure. This will be more fruitful than trying to find the exact location of the Sea of Reeds or Mount Sinai, or the "Lost Ark," or Moshe's burial site—of whose location "no man has knowledge until this day" (Deut. 34:6). These have all receded into archeological oblivion. What has survived of ancient Israel is its approach to history and to life, and its literature. In that sense, the book of Exodus is an attempt to distill history and to learn from it, using echoes from the past to shape the present and the future.[53]

What this quotation means for us is that if one reads a book of the Bible with the documents model, one must acknowledge that its contents differ as to the type of documents that they are. Also, very few passages in the Bible represent

---

52. John Paul II, "Address on *The Interpretation of the Bible in the Church*," §8 (Béchard, *Scripture Documents*, 174–75).

53. Fox, *Five Books of Moses*, 243.

documents that can identify the actual places and times in which the narrated events occurred.

When students are exposed to the academic Bible, they realize how the historical critics view the Bible as a collection of documents that reflect a culturally and historically limited perspective. Students will notice when their professor points out that the number of people who followed Moses out of Egypt (Exod 12:37) is exaggerated and when their professor wonders out loud whether the walls of Jericho fell as Joshua 6 describes. This can lead some students to a crisis of faith. Such crises can occur among all readers of the Bible.[54] We Christians need to remember that our faith is based on the resurrected Jesus, the Son of God. We encounter Jesus in the church and in Scripture. Our faith in Christ is not in the first place based on our preconceptions of how Scripture communicates truth. Our ancestors in the faith, faithful Jews and Christians, have passed on our Scripture to us. We can trust that God inspired Scripture's authors and guided the editors and scribes responsible for giving us the Bible in the form we have it today, and we continue to hear the God of Israel and this God's Son, Jesus, speak to us in Scripture, whether the number in Exodus 12:37 is inflated or not, and whether a prophet named Jonah was really inside a great fish for three days or not.

Historical criticism is one lens among many that we use to read the Bible. It is useful for impressing on the reader how the books in our Bibles were addressed to a people different from us, in cultures and times different from ours. It helps us recognize that the presuppositions of Scripture's authors are not always the same as ours.[55] It is useful and must be employed, because we inevitably do ask questions like "Did this really happen?" when reading texts that originate from outside our frame of reference. But in the academic study of the Bible, one encounters authors who treat the Bible as though it can only be studied through the lens of historical criticism. This is inconsistent with the reasons that the texts of the Bible have been read and treasured for generations. For all people of faith, the Bible is a witness to humanity's encounter with the transcendent. It must be respectfully regarded as more than simply a collection of documents that do not satisfy current expectations for historical and scientific reportage. In this regard, historical criticism has been rightly indicted as inadequate as a single way to read the text of the Bible. Here is what Friedrich Schlegel, a German poet and philosopher who lived from 1772 to 1829, wrote

---

54. For realistic novels that describe a crisis of faith arising out of questions regarding the Bible's truth for an Orthodox Jew, see Potok, *In the Beginning*, or for a Pentecostal Christian, see Gardner, *Flight of Peter Fromm*.

55. Jenson, *Systematic Theology*, 2:278.

about historical criticism: "The two main principles of the so-called historical criticism are the Postulate of Vulgarity and the Axiom of the Average. The Postulate of Vulgarity: everything great, good and beautiful is improbable because it is extraordinary and, at the very least, suspicious. The Axiom of the Average: as we and our surroundings are, so must it have been always and everywhere, because that, after all, is so very natural."[56] Schlegel's evaluation thus faults historical criticism for devaluing or rejecting anything in texts that it considers improbable owing to the historical critic's limited standards.

So in any study of Scripture, it must always be remembered that historical criticism is a necessary mode of reading, because it takes seriously the human authors behind the books. Some components of historical criticism were used by ancient commentators on Greek classics and by church fathers Origen, Augustine, and Jerome.[57] The quest for the literal sense of Scripture is a quest worth pursuing, and the historical-critical method is necessarily used in finding the literal sense, since this method helps to ascertain a diachronic understanding of how the text developed.[58] The reason it cannot be the only way of reading Scripture is that from the outset it ignores the main reason that the texts were written, copied, edited, and canonized, their witness to humanity's encounter with the transcendent and the church's conviction that within the Scripture, God still speaks to us.

Three Principles to Accompany Historical Criticism

If historical criticism is necessary and yet not sufficient as the only way to read Scripture, what perspectives are necessary to supplement it? In the Catholic tradition, the following three guidelines have been articulated. First, one must read Scripture as a unified whole. Second, one must take into account how the life-sustaining tradition of the church throughout the world reads Scripture. And third, one must respect the rule (sometimes called "analogy") of faith.[59]

The first of these principles means that we cannot allow one text in Scripture to function as our only explanation of a particular topic when other parts of Scripture address that topic differently. For example, Tyconius, at the beginning of his section titled "The Promises and the Law" in his *Book of Rules* for

---

56. Friedrich Schlegel, Critical Fragment no. 25 (1797), quoted in Legaspi, *Death of Scripture*, iv.

57. Pontifical Biblical Commission, *Interpretation of the Bible in the Church*, I.A (Béchard, *Scripture Documents*, 249).

58. Pontifical Biblical Commission, *Interpretation of the Bible in the Church*, I.A.4 (Béchard, *Scripture Documents*, 253).

59. Benedict XVI, *Verbum Domini* §34.

interpreting Scripture, writes, "Divine authority has it that no one can ever be justified by the works of the law. By the same authority it is absolutely certain that there have always been some who do the law and are justified."[60] Tyconius derives the first sentence from texts like Romans 3:28 within Paul's letters. He derives the second sentence from texts like Luke 1:6 and John 1:47 that describe people as righteous keepers of God's law.[61]

The second principle is illustrated by the church's traditional ways of reading the words Jesus spoke while on the cross to his mother and the beloved disciple (John 19:25–27). Beyond a documentation of words Jesus spoke before his death, the church has taken these words as significant not simply for the historical person known as the beloved disciple but for the church as a whole. So Mary's relationship with the church is one of mother to son, in a way consistent with how Revelation shows the dragon at war against "the rest of the offspring" of the Messiah's mother (Rev 12:17a).

The third principle, reading in accord with the rule of faith, is similar to the second, except that it involves reading according to traditions that have been codified by church councils or other rulings. When reading descriptions of God creating or giving birth to wisdom in Proverbs 8:22–25, then, the church does not hear the Son of God speaking, as Arius did, but rather simply personified wisdom. Similarly, to read "the Word was God" in John 1:1, as "the Word was a god," as the Jehovah's Witnesses do, is contrary to the church's rule of faith.

The Documents Model in the Classroom

If you are an undergraduate theology major or a seminary student, you will be exposed to the documents model, whether in positive or negative appraisals of the historical-critical method or in attempts to prove the historicity of given sections of the Bible. A workable response to your academic engagement with this model is to take a balanced and long-term view of how this model has been used and to understand what value the church places on Scripture viewed in its function as a collection of documents.

The historical-critical method is useful in that it helps provide answers to the sorts of questions that modernity poses to the text: Did this happen? If so, did it happen as it is narrated in Scripture, or could someone have embellished the story? If the story got embellished, what was the motiva-

60. Tyconius, *Book of Rules*, 21 (Section III).
61. Tyconius, *Book of Rules*, 23 (Section III).

tion? But the historical-critical method is not the only or the best way to read Scripture. In his 1980 article "The Superiority of Pre-critical Exegesis," David Steinmetz argues against the presupposition of many historical-critical readers that what the original human author of a text intended is the only legitimate interpretation of a text. Steinmetz observes how many medieval exegetes did not consider the intended meaning of the human author to be the best meaning of a text.[62]

Long before the middle ages, Origen had questioned the equation of the literal sense of a narrative with actual history. His examples were certain glitches in the six days of creation (Gen 1) and in the anthropomorphic descriptions for God in Genesis 2. He did not think a godly reader was bound always to assert that the literal reading of Scripture was an accurate photo of what actually happened on earth.[63] Origen's openness to hidden truths means that he does not expend his exegetical skills in explaining how something read literally in Scripture's narratives must have happened. Rather, he looks for principles or truths that are underneath the surface of the narrative.

The church recognizes a definite sense in which Scripture is a collection of documents. But the orientation of these documents is to provide readers with what we need for salvation, not necessarily with a record of history as it happened. Thus *Dei Verbum* tells us, "We must acknowledge the Books of Scripture as teaching firmly, faithfully, and without error the truth that God wished to be recorded in the sacred writings for the sake of our salvation."[64]

Dei Verbum's insistence that Scripture must be read in ways appropriate with each text's literary genre also helps preserve the advantages and avoid the pitfalls present when one reads Scripture only as a collection of documents.[65] When we can employ the participatory view of history, in which God and humanity are actively at work to redeem this world, then we can apply a historical-critical method that is respectful of Scripture. Of course, this method will not be the same as the historical-critical method that secular academics use. But it will allow us to communicate with the secular academics. Thus, as Matthew Levering says, "history as understood biblically is saturated with the divine realities of salvation and requires interpretation that can gain purchase on such realities." Also, the historical-critical method

62. Steinmetz, "Superiority of Pre-critical Exegesis," 27.
63. Steinmetz, "Superiority of Pre-critical Exegesis," 29. Origen, *On First Principles* 4.3.1 (Butterworth, 383–84).
64. *Dei Verbum* §11 (Béchard, *Scripture Documents*, 24).
65. *Dei Verbum* §12 (Béchard, *Scripture Documents*, 25).

should be applied to Scripture as one reads it within the church: "Biblical interpretation is a sharing in the Church's reception of inspired Scripture."[66]

THE DOCUMENTS MODEL IN MINISTRY

Whether you enter Catholic, Orthodox, or Protestant ministry, you will encounter people in your flock who will be checking on the way you view Scripture's books as documents. If they sense that you employ the documents model differently than they do, take pains to de-escalate the confrontations they might attempt. Do not invest significant time or energy in your pastoral ministry to Scripture apologetics—for example, arguments in favor of or against a week of creation less than ten thousand years ago, a panterrestrial flood, or a specific date for Israel's exodus from Egypt. The reason it would be unwise to prioritize Scripture apologetics on either side of these issues is that such efforts inevitably adopt modernist assumptions of what constitutes historical truth. It is analogous to employing a virus-infected laptop or tablet to communicate with and defeat hackers trying to raid the laptop. When you rely only on "scientific" arguments for Scripture's historical value, you may think you have won a given battle, but you will be planting a mindset in others that can prompt them to stop reading the Bible. It is foolish to adopt a modernist mindset that actually believes one can prove that something occurred in the past in a way that all must accept. This ignores how all discourse is embedded in community and occurs with unstated assumptions in the author and original audience that we cannot recover. So, when employing the documents model, always be sure to accompany any defense of Scripture with a word that calls your congregation to consider the community that first accepted the text as Scripture and the church that now reads and follows it as Scripture. And when considering and discussing a challenging or puzzling text of Scripture, it can be especially valuable to survey the variety of responses that church fathers give.

It will be to everyone's benefit to point out how a given document in the Bible, a narrative in Genesis or John and a genealogy in 1 Chronicles or Luke, can also be read as a story or even a prayer. To cite a specific example, Charles Bobertz's reading of the Gospel of Mark illustrates how that gospel makes a lot of sense when read with the prayers model.[67] As we will see in the following

---

66. Levering, *Participatory Biblical Exegesis*, 143.
67. Bobertz, *Gospel of Mark*.

chapters, considerations of the communities that first accepted the text as Scripture or now read the text as Scripture inevitably involve an appreciation of the other models of Scripture.

Everyone who comes to the Scriptures must decide in what sense its books are documents. Since reading is a social activity, it is best always to read Scripture with one's communities in mind. There is first of all the community of people who wrote, edited, copied, and preserved the texts that are now in our Scriptures. Their understanding of Scripture must always be respected. Then there is the faith community in which one lives. The Catholic Church is blessed with a long tradition of Scripture exegesis. The variety among those who have provided exegesis within the Catholic tradition and the acknowledgment that Scripture includes a literal sense and a threefold spiritual sense (allegorical, moral, and anagogical) allows for plenty of flexibility in one's interpretation. Still, some find the church's tradition wanting. In Gundry's commentary that I referred to at the beginning of this chapter, he faults the Catholic approach to Scripture as follows:

> Because they appreciate the development of tradition in the church, Roman Catholics have thought themselves able to uphold biblical authority even in the face of higher-critical demonstrations that the Bible has many human traits. For them, these traits help make up ecclesiastical tradition, which has authority both inside and outside the Bible. Then, however, biblical authority starts dissolving in the ocean of ecclesiastical tradition, especially in its postcanonical developments. This tradition depends, moreover, on an authority increasingly difficult to maintain, that of the institutional church. In effect, refusing to draw the boundary of authority at the limits of the biblical canon dilutes the very idea of a biblical canon. Thus it was only a matter of time before the orthodox Roman Catholic view of biblical inspiration fell prey to historical-critical study, complete with the same attempts at rehabilitation that liberal Protestants had futilely put forward. The traditionalism that prolonged the orthodox view proved to be a Trojan horse.[68]

Gundry's statement that the Catholic Church's authority over Scripture, outside the canon, actually "dilutes the very idea of a biblical canon" is too incomplete to be helpful. No canon is self-formed, so all canons of Scripture must have some outside authority in their genesis. If one were to limit one's

68. Gundry, *Matthew*, 624.

authority to the canon of Scripture, as Gundry seems to advocate here, one would be left with what we have experienced in the last half millennium, a proliferation of Christian groups, all insisting on their authentically Christian identity. But their very existence as distinct communities and their insistence on their Christian authenticity, along with the illegitimacy of other Christian groups, sabotage the unity to which Christ called his followers. It is inconsistent of Gundry to attack a Catholic idea of tradition and authority when all Christians—even those claiming to read on a "Scripture alone" basis—employ tradition as a guide for their reading. These groups definitely employ authority, a de facto magisterium, as well, as many can attest who have tried to argue against a given interpretation of Scripture in a "Scripture alone" church.

When using Scripture as a document, then, we should always seek to listen to how the document has been heard in the past and listen to it from within the Christian community. An interpretation that isolates the interpreter from ways that Christians have traditionally read a text must only be embraced if one can show how the new interpretation solves dilemmas inherited from past generations and fosters unity in our fragmented family.

STORIES

*Religious tradition has by and large encouraged us to take the Bible seri-
ously rather than to enjoy it, but the paradoxical truth of the matter may
well be that by learning to enjoy the biblical stories more fully as stories,
we shall also come to see more clearly what they mean to tell us about
God, man, and the perilously momentous realm of history.*

—ROBERT ALTER[1]

The story we construct to understand a given passage of Scripture can be
very significant in determining that text's meaning. One of the most hotly
contested cases in Scripture is the backstory to the Letter to Philemon. We
are nowhere told why the slave named Onesimus left his home. We are never
specifically told whether it is Philemon or someone else addressed in the letter
who once had a close relationship with Onesimus, which is now strained. The
"knowing you will do more than I say" phrase in the letter's final paragraph
(Phlm 21) projects another chapter in a story unrecoverable to us. But even
with these missing details, we need to construct a story in order to understand
the letter.

The traditional story has been that Onesimus ran away from his owner,
Philemon, after stealing or vandalizing some of Philemon's property. In Rome
or some other city outside the Lycus Valley, Onesimus came into contact with
Paul. Paul sends Onesimus back with the letter we know as Philemon, asking
Philemon to accept Onesimus as a Christian brother and to allow Onesimus
to join Paul's ministry team.

This story was adjusted by John Knox, who suggested that since Paul elsewhere tells Archippus to complete the ministry to which he is called, it is
Archippus who is the owner of Onesimus and the one mainly addressed in
the letter called Philemon (Col 4:17; Phlm 2). Since the bishop of the church of
Ephesus in the early second century is named Onesimus, Knox suggested that

1. Alter, *Art of Biblical Narrative*, 189.

Archippus indeed freed Onesimus and that this former runaway slave became bishop of that significant church.[2]

More recently, Allen Dwight Callahan has revived an alternate story that was current among some abolitionists in the mid-nineteenth century. In this story, Onesimus and Philemon were brothers who had a serious rupture in their relationship. Onesimus leaves his family after this rupture and meets Paul when Paul is imprisoned elsewhere. Paul then sends Onesimus back to his brother Philemon, asking Philemon to accept him back, no longer simply as a biological brother but as a brother in the Lord.[3]

The story offered for the Letter to Philemon in the mid-nineteenth century was intimately related to the position one took on slavery. The backstory also has the potential to touch on the question of reparations to slaves. We can see from this example that in some cases a story is necessary to understand the Bible, and the story one constructs has weighty consequences in one's subsequent exegesis.

Definition and Characteristics of Stories Model

The stories model views Scripture, sometimes even those genres within it that are not considered narrative literature, such as law, genealogy, poetry, epistle, and apocalyptic, as primarily an integral part of a narrative. For someone using this model, every part of the Bible is potentially a story or a chapter in a story. As a consequence, the person reading with the stories model considers a narrative template to be essential for understanding the meaning of Scripture. This model sometimes fits all it sees in the Bible into one long narrative—a metanarrative—or it may consider the stories it sees everywhere in the Bible as separate and unconnected to a single narrative. The model derives meaning from a text of Scripture by fitting the text into a story.

In relation to the senses of Scripture, the narrative model can be the primary model when someone is explaining the text's literal, allegorical, or anagogical senses. Since much of the Bible is composed of stories, this model is readily activated when reading for the literal sense of narrative material, whether in Exodus or one of the Gospels. Because the allegorical sense looks for correspondence between a given text and a different story, the stories model is employed here, since this interpretation of the text depends on con-

2. Knox, *Philemon among the Letters of Paul*, 25–34, 51–56; Knox, *Chapters in the Life of Paul*, 6. Ign. *Eph.* 1:3; 6:2.

3. Callahan, *Embassy of Onesimus*.

nections to another story. And since the anagogical sense points toward an eschatological horizon, it too can readily employ the stories model, offering a heavenly antitype to a biblical character or a celestial view of terrestrial discourse in the Bible.

You know that the stories model is operating . . .

. . . when your professor, textbook, or a homily you hear situates a theological idea into a comprehensive narrative. Narrative theology will take an idea such as the election of Israel and explain it in terms of a story. Or, to offer another example, if a given explanation of a New Testament text retells an Old Testament story not cited in the New Testament text, the stories model is activated.

. . . when your professor, textbook, or a homily you hear offers a plot underlying a given law code, psalm, prophetic oracle, letter, or apocalyptic section of Scripture as though this plot is necessary to understand the text in question. The appeal to a narrative, often accompanied by an unstated assumption that the narrative must be recognized and kept in mind to understand the passage, is a sign that an interpreter of Scripture views narratives as the mitochondria that give Scripture its dynamism or life-giving force.

. . . when an exegete pays very close attention to literary style, highlighting conventions such as wordplay, catchword, and inclusio. Robert Alter's English translations of the Hebrew Bible and his book *The Art of Biblical Narrative* are examples of this approach to texts in the Hebrew Bible. Alter writes that "the narrative prose of the Hebrew Bible . . . cultivates certain profound and haunting enigmas, delights in leaving its audiences guessing about motives and connections, and above all, loves to set ambiguities of word choice and image against one another in an endless interplay that resists neat resolution."[4]

Though the stories of Genesis are famously compact and laconic, with few details of background provided, they are masterfully constructed narratives.[5] The narrative regarding Joseph, for example, has been thoroughly explored

4. Alter, *Genesis*, xi.
5. See Auerbach, "Odysseus' Scar," for a comparison between the narrative techniques in Homer's *Odyssey* and the book of Genesis. Robert Alter's chapter "Characterization and the Art of Reticence" is also a masterful survey of how Old Testament narrative is able to portray character with a minimum of words (*Art of Biblical Narrative*, 114–30).

by James Kugel in light of later interpretations and retellings. It is the stories model of Scripture that is most suited to explaining why, in the middle of the Joseph stories (Gen 37–48), we encounter a different narrative, the story of Judah and Tamar (Gen 38).[6]

SPECIFIC APPLICATIONS OF THE STORIES MODEL

There are different kinds of stories. When at a family reunion, some relatives will claim to tell a story of "what really happened." Others will tell stories that contain adjustments in plot, added details, and exaggeration to make a point. Family members will gather around both sorts of storytellers, since both convey meaningful truths in the family.

Stories as History

The former type of story, presented as "what really happened," appeals to many people's expectation that we can know what really happened, an approach to history that is associated with Leopold von Ranke (1795–1886) and other modernist historians. Those employing this approach to history may read some or all of Scripture's stories (except perhaps parables) as communicating exactly how things happened.

The challenges to this approach come both from within the text and from outside the text. From within the text, we wonder how light was created before there was a sun and moon, how Adam and Eve's children found spouses, and how to understand parallel passages that tell stories in different ways. From outside the text, we wonder why the text of Genesis describes Abraham as owning camels, when camels were not introduced into the land of Canaan until the first millennium BCE, or whether the conquest of Jericho happened as narrated in Joshua, since the archaeological evidence is ambiguous. We wonder what to do with large numbers in some passages of the Bible, which either seem larger than appropriate for their referents or different from parallel accounts.

Stories as Stories

Others do not read Scripture's narratives as offering the precise correspondence between event and record that modernity expects in the genre of history. At least since the days of Augustine, readers have wondered how to understand

---

6. Kugel, *In Potiphar's House.*

the creation story in Genesis 1, for example. Augustine interprets the days of creation as signifying the progress of the human person, who can rise from the merely physical to a spiritual level, and the spread of the gospel throughout the world through the evangelists and other ministers of the church.[7]

In 1963 the Pontifical Biblical Commission issued a statement regarding the historical accuracy of the Gospels. In it, the commission affirms that one should not press differences in the order of events narrated or in the precise wording of Jesus's teachings in ways that emphasize the historical precision of these gospel accounts.

> And since the meaning of a statement depends, among other things, on the place which it has in a given sequence, the Evangelists, in handing on the words or the deeds of our Savior, explained them for the advantage of their readers by respectively setting them, one Evangelist in one context, another in another. For this reason the exegete must ask himself what the Evangelist intended by recounting a saying or a fact in a certain way, or by placing it in a certain context. For the truth of the narrative is not affected in the slightest by the fact that the Evangelists report the sayings or the doings of our Lord in a different order, and that they use different words to express what he said, not keeping to the very letter, but nevertheless preserving the sense.[8]

For example, someone reading the Gospels might say that since John describes Jesus cleansing the temple early in his ministry and the Synoptic Gospels describe the temple cleansing near the end of it, there must have been two temple cleansings.[9] But in light of the Pontifical Biblical Commission's statement, it is perfectly legitimate to say that Jesus cleansed the temple once, probably shortly before his arrest, and that John has moved the event forward in his narrative in order to drive home his idea that Jesus replaces the temple.

As we saw in the quotation from Joseph Fitzmyer's Luke commentary in the previous chapter, there are different genres of truth.[10] No one questions the truth of the parable of the good Samaritan, for example, although as a parable it is not presented as historical reportage of an event that actually happened. Distinguishing between different genres of truth and not expecting every narrative in the Bible to reflect historically verifiable events is very similar to what the Pontifical Biblical Commission affirmed in its 1993 document,

---

7. Augustine, *Confessions* 13.12.13–13.34.49 (Boulding, 350–79).

8. Pontifical Biblical Commission, *Instruction on the Historical Truth of the Gospels* (= *Sancta Mater Ecclesia*) §9 (Béchard, *Scripture Documents*, 230–31).

9. Matt 21:12–13; Mark 11:15–17; Luke 19:45–46; John 2:13–17.

10. Fitzmyer, *Gospel According to Luke I–IX*, 18.

The Interpretation of the Bible in the Church, a document with which Cardinal Ratzinger was deeply involved. The document criticizes fundamentalist exegesis as follows: "Fundamentalism also places undue stress upon the inerrancy of certain details in the biblical texts, especially in what concerns historical events or supposedly scientific truth. It often historicizes material that from the start never claimed to be historical. It considers historical everything that is reported or recounted with verbs in the past tense, failing to take the necessary account of the possibility of symbolic or figurative meaning."[11]

A balance must therefore be maintained in the reading of the Gospels. While the church affirms their "historical character," this does not mean that the believer is expected to believe that everything they narrate happened in history.[12] Jesus probably did cleanse the temple at the end of his ministry as the Synoptics portray and not at its beginning as John narrates.[13] And Jesus probably was mocked and persecuted by Roman soldiers as Matthew, Mark, and John tell us and not Herod's soldiers as the pro-Roman author Luke narrates.[14]

The contents of early definitions of the gospel, such as in 1 Corinthians 15:3–8 or early creeds, must be affirmed as historical truth. Beyond that, readers of Scripture are free to differ on whether a given narrative of Scripture communicates both historical and theological truth, or mainly theological truth.

Those who apply the stories model in the "stories as stories" way will typically point out inconsistencies in parallel accounts or details that seem to stretch the bounds of credulity. An example of inconsistency is that David pays fifty silver shekels for the temple site and the seller Araunah's oxen in 2 Samuel 24:24, and he pays six hundred gold shekels for the temple site in 1 Chronicles 21:25 to Ornan. A detail that seems difficult to accept is the 600,000 Israelite men leaving Egypt, according to Exodus 12:37. According to this record, there would have been well over one million people moving through the wilderness in the exodus experience. This high number prompts some students of Exodus to conclude that the biblical account of the exodus offers an inflated count of the people, perhaps because the narrative fuses together several migrations of peoples out of Egypt.[15]

One challenge to the "stories as stories" application of this model is that some people have difficulty trusting a Bible when they hear that it contains

---

11. Pontifical Biblical Commission, *Interpretation of the Bible in the Church*, I.F (Béchard, *Scripture Documents*, 274).

12. *Dei Verbum* §19.

13. Matt 21:12–17; Mark 11:15–19; Luke 19:45–48; John 2:13–25.

14. Matt 27:27–31; Mark 15:16–20; John 19:1–3; Luke 23:11.

15. Collins, *Short Introduction*, 66. If the number of migrants leaving Egypt is inflated at Exod 12:37, then the census counts in Num 2:32 and 26:51 are also inflated.

narratives or details within narratives that may not have happened. Thus, they throw out the baby with the bathwater and decide that if one story did not happen, then all its stories are suspect. But for millennia, both Jews and Christians have read some of the Bible's stories figuratively, maintaining that they teach truth while not narrating something that actually happened. For example, in the Bible's accounts of Israel's genocide of Canaanite cities, both Jewish and Christian interpreters have been ready to say that these stories teach spiritual truths but do not communicate what actually happened.[16]

Old Testament Texts Often Read as Stories

The stories model—reading any part of the Bible as a story or a chapter of a story—makes a lot of sense, given the Bible's contents. The creation accounts in Genesis 1 and Genesis 2–3 are stories. Once the story of Adam and Eve ends with their expulsion from the garden, we encounter a story of their sons Cain and Abel. The stories, augmented in places with genealogies and punctuated occasionally by poetic codas, continue unabated until we get to the laws that Moses receives at Mount Sinai and on the rest of his journey. But even the law sections have stories that introduce or frame them.[17] In other sections where we would not expect stories, such as the Psalms, the human instinct for arranging data into stories with plots emerges, whether in the superscriptions added to individual psalms or in the arrangement of the Psalms into five books.[18] The stories inserted into the prophets' books give context to their oracles, beginning with their call narratives and including other events in their lives.[19]

The "stories as history" approach, a particular application of the stories

16. Kolbet, "Torture," 558–62, describes how Origen, following Justin Martyr, *Dialogue with Trypho* 75.1–3, 89.1, 90.4, sees Joshua as representing Christ. And the Canaanites whom the book of Joshua presents as the enemies to be annihilated represent sins or vices inside us (Origen, *Homilies on Book of Joshua, [Son] of Nun* 1.7 (*Origenes Werke VII*, 294.28–295.5). N. MacDonald, *Deuteronomy*, 112, argues for a figurative reading of the annihilation of Canaanites commanded in Deut 7 on the basis of the archaic, stylized names for the Canaanite nations, the prohibition against intermarriage with the Canaanites (pointless if Canaanites were to be actually annihilated), and comparison with Exod 23:20–33; 34:11–16 (the angel of the Lord or the Lord himself will drive out the Canaanites; Israelites are commanded only to destroy cult objects). I am indebted to Gary Anderson for sources cited in this footnote.

17. Sailhamer, *Pentateuch as Narrative*, 33–59.

18. Psalm superscriptions that set the psalm into a narrative framework include those for Pss 3, 7, 18, 30, 34, 51, 52, 56, 57, 59, 60, 63, 90. There are also lines within some psalms that provide narrative context; see Pss 74:3–9; 79:1; 126:1–2; 137:1–3.

19. Call narratives that the prophets provide include Isa 6:1–13; Jer 1:1–19; Hos 1:1–9. Other

model, might view Genesis 1 as an accurate description of how God created the earth, whether interpreted as twenty-four-hour days or "days" of longer periods of time. This approach views Adam and Eve as the first ever humans, and the conversation between the serpent and Eve, as well as the ones between God and the humans in Genesis 2–3, as accurate descriptions of discourse that actually occurred in humanity's past. The Hebrew people's occupation of the land of Canaan is viewed primarily as accomplished through military conquest, such as the almost complete annihilation of Jericho and Ai described in Joshua. Parallel accounts within the Bible are harmonized or considered as referring to separate events. Thus, the different prices in the narratives of David's selection of the temple site are harmonized by suggesting that the more expensive price in 1 Chronicles is due to an adjustment for inflation.

When reading the early chapters of Genesis, those applying the stories model in a "stories as history" way will not look to comparative accounts from the ancient Near East of creation or a great flood, for they will look at the Bible's creation accounts and flood narratives as singular happenings, whose records in the Bible can be perceived on their own terms. They will certainly be sensitive to the characterization given to Adam, Eve, Cain, and Noah while continuing to assert that such characterization fits with these figures' identities "in real life."

The "stories as history" readers view the Bible as a set of closely entwined stories, so that if any single story is discredited, the entire structure falls, unlike the Jenga game, in which pieces can be removed from a structure without a collapse. The "stories as history" proponents would say that if Jonah was not really swallowed by a great fish and spewed out three days later, then other narrative material in the Bible becomes suspect, including Jesus's citation of this part of the Jonah story (Matt 12:39–41; Luke 11:29–32). These readers tend to view scriptural narratives as one-of-a-kind stories, all narrating history as it actually happened.

In contrast, the "stories as stories" approach to the Bible will not consider the creation accounts found throughout the canon as transcripts of exactly how creation happened. Instead, this application of the stories model looks to these accounts as asserting particular ideas that respond to creation accounts from the cultures of the ancient Near East. Thus, in distinction from the Babylonian creation story that describes how Tiamat, the goddess of the sea, was cut apart by Marduk, the creation story of Genesis 1 makes a special point of

---

narrative interludes that provide context for prophetic oracles include Isa 36:1–39:8; Jer 20:1–6; 37:11–39:14; 52:1–34; Hos 3:1–3; Amos 7:10–17.

stating that God created the sea monsters (1:21), as though such monsters are no threat to God. The creation story in Genesis 1 takes a perspective similar to Psalm 104:26, which states that God created Leviathan to play in the sea. This is different from references to Leviathan in other biblical descriptions of creation, which treat Leviathan as a formidable enemy of God (Job 40:25–32; Ps 74:13–14).[20]

This application of the stories model looks to other narratives from the ancient Near East or the Mediterranean world and then considers how the Bible's narratives have adapted those stories to make a point. For example, when one realizes that the Babylonian creation story says that only the king's family is created in the image of Marduk, god of Babylon, then one can appreciate how the creation story of Genesis 1 uses repetition of the words "image" and "likeness" to emphasize that all humanity, male and female, are created in God's image (1:26–27). Similarly, when one realizes that the Babylonian account of the creation of humans is that we humans were made so that the gods would not have to work, it is significant that God rests on the Sabbath day, as though the God of Israel wants all to rest one day a week (Gen 2:2–3).[21] Someone applying the stories model in a "stories as stories" way will explain Scripture's creation accounts and descriptions of the flood as representing Israel's versions of the creation and flood stories of the ancient Near East, in light of Israel's understanding of God.

New Testament Texts Often Read as Stories

The paradigmatic instance of "story" in the New Testament is embodied in each of the four Gospels. While scholars have debated what literary genre the Gospels precisely exemplify, all agree that they are narratives, focusing mostly on Jesus's public ministry, whether presented as lasting for three years or for an undesignated length of time.[22] Insofar as Christianity highlights the gospel story as a preeminent story within Scripture, the Gospels are hon-

---

20. Levenson, *Creation*, 53–65.

21. Levenson, *Creation*, 100–120.

22. The Synoptic Gospels do not specify how long Jesus's public ministry lasted. For example, within Luke's extensive travel narrative, there are no indications of how long it took for Jesus, healing and teaching as he went, to move from Galilee to Jerusalem. John presents Jesus's ministry as lasting for about three years, because of this gospel's references to Passovers. John mentions the annual feast of Passover not simply to mark the passage of time but to build suspense for the final Passover he narrates, when Jesus the lamb of God is sacrificed.

ored when read in Christian assemblies. The record of Jesus's incarnation, life, death, and resurrection is considered the most significant part of Scripture by many Christians, and this necessarily means that the stories model plays a significant role in Christian exegesis.[23] In the Gospels, when Jesus seeks to define the kingdom of God that he is announcing, he tells stories in the genre of parables.[24] Parables therefore function as stories within the overarching gospel story.

Acts provides stories of the apostles, especially Peter and Paul, to address the challenges of reading the Pauline letter collection with little to no context. We do not have stories for some of the other letters and only a minimal story for the author of Revelation, but readers readily latch onto any piece of the text that gives us some indication of the text's backstory.[25]

In the Gospels, the stories model pays attention to how the gospel authors constructed their stories. Frank Kermode observes that the authors of Matthew, Mark, Luke, and John all had a fairly fixed account of Jesus's last days on earth, but that their resources for the first part of their gospels were not organized into story form, coming to them rather as anecdotes, records of miracles, and sayings of Jesus. The challenge for each of the gospel authors, therefore, was how to get these resources regarding what preceded Jesus's passion and resurrection into a narrative format. Kermode thinks that each of the four evangelists meets this challenge in a different way, and that none completely "overcomes" the problems that come with putting nonnarrative discourse into narrative form.[26]

It is especially the ending of Mark that some readers find literarily deficient, if, as the earliest manuscripts indicate, it ended with "for they were afraid" at 16:8. It is no wonder that others would come along and, using the other gospels and the book of Acts, add endings that bring more resolution to the narrative.[27]

Authors who apply the stories model to New Testament letters suggest narratives that they think will provide an explanatory substructure that makes one or more of the letters more understandable. N. T. Wright offers a story that he thinks represents how Paul thought about Israel, the messiah, and the church. In this story, Israel was called to represent God to the world. Wright thinks that

23. *Dei Verbum* §18 attributes "special preeminence" within all of Scripture to the Gospels.

24. Ryken, *Bible as Literature*, 9, describes how Jesus answers questions with parables.

25. See, e.g., 1 John 2:19; Rev 1:9–11.

26. Kermode, "Matthew," 387.

27. See Kelhoffer, *Miracle and Mission*; Kelhoffer, "Eusebius' *ad Marinum*."

Paul views Israel as failing in this calling, and that Jesus then replaces Israel in the role of bringing God's truth to the world. The family of Israel, then, in Wright's view, is redefined so that it includes all those, Jews and non-Jews, who identify with Messiah Jesus.[28] Stories such as these are not innocuous, academic exercises. Wright's idea of the story that was in Paul's mind as he wrote his letters carries some elements of the anti-Judaism that prompted Christians to allow Hitler to come to power in the twentieth century, and thus must not be completely accepted.[29]

Another case of the stories model engaged with a New Testament letter is Richard Hays's book *The Faith of Jesus Christ*. Against others who think that the Letter to the Galatians is driven by Paul's own conversion experience or a single idea such as justification by faith, Hays argues that the core of Galatians is based on the story of Christ—that is, Christ's own faithfulness in the incarnation and crucifixion.[30]

Key Issues in the Stories Model

We need stories to help us make sense of our experience in this world. Yet stories can relate to our experience in different ways. In what follows, we consider a key shift, beginning in the sixteenth century, in how Christians read the Bible's narratives. Then we explore three major categories for reading Scripture's narratives. Finally, we look at some of the key ideas embedded in these narratives.

Western Civilization's Approaches to Scripture's Stories

We often regard ideas, people, or stories as under the influence of cultural forces and traditional constructs that operate beneath our consciousness. If you are wondering how it came to be that Western civilization questioned certain narratives in the Bible, or how the Bible's stories weathered the Enlightenment, this section is for you.

Traditionally, the Bible's narratives were read along the dual lines of the literal sense and the spiritual sense. Within the spiritual sense, one could read the Bible morally, allegorically, or anagogically. If we think of the parable of the good Samaritan, the moral sense is this: we should be a neighbor to anyone

28. Wright, *Paul and the Faithfulness of God*, 774–1042.
29. Kaminsky and Reasoner, "Israel's Election."
30. Hays, *Faith of Jesus Christ*, 166–83.

we encounter who is in need. The allegorical sense is this: as the wounded man was taken to the inn, so we as sinners are taken by Christ to the church. And the anagogical sense is this: as the wounded man was taken to the inn, so believers will be received into heaven at the end of time.[31]

A key development in the history of biblical exegesis was Luther's insistence that the Bible be read as history, and "not just any history; it was a special and particular history, the history of the church as the people of God."[32] For example, the narrative of the call of Abram out of Ur was a thumbnail sketch of the history of the church, and Abraham's genealogy was a history of the earliest church. Pelikan explains that Luther resisted the label of allegory while treating the Bible's stories as a history of the church by always keeping in mind that while the Jews were the people of God at the time of the Old Testament's composition, Israel would later be rejected as the people of God: "Luther was always careful to expound the passages citing Israel's status in such a way as to make room, ex post facto, for Israel's rejection and for the creation of the new Israel; the prerogative of the Jews was that God manifested Himself to them in His Word. Thus Luther could give them all due honor as the people of God and at the same time lay claim to that title for the church. And he maintained that this had been the intention behind the establishment of the people of God all along."[33]

This was not the right move, since Paul affirms in Romans 9–11 that even after the birth of the church, Israel remains God's people. It is necessary to affirm Israel's ongoing status as the people of God in order to respect God's faithfulness and Paul's teaching on Israel in Romans 9–11 as well as to avoid another Holocaust.[34]

Because of the claim that the Bible represents God's word for humanity, and because of the higher expectations put on the Bible once the *sola Scriptura* principle gained influence and the four senses of Scripture used by the church fathers and medieval exegetes lost currency, readers of the Bible began articulating how the Bible's narratives made sense in the eighteenth and nineteenth centuries, as described by Hans Frei in what follows.

---

31. For more discussion on the senses of Scripture, see chap. 8 below.

32. Pelikan, *Luther the Expositor*, 89.

33. Pelikan, *Luther the Expositor*, 91 (Luther's interpretation of the call out of Ur and the genealogy), 92 (quotation).

34. For further discussion on the biblical basis for the Christian affirmation of Israel as the people of God, see the declaration of Vatican II *Nostra Aetate*; the Pontifical Biblical Commission's document *The Jewish People and Their Sacred Scriptures in the Christian Bible*; and Kaminsky and Reasoner, "Israel's Election."

Spaciotemporal Referentiality

First of all, there were those who found the meaning of biblical narrative in the circumstances occurring in time and space, in the world to which the narratives refer. This category includes the supernaturalists, who accepted the supernatural events described in the Gospels at face value, affirming that the angelic appearances and miracles all actually happened. This approach is basically the same as the "stories as history" application of the stories model described earlier in this chapter. Luther and Calvin are among the supernaturalists, for they taught that the text meant what its literal sense communicated, unless something in the wider context mitigated against this. The general category of spaciotemporal referentiality also includes the naturalists, who correlated biblical narratives with what happened in time and space, but sought natural explanations for the supernatural events narrated in them. An example of a naturalist reading of Jesus walking on the water is the explanation that Jesus walked on stones that were just beneath the surface of the water.

These first two subsets of the spaciotemporal readers, the supernaturalists and the naturalists, would be reading the text for its literal sense. A final subset within this category of spaciotemporal referentiality is the approach that views the biblical narratives as written intentionally to deceive readers. In this mode of referentiality, the authors of biblical narrative think that what they write did not happen, but write so as to trick readers into believing their stories correspond exactly with what happened.[35]

Rationalism

Another approach to biblical narrative was pursued by rationalists who found the meaning of biblical narratives in the ideas contained in them. Within this category, some thought that the authors had intentionally composed stories of events that did not happen in order to teach moral or spiritual truths. Those who regard some of the narratives in the Gospels as historical fiction would be in this category. Others, notably Immanuel Kant, looked only at the narratives themselves and sought to distill from them some timeless ideas, with no consideration of the human author's possible intentions.[36] If the truths within a given story can be found throughout the whole Bible, then this category can be the seedbed for metanarratives that explain an underlying idea as a key to

35. Frei, *Eclipse of Biblical Narrative*, 23–24, 256–61.
36. Frei, *Eclipse of Biblical Narrative*, 261–64.

the whole Bible. Northrup Frye's description of how the pattern in the book of Judges (rebellion → misfortune → repentance → blessing) is really the pattern of the whole Bible illustrates this application of a rationalist approach.[37]

An example of the rationalist approach is the outright rejection of some elements within biblical stories. This rejection usually happens on the basis of a modernist assumption that the evidence available for such details indicates that they are merely created out of the imaginations of human authors. For example, the archaeological evidence for Israel's military conquest of Canaan as narrated in the book of Joshua is nonexistent. This leads Catholic scholar John J. Collins toward the conclusion that the conquest did not happen as narrated in Joshua. He offers a model for the Israelite occupation of the land that matches the current results of archaeological research, that the Israelites gradually emerged as a people from among the Canaanites, who moved from the lowlands up to the central highlands.[38]

Myth

A third category is composed of the mythophiles. They understood the meaning of biblical narratives to lie neither in the events to which the narratives refer, nor in the moral or spiritual truths recoverable in the stories, but in the mindset or worldview that the narratives communicate. Schleiermacher's participation in this approach to Scripture's narratives led him to assert that Jesus only appeared to die on the cross, since an actual death would mean a break in the consciousness of Jesus, which he understood to be the consciousness specifically conveyed in the passion and resurrection narratives.[39] This of course is a problem in the light of Christian tradition, which considers docetism a heretical way to describe Jesus's death.

In the case of the military conquest of the land, the mythophile approach would be compatible with the spiritual sense that Origen saw in the holy war narratives of the book of Joshua. Since the moral difficulties of the complete slaughter of a given population seemed to preclude the possibility of a literal reading for him, he wrote that the point of the narratives is to teach how God's people must battle against sin in their lives.[40]

37. Frye, *Great Code*, 169.

38. Collins, *Short Introduction*, 116–20.

39. Frei, *Eclipse of Biblical Narrative*, 264–66, 311–13.

40. On the moral problems inherent in the Bible's holy war narratives, see Collins, *Short Introduction*, 121–22. On Origen, see discussion and note at end of "Stories as Stories" section above.

The Perspectives of Scripture's Stories

It is worthwhile considering the perspectives from which Scripture's stories are told. The disparate stories within the Bible share common assumptions or ideas that recur in the layers upon layers of stories in Scripture. There are several characteristics that recur in Scripture's stories that definitely account for the Bible's status as classic literature.

Good versus Evil

There is first of all the recurring plot of moral good versus moral evil. Yes, the Old Testament can present God as the cause of natural evil, but God's character of steadfast love and faithfulness is repeatedly emphasized in our Scriptures.[41] Even in a case where God is accused of breaking a promise, God's lovingkindness and faithfulness are celebrated and considered nonnegotiable for a genuine understanding of God.[42]

The God Who Speaks

Among the characters who appear in Scripture's plot of good versus evil, the main protagonist is the God of Israel. Readers familiar with the Christian Scriptures may take the portrait of God for granted, but do well to appreciate how permeable and thin the boundary is between the divine and human worlds, according to both Old and New Testaments. Yes, the transcendence of God is maintained in all sections of the Bible, but the immanence and communicative nature of God and God's messengers are remarkable. From the Genesis narratives of God questioning Adam, confronting Cain, and calling Abram to Revelation's portrait of "one like a son of man" who tells John to write what he sees, our Scriptures are replete with close encounters that God initiates with humanity.

Human Agency

Alongside God's leading role in Scripture, people figure prominently, and their decisions are essential in the flow of the story and for their own roles in the various stories the Bible tells. There have been Scripture readers, often when

41. Gen 24:27; 32:10; Exod 34:6; 2 Sam 2:6; 15:20; Pss 25:10; 57:4; 61:8; 85:11; 86:15.
42. Ps 89:3, 15, 25, 34, 40, 50 (2, 14, 24, 33, 39, 49 in translations that do not number "Maskil of Ethan the Ezrahite" separately as verse 1).

living in situations in which they consider themselves to be true believers vastly outnumbered by heretics and unbelievers around them, who view the world as an arena in which God actively determines human actions and all events. But in general, both the rabbis and the church fathers read Scripture as a record of human actions freely made, which have real consequences in the lives of others.

Intersecting Worlds

The Bible's stories typically view reality as an interplay between the unseen, spiritual world and the visible, material world. The former brings a sense of mystery and transcendence to the Bible's stories, a sense that can then grow in the reader's own consciousness of reality. Because the unseen, spiritual world can enter into the visible, material world, the Bible's stories at times lead to a sacramental view of the world, in which ordinary objects and events glow with ultimate significance. This illustrates a purpose for the stories: they teach about God and about what it means to live in this world, whether among the elect, the people of Israel, or among the non-elect, with whom God also wants a relationship.[43]

Critique from Inside the House

The narrative framework for the prophet Amos portrays him as standing in Bethel, a significant city of Israel's Baal worship. Amos first criticizes other nations and then criticizes neighboring Judah and finally Israel, the country in which he is speaking. Amos is originally from the country of Judah, so he is a Hebrew neighbor of the Hebrews in Israel, and Amos's messages are preserved by Israelites and Judeans. The narrative is thus an in-house critique and call from within the nation for renewed commitments to justice.[44]

An integral part of the Christian Scriptures' narrative DNA is this in-house critique and call for justice. In the Old Testament, the critique includes the Hebrew people's reflection on times when they have not worshiped their God exclusively nor treated their fellow citizens according to the love of neighbor mandated by Mosaic law. The Deuteronomistic Historians responsible for the books of Joshua, Judges, and 1 Samuel to 2 Kings are locked in on narrating

43. Ryken, *Bible as Literature*, 178–81. On the Bible's didactic role in teaching how to live as elect or non-elect, see Kaminsky, *Yet I Loved Jacob*.

44. R. M. Brown, *Unexpected News*, 47–48.

their kings' and their people's mistakes as a way of explaining Israel's exile to Assyria and Judah's exile to Babylon.[45] The narrative template behind the Prophets section of the Old Testament regularly includes the sins of Israel's people, including those of the prophet himself, as an integral part of the story that needs to be told.[46]

The New Testament's narrative context that highlights the sins of Israel and the sins of Christ-followers is indebted to this characteristic of the Hebrew Bible. In the Gospels, this includes Jesus's critiques of the Pharisees and other leaders, as well as the descriptions of the apostles' mistakes and unbelief.[47] In the letters of the New Testament, these narrative characteristics of internal critique and calls for justice form part of the narrative substructure.[48]

The narratives of Scripture also include accounts of people questioning God about apparent injustices. Jeremiah accuses God of seducing him and goes on to curse the day on which he was born (20:7–18). God is a God who can be petitioned for justice (Gen 18:22–33; Job 23:1–17; Ps 89:38–51; Hab 1:1–17; Rev 6:9–11).

Choice of the Underdog

Another narrative characteristic of much of the Bible's stories is that the underdog gets to be divinely chosen and blessed. Joel Kaminsky has helpfully written about what the stories of Cain and Abel, Isaac and Ishmael, Jacob and Esau, and Joseph and his brothers all tell us about God's choice of choosing some people over others. From these stories we learn that there is not always a clear reason why one is chosen over another, that the chosen one often must pass through suffering or a brush with death, and that God's choice of one does not mean that God's relationship with the non-chosen one has ended.[49] Ancient Israel may have treasured these stories because the people of Israel saw themselves as the younger brother, who would in most cases get the smaller por-

---

45. Josh 7:1–26; 9:3–27; Judg 19:1–20:48; 1 Sam 13:8–15; 15:1–35; 2 Sam 11:2–27; 1 Kgs 21:1–26; 2 Kgs 21:1–16.

46. Critiques of the people: Isa 58:1–14; Jer 7:1–15; Ezek 16:1–63. Critiques of the prophet himself: Isa 6:5; Jonah 1:1–3; 4:1–9.

47. Words of judgment on area towns and religious leaders: Matt 11:21–24; 23:2–36. Critical portraits of apostles: Matt 16:5–12 // Mark 8:14–21 // Luke 12:1; Matt 26:69–75 // Mark 14:66–72 // Luke 22:56–62 // John 18:25–27.

48. Rom 1:18–3:20; 13:12–14; 1 Cor 3:1–4; 5:1–8; 6:1–20; 8:7–13; 10:14–33; Heb 5:11–13; 10:23–27; Jas 2:1–7; 4:1–10; 5:1–6; Rev 2:4–5, 14–16, 20–23; 3:2–3, 15–19.

49. Kaminsky, *Yet I Loved Jacob*, 23–25, 41.

tion of an inheritance. They would consider themselves the younger brother because they existed among civilizations much older and more powerful.[50]

Besides God's choice of the younger sibling, many stories in the Scriptures describe God bringing down the proud and self-sufficient ones while supporting the poor and marginalized. Thus, for example, in the Magnificat of Mary we find descriptions of God dispersing the proud, bringing the powerful down, and turning the rich into empty-handed, needy people (Luke 1:51b–52a, 53b). And concurrently with these descriptions, the poem celebrates how the God of Israel raises up the lowly and feeds the hungry (Luke 1:52b–53a). These themes are commonplace in the Old Testament. Robert McAfee Brown says that Luke cannot adequately narrate the birth of a Hebrew without including these themes in the story. Mary's Magnificat thus emerges as a politically charged prayer. And while our familiarity with the Magnificat may cause us not to hear all it expresses, it is worth noting that God's support for his servant Israel indicates how power structures are reversed within the kingdom of God.[51]

Strengths of the Stories Model

In the metanarratives chapter later in this book, we will focus on how readers have tried to weave all of the Christian Scriptures into a single story. Here we are focusing on those whose default approach to all the genres within Scripture is to read them as stories.

The stories model values alternate tellings of a single narrative. It is part of the genius of the Hebrew Scriptures that Christians have inherited and followed in the canonization of the New Testament that different stories are preserved within the canon. It might be a relatively minor question whether David paid fifty shekels of silver or six hundred shekels of gold for the temple site. But it is a more significant question whether the episode of the census that David took was David's own mistake or whether an enemy (the Hebrew word for enemy is *satan*) prompted the misstep. In 2 Samuel 24:1 the Lord, whose anger is kindled, incites David to take a census, while in 1 Chronicles 21:1 we read that *satan* stood up to incite David (same verb as in 2 Sam 24:1) to initiate a census. Since *satan* can denote either a rival nation or the prince of evil, one's exegesis of 1 Chronicles 21:1 is intimately related to one's metaphysics.[52] Then the alternate viewpoints of the different versions of the story

---

50. Collins, *Short Introduction*, 15–17.
51. R. M. Brown, *Unexpected News*, 76, 79–81.
52. The Hebrew word *satan* can refer to an enemy nation (1 Sam 29:4; 2 Sam 19:23;

provide the reader with another choice: Does one believe that God causes our mistakes (as in 2 Sam 24:1) or that it is an enemy that is the real cause (as in 1 Chr 21:1)?

The stories model of Scripture allows people to plumb the depths of biblical narrative for the key ideas it contains. Near the end of a lengthy exegesis of the chapters in Genesis on Joseph, soon after quoting the speech of Judah, who formerly had sought to kill Joseph and now asks Joseph to respect their father's love for Benjamin (Gen 44:18–34), Robert Alter writes, "A basic biblical perception about both human relations and relations between God and man is that love is unpredictable, arbitrary, at times perhaps seemingly unjust, and Judah now comes to an acceptance of that fact with all its consequences."[53] These ideas about love are communicated with a poignancy and relevance by narrative in ways that simple description cannot match. The stories in the Bible make sense of what our human lives mean in a world ruled by one God, the God of Israel. They help us explore how God's purposes intersect with our human desires and decisions.[54]

Aside from communicating key ideas and exploring complex relationships, a reader's appreciation of and attention to the stories of the Bible provide a context, whether cultural or religious, for one's own life. The Bible's stories provide a panoramic view of all peoples of the earth, at least in places like the flood story of Genesis and the stories of Israel's interactions with other nations. Once written, these stories allow entry points for all peoples of the earth to find themselves in the overall narrative of how God relates to humanity. This overall narrative can be summarized in different ways, as we will see in the chapter on metanarratives below. But even with the verbiage about God's choice of Israel, the sheer number of stories in the Bible offer connections into how God relates to humanity that cannot be replicated in models that view the Bible as something other than story.

This is, first, because stories can provide a context that other forms of literature cannot. Once we can locate ourselves within a story, we can then understand our relationships with our contemporaries. It is also because the Bible's narratives include a universal horizon behind their emphasis on the chosenness of Israel. In a way that might seem counterintuitive to some, the Bible's emphasis on the special love God has for Israel, God's elect, played out as it is

---

Ps 109:6) or to the prince of evil (Zech 3:1–2). Hebrew does not have a script of capital letters, so only the context can determine what *satan* means in the Hebrew Bible.

53. Alter, *Art of Biblical Narrative*, 174–75.
54. Alter, *Art of Biblical Narrative*, 176.

on a stage that also includes non-elect and anti-elect peoples, allows readers to see that all peoples are encompassed in God's dealings with the world.[55]

The Christian Scriptures as stories pull the reader toward recognizing the world of these stories as the real world. A network of interlocking images provides a topography of landmarks and reference points for this world. Land as distinguished from sea or wilderness, expulsion and return to the land, covenants between God and those who dwell in the land, a place for worshiping God within the land, kings who rule those in the land, prophets who instruct them and priests who facilitate worship in the land are all part of the network of shared images that build a world for the readers of Scripture.[56]

The contexts that the narratives of the New Testament provide for Christian readers are ecclesial and sacramental. We understand who we are as members of the church through texts within the Gospels and Acts (Matt 16:15–20; 18:15–22; Luke 24:13–53; Acts 2:1–47; 4:32–35; 13:1–3) and narrative-embedded commands within the letters (1 Cor 5:1–11; 11:17–32). The sacramental context the New Testament provides builds on the representation of intersecting worlds mentioned above. In the New Testament, the Gospels' portraits of baptisms, healings, and Jesus's institution of the Eucharist focus the perspective of intersecting worlds into a Christocentric vision of our embodied existence.

LIMITATIONS OF THE STORIES MODEL

The stories model is attractive because of our human need for stories. We need narratives to make sense of our lives and to understand the big ideas by which we live. But the stories model cannot capture all that our Scriptures offer people.

First of all, the stories model does not fully capture the way in which the Scriptures function as a thesaurus of prayer for readers. Yes, there are some narrative connections that the superscriptions of the Psalms offer, and there are occasional connections in the Psalms to events in history, such as the destruction of Solomon's temple or the return from exile.[57] But the superscriptions and the few connections to history offered within some psalms cannot encapsulate the spiritual energy awakened by the prayers of the Psalms.

---

55. See Kaminsky, *Yet I Loved Jacob*, 111–19 (on the anti-elect) and 121–36 (on the non-elect).
56. Ryken, *Bible as Literature*, 186.
57. See, e.g., the superscriptions to Pss 3, 34, 51, 56, 57, 59, and 60. On the destruction of Solomon's temple, see Pss 73:3–7; 79:1. On the return from exile, see Pss 126 and 147.

Next, there is a profound sense of law that the Scriptures offer, a sense that cannot be erased even by an antinomian reading of Pauline letters. The stories model cannot capture the awareness and challenge of a divine call to obedience that the Scriptures evoke.

The stories model includes differing accounts of the historiography in the Christian canon. An exclusive use of the stories model that offers no historical connection or documentation—the "stories as stories" application of this model—will result in an emaciated Bible that cannot fulfill people's need for a link to the past that informs them of how the transcendent God enters the world in which we live.

It is true that some people, such as John Chrysostom, considered gospel narratives to be prophetic for later generations, but in most cases those who employ the stories model do not find the stories to be predictive. The model therefore does not address many readers' expectations to find a prophetic word within the Scriptures. So the stories model must be used alongside other models.

Finally, a methodological challenge to the "stories as history" application of the stories model is that sometimes the apologetic task of arguing that a passage in the Bible is accurate, historical reportage eclipses major truths that others find in the same passages. For example, one might spend one's energy explaining how Genesis 1 matches the geologic and fossil evidence on our planet while unconscious of how this creation account emphasizes God's mastery over evil. One might spend one's energy explaining how a human could survive an extended stay inside a large fish or a whale without being aware of all the ways that the book of Jonah emphasizes God's engagement and mercy toward outsiders. So even if one applies the stories model in the "stories as history" way, one should definitely acknowledge and communicate the deeper ideas that these stories communicate, beyond simply trying to prove that things happened exactly as these stories indicate.

The Stories Model in the Classroom

You will be exposed to narrative theology and the stories model of exegesis in your theology or biblical studies classes. At all times it is good to ask, "Has my professor/textbook shown that the story he or she presents as behind this text or theological idea is necessary for understanding it?" and "Is the narrative used to explain this biblical text or theological idea the best narrative for understanding it?"

Dennis Ronald MacDonald is known for promoting the stories of Homer as explanatory companions of the Gospels and Acts.[58] Marianne Palmer Bonz compares Luke-Acts with Virgil's *Aeneid* and finds similarities significant enough to lead her to conclude that the author of Luke-Acts was influenced by the *Aeneid* when composing his gospel and its sequel. The result of Bonz's study is an awareness of the reconceptualization that Luke offers in his gospel. "Luke appears to have been inspired by Virgil in his presentation of the church as the natural and, indeed, the only legitimate successor to ancient Israel. Seizing upon the divine origins of the Trojan people, long established in legend, Virgil's epic extends those claims to encompass Rome and its inhabitants. The promise of ancient Troy reaches its fulfillment in the creation of the Roman people, just as, in Luke's narrative, the promise of ancient Israel reaches its fulfillment in the establishment and growth of the new community of believers."[59] And as mentioned above, Richard Hays published his dissertation on how the story of Christ's faithfulness animates the heart of Paul's Letter to the Galatians.[60]

Whether you are being told that the Gospel of Mark is based on stories from Homer's *Odyssey*, that Luke-Acts is mirroring Virgil's *Aeneid*, or that a particular story is behind the heart of Paul's Letter to the Galatians, never accept the explanatory story being offered without questioning whether another story might be better considered in its place. That process of questioning the choice of an explanatory story will help you better understand what the biblical author is claiming in each case and will help you learn from the points of contact presented.

The Stories Model in Ministry

When ministers prepare to speak to their audiences, they tend to look to Scripture for a story in which they and their audiences can find themselves. In his analysis of sermons preached by Protestant pastors in the North at the time of Lincoln's assassination, David Chesebrough notes that most of their sermons were based on the Old Testament, since the Old Testament contains stories of war, leaders who are put to death, a chosen people, and a wrathful God who executes vengeance. Chesebrough considers these aspects of the Old Testa-

---

58. D. MacDonald, *Homeric Epics*; D. MacDonald, *Does the New Testament Imitate Homer?*
59. Bonz, *Past as Legacy*, 192–93.
60. Hays, *Faith of Jesus Christ*, 119–83.

ment's stories to be more appealing to Northern Protestant ministers at the time of Lincoln's assassination than anything from the New Testament.[61]

Lutheran minister Joseph Seiss offered an extended comparison between Moses and Lincoln in a sermon, since the story of Moses's life seemed a fruitful analogue to the life of Lincoln.[62] This fits the pattern noted by Mark Noll, who mentions how white ministers in America read the exodus as a type for the American quest for independence from Britain, while black ministers read it as a type for their own emancipation. Noll summarizes the attraction of the stories model and the assumption supporting its use in eighteenth- and nineteenth-century United States as follows: "The Bible was not so much the truth above all truth as it was the story above all stories. On public occasions Scripture appeared regularly as a typical narrative imparting significance to the antitypical events, people, and situation of United States history. That is, ministers preached as if the stories of Scripture were being repeated, or could be repeated, in the unfolding life of the United States."[63]

Pastors in other nations can also find parallels between Scripture and their national or ethnic experiences. Just as Americans need to beware of equating their national history with biblical accounts of God's election of Israel, so Christians in every political and ethnic situation need to remember that the election of Israel as portrayed in the Bible is unique, and that no wholesale transfer of significance can be made between Israel's history as described in Scripture and any political entity on the earth today.

When you minister, people in your congregation will sometimes seek to discern how you are interpreting the stories of the Bible. In their minds, a question such as "Does my pastor think these stories are records of what actually happened, or is my pastor treating the stories as fiction?" will be motivating them to listen closely to your exegesis of Scripture. We have dealt with related questions in the "Stories as Stories" section above, but here we will consider what is the best way to preach when some in our audience are focused on this question.

In the homily or sermon, it is best to set before your audience the deep truths that your text is teaching and not spend time discussing whether the narrative you are reading is an exact depiction of something that happened

---

61. Chesebrough, *"No Sorrow like Our Sorrow,"* xvii–xviii.

62. Seiss, *Assassinated President*, cited in Chesebrough, *"No Sorrow like Our Sorrow,"* 83–84.

63. Noll, "Biblical Nation," 43.

or not. There is only so much energy that an audience will invest in what you express in the homily. If you begin by trying to prove that Jonah really was in a fish for three days and three nights, or that the story is a parable, your audience will exhaust their attentive energy on whichever of these points you attempt to communicate, and they will have little left for the main point of Jonah: the possibility of repentance for all and God's ever-present offer of mercy. Also, in speaking during the homily or sermon about either the historicity or the mythic character of a given narrative, you will inevitably lose some in the audience. The question of historicity versus mythic character is one best left for those in the congregation to ask. When they ask, answer them privately. Don't use the homily or sermon for this sort of preliminary question. Instead, show your audience what the text is saying about repentance and mercy.

In your ministry of preaching and teaching Scripture, the historical veracity of the virgin birth, life, death, and resurrection of Christ must be vigorously upheld. Outside of those events, it is best not to spend time and energy convincing an audience either that something really happened as it is written or that it happened differently or did not happen. As Peter Enns argues, defending the historicity of the Bible can be a rabbit trail that distracts you and your audience from the big ideas that the Bible is trying to communicate.[64] What will happen if you try to prove either that a fish actually swallowed Jonah and vomited him up on land three days later or that this did not happen? No matter which view you choose to prove, you will distract most of your audience from the main message of the book of Jonah and you will alienate some in your audience. It is far better to enter into the world of the text and proclaim the main ideas that it is communicating. Here is how I think this section of Jonah can be effectively presented.[65]

> The narrative of Jonah now shows God intervening by sending a large fish to swallow Jonah. Jonah's prayer is a prayer of thanksgiving. He seems to be thanking God for a deliverance before it happens. His prayer also seems to represent his own decision to follow God's will. He is no longer running from God as in the first chapter, and sleeping while the sailors were praying. Now he is praying, and promising to keep promises he has made (2:9). This is the second of three descriptions of repentance in this book. First the sail-

64. Enns, *Bible Tells Me So*, 87–99.
65. What follows is my example for preaching on Jonah. For a consideration of how the Gospels' different ways of telling stories relates to preaching, see the section "How Biblical Stories Preach" in Goldingay, *Models for Interpretation*, 73–76.

ors turned from calling on their gods to worshiping the Lord (1:5, 16), here Jonah is turning to thank God and announce his close dependence on God (2:2–9), and in the next chapter we will see the city of Nineveh repenting and God's merciful response (3:5–10). The whole book is trying to say that God stands ready to forgive and respond to all who are ready to repent, whether they are random pagans like the sailors, religious hypocrites like Jonah, or the enemies of God's people—like the city of Nineveh. It becomes an invitation to us to reach out to God—we can pray what Jonah prays—and acknowledge God's powerful presence on earth, pray for deliverance, and thank God for responding to us.

Because we understand our lives only in terms of how they fit into a narrative, the stories model is very useful in ministry and should be regularly used alongside the models of prayers and oracles.

PRAYERS

We give you thanks, Holy Father, for your holy name, which you have caused to dwell in our hearts, and for the knowledge and faith and immortality that you have made known to us through Jesus your servant; to you be the glory forever. You, almighty Master, created all things for your name's sake, and gave food and drink to humans to enjoy, so that they might give you thanks; but to us you have graciously given spiritual food and drink, and eternal life through your servant.

—DIDACHE[1]

In my first semester of teaching at a Catholic school, I asked students to read half of the Gospel of Matthew and tell me what they learned or what questions the text prompted for them. One student related his discovery: "Now I know where 'Lord, I am not worthy to enter under your roof, but only say the word and I shall be healed' comes from!" He had been accustomed to saying these words at Mass, in the act of humility within the invitation to Communion.[2] He had not realized that he was praying Scripture every time he said these words at Mass.

DEFINITION AND CHARACTERISTICS OF THE PRAYERS MODEL

No one, whatever their model of Scripture, will deny that Scripture contains many prayers. After all, the title of the book of Psalms in Hebrew, *Tehilim*, means "praises," or "praise songs," denoting a subset of prayer discourse. But the prayers model does not only refer to how people can pray certain prayer texts that are in the Bible. The prayers model reads all genres of text within the Bible—narrative, law, poetry, apocalyptic, genealogy, and parable—as potential prayers to be spoken to God.

1. *Didache* 10:1–3 (Holmes, 359).
2. Matt 8:8; *General Instruction of the Roman Missal* §84.

You know that the prayers model is operating . . .

. . . when someone prays a phrase or more from Scripture by actually quoting it in a prayer. Every time we pray or sing a psalm from the book of Psalms or pray the Lord's Prayer (Matt 6:9–13; Luke 11:2–4), we are activating the prayers model. Other examples can easily be identified from the Liturgy of the Hours. In morning prayer we pray the Benedictus with Zechariah, John the Baptist's father (Luke 1:68–79). In evening prayer we pray the Magnificat with Mary (Luke 1:46–55). In night prayer we pray the Nunc Dimittis with Simeon (Luke 2:29–32). The Hail Mary is built on the words with which Gabriel and Elizabeth addressed Mary (Luke 1:28, 42). The "have mercy on me" phrase of the Jesus Prayer, commonly taught in the Orthodox Church, has many precedents in the Old Testament.[3]

. . . when someone structures a prayer around a Scripture text. I was once asked to give a closing prayer at a baccalaureate service. I had a deep desire to pray with Psalm 90 as my template, since that psalm gets at the deepest characteristics of human existence. So I quoted lines from that psalm and then added related descriptions and petitions that fit the graduating class's experience.

. . . when the words of Scripture are pronounced in a liturgical or worship setting. "What God has joined, let not man separate" are words pronounced when a minister is performing a wedding ceremony. They come from Matthew 19:6b. When spoken during the sacrament or ordinance of marriage, they are opening the audience's perspective to God's presence in the marriage that has just occurred and asking for the audience's prayerful support for the union begun that day. In this way, this can be an example of the prayers model.

Specific Applications of the Prayers Model

To read Scripture in its entirety as the triune God's word to humanity requires reading within the tradition of the body of Christ, the church. This social context for reading Scripture coheres with the prayers model, for prayer in the Judeo-Christian tradition is significantly a communal activity. This can be seen in the community laments and hymns in the book of Psalms, the first-person

3. Neh 13:2; Pss 27:7; 30:11; 51:3; 56:2; 57:2; 119:58.

plural verbs and pronouns in the Lord's Prayer, and the corporate prayers in the books of Acts and Revelation.[4]

The prayers model understands Scripture as God's word to the church, a word continually calling for a response. The texts of Scripture are not simply laboratory specimens to be dissected, as they can be viewed in the documents model. They are instead God's words of invitation to relationship, complete with possible scripts for readers' responses to this invitation.

The core text, the nerve center of the prayers model, is the book of Psalms. The care and intensity that the church has traditionally invested in praying the Psalms is well exemplified in the *Rule of Saint Benedict*. In a section of twelve chapters, St. Benedict identifies which psalms are to be prayed, explains how the praying of psalms might change depending on the time of year, and describes the manner in which those following his rule are to pray them. The *Rule of Saint Augustine*, followed by Augustinian and Dominican orders, is more brief on praying the Psalms but equally profound: "When you pray to God in psalms and songs, the words spoken by your lips should be alive in your hearts."[5]

The church fathers Athanasius and Augustine provide two ways of praying the Scriptures. Both are helpful, and one can move between the two when praying the Psalms.

Reading Scripture's Prayers as a Mirror

Athanasius, knowing that his sick friend Marcellinus was reading Psalms as a response to his illness, wrote to him and described how the Psalms are like a mirror: "It seems to me that these words become like a mirror to those singing them, so that he might perceive himself and the emotions of his soul, and thus affected, he might recite them . . . so that in these same words . . . the stirrings of our souls might be grasped, and all of them be said as concerning us, and the same issue from us as our own words, for a remembrance of the emotions in us, and a chastening of our life."[6] Athanasius and much of Christian tradition thus existentially reads Scripture as providing prayers one can pray. Most who pray the Divine Office are reading the Psalms with this particular use of the prayers model: they pray the Bible's words as their own prayers.

---

4. Pss 44, 74, and 89 are communal laments. Pss 33, 65, and 67 are communal hymns. The corporate nature of prayer is evident in these New Testament texts: Matt 6:9, 11–13; Luke 11:3–4; Acts 5:24–30; 13:2–3; 16:25; Rev 4:8–11; 5:8–14; 6:9–10; 11:16–18; 15:2–4; 19:1–4, 6–8.

5. *Rule of Saint Benedict* §§8–19 (pp. 20–28); *Rule of Saint Augustine* §2.3 (p. 13).

6. Athanasius, *Letter to Marcellinus* 12, as quoted in Murphy, *Experiencing Our Biblical Heritage*, 124–25.

In the Orthodox Church, hesychasm, a means of preparing for God's kingdom to come inside oneself (Luke 17:20–21), is oriented around repetition of a divine name. This repetition is based on the Hebrew idea that a name is a doorway into a person's essential character. A name of the divine that is revealed in Scripture is a theophany in its own right. So repeated calling on a divine name, in Orthodox tradition, is a way of coming into closer communion with God: "By invoking the Name of Jesus, with faith and love, the worshiper ascends Mount Sinai in the grace and power of the Holy Spirit, to stand in awe before the divine Presence."[7]

The Spiritual Exercises of Ignatius potentially offer a Western analogue to hesychasm. They also can help us internalize God's presence, as we place ourselves into biblical discourse in which God encounters humanity.[8] When we place ourselves into a biblical scene, meditate on it, and by means of such meditation find our identity, we are applying the prayers model as a mirror.

Reading Scripture's Prayers as a Window

In contrast to Athanasius's existential orientation toward the Psalms, Augustine's orientation is christological and ecclesiological.[9] Augustine identifies certain people, such as the "blessed" person who meditates on God's law day and night in Psalm 1, as Christ. He identifies references to the "congregation" or the "people" in various psalms with the church.[10] This way of engaging with Scripture's prayers is likened to a window, since through a prayer text of Scripture it sees someone outside oneself—usually Christ or the church—as the one who is praying. The basis for this application of the prayers model can be found within the New Testament itself. Paul identifies Christ as the speaker of Psalm 69:9 in Romans 15:3. This text in Romans, as well as passion narratives of the Gospels, depict Jesus as praying the Psalms. Besides historical figures such as David or the historical pre- and postexilic congregations of Israel, the New Testament is thus offering another implied speaker of the Psalms. Jesus is depicted as praying the Psalms in scenes related to his passion:

---

7. Breck, *Scripture in Tradition*, 215–18, quotation from 218.

8. See Martin, *Jesuit Guide to (Almost) Everything*, 19–21.

9. As is already evident, I am relying on Murphy's *Experiencing Our Biblical Heritage* for examples of reading the Bible's prayers as a mirror into our own lives or as prayers that Christ or the church prays. For the terminology of mirror and window, I am indebted to Harry Hagan, OSB, in personal correspondence of September 28, 2017. He uses these terms to offer alternatives in how one can pray the Psalms, when some seem so far removed from our life situations.

10. Murphy, *Experiencing Our Biblical Heritage*, 125.

Mark 14:34 (Ps 42:6, 12); Mark 15:34 (Ps 22:1); Luke 23:46 (Ps 31:5). There are attributions of psalm prayers to Jesus at times other than his passion as well: John 2:17 (Ps 69:9); Rom 15:8–9 (Ps 18:49); Heb 2:10–13 (Ps 22:22); Heb 10:5–7 (Ps 40:7–9).[11] The New Testament basis for viewing the church as the speaker of a psalm can be found in Romans 8:36, which quotes a communal lament of Israel (Ps 44:22).

It is worth noting how Augustine's *Confessions* exemplifies the prayers model in a subtler way than simply repraying the Bible's prayers. As Augustine prays to God through his entire *Confessions*, he identifies with various characters from the Bible while forming his own prayer. In the following quotation, Augustine identifies with each one of the three parables found in Luke 15.

> You too, merciful Father, yes, even you are more joyful over one repentant sinner than over ninety-nine righteous people who need no repentance. And we likewise listen with overflowing gladness when we hear how the shepherd carries back on exultant shoulders the sheep that had strayed, and how the coin is returned to your treasury as neighbors share the glee of the woman who found it, while the joy of your Eucharistic assembly wrings tears from us when the story is read in your house of the younger son who *was dead, but has come back to life, was lost but is found.*[12]

Murphy, after contrasting these two patristic approaches of mirror and window, seems to advocate a compromise. He recommends that a reader view the psalmist and herself as reader as standing before God. In this position, the Spirit of God can bring truths to mind. Despite the wide variety of mental states reflected in the book of Psalms, all of them are prayers spoken out of an attitude of trust in God. They thus model for us a way to bring our frustrations, griefs, and deepest fears to God while trusting in God's lovingkindness and faithfulness.[13]

OLD TESTAMENT TEXTS OFTEN READ AS PRAYERS

The prayers model mines Scripture for the names for God so that the reader may invoke God through names that have long been used in prayer. In this sense, Scripture is a thesaurus of names by which to address the divine in prayer. The implied authors of the Old Testament show a concern for how

11. Hays, "Christ Prays the Psalms," 123–27.
12. Augustine, *Confessions* 8.3.6 (Boulding, 189), citing Luke 15:4–32.
13. Murphy, *Experiencing Our Biblical Heritage*, 126.

God is addressed. Thus, we read in Exodus 3:13–15 how Moses asked the God of Israel's name and learned that the name means that God exists and defines who God is only by God's own intention, by no other experience or expectation we have.[14] And in Exodus 6:2–3 we read, "And God spoke to Moses and said to him, 'I am YHWH: I appeared to Abraham, to Isaac, and to Jacob as El-Shaddai, but by my name YHWH I was not known to them.'" The name YHWH, which is an English transliteration of the proper name of the God of Israel used in the third commandment, is not to be used in vain (Exod 20:7) and thus is not vocalized in the Masoretic Text of the Hebrew Bible. The first person to name the God of Israel in the Old Testament is Hagar, the Egyptian slave-woman of Abraham and Sarah. It is significant that Scripture records how this oppressed and ostracized woman names God as the "God who sees" (Gen 16:13).

Within the opening chapters of the Old Testament, someone reading with the prayers model in mind would inevitably be drawn to some of the programmatic lines, such as the repeated descriptions of humans in God's image, the command to be fruitful, and the description of God's provision of Eve to Adam (Gen 1:26–27; 1:28; 2:18–24). Lines from these texts are easily included in one's personal prayers or in public liturgies.

One reading with the prayers model would note how 2 Samuel 24 is focused on the location of the temple. Its fixation on telling the details of how the temple site was chosen shows the priority its authors placed on worship at the temple. David's own decision to place himself under a merciful God rather than under human judgment is also valuable to those using the prayers model (24:14). And finally, David's insistence on paying a full price for what is involved in his selection and dedication of the temple site is eminently applicable for one who seeks to prioritize prayer in one's own life (24:24).

Those reading Scripture from the perspective of the prayers model will almost instinctively accept the conversational relationship that the God of Israel and Jonah have as a possibility for all believers to have. Jonah's prayer from the fish (2:1–9) becomes a model for how to pray in times of distress. Jonah's reaction to God's mercy is a negative example—how not to respond when God shows mercy to others (4:1–8). For those applying the prayers model in an existential way to their own lives, the book of Jonah is a powerful impetus to seek God's will in the details of life, to obey God's call, and to celebrate God's mercy on all.

Among the various genres of psalms, those known as the penitential psalms become a model of repentance for readers employing the prayers model.

---

14. Janzen, *When Prayer Takes Place*, 33.

Whether one reads a penitential psalm as a prayer of the whole church or an individual prayer, it is ideal discourse when one seeks to turn from sin toward God. Even though Augustine is known for reading the psalms as though Christ or the church is praying them, at the end of his life Augustine prayed four penitential psalms of David as though he himself were the speaker. In other words, he applied these psalms as a script for his own relationship with God. We know this because he put the penitential psalms on the walls of his room in the last two weeks of his life, preferring to pray them over seeing visitors.[15]

In the prayers model of Scripture, priority is given to the prayer book of Israel and the church, the book of Psalms. The Psalms form the backbone of the Liturgy of the Hours, the prayers that many pray at set times throughout the day. The basis for praying in this way can be seen in how Psalm 119:55, 62, 147–48 portrays one praying both early in the morning and late at night, presumably as a way to show how prayer is a high priority. Specific grounding for the original format of the Liturgy of the Hours may be seen in Psalm 119:164, with its picture of praising God seven times per day.

Most of the psalms are complaints, also called laments. They represent the honest pleas and cries to God from people in a wide variety of situations. Robert Alter calls this genre of psalm a "supplication" and notes that this genre and the genre that could be called "praises" together account for over two-thirds of the 150 psalms in the Bible's Psalter.[16] But the fact that other genres of psalm can also be prayed to God provides an opening for us to understand that other forms of discourse within the canon of Scripture can also be prayed.

Though there are more laments than any other genre within the book of Psalms, the title of the book and its organization make a powerful statement. Many of the lament psalms conclude with a statement of trust or a description of a future in which the plaintiff will be praising God.[17] The very act of complaining to God thus becomes an acknowledgment of God's power and segues into a trusting statement of hope. The title of the book, as noted above, is *Tehilim* (praises) in Hebrew. The last six psalms are definitely songs of praise, and every one of the last five begins with "Hallelujah." So it seems that in the composition of most of the lament psalms, the title for the whole book, and the arrangement of the final psalms, the editors are telling us that the essence of discourse toward God is praise. And the immediate and necessary compulsion

---

15. P. Brown, *Augustine of Hippo*, 436, citing Possidius, *Vita* 31.1–3. The psalms Augustine prayed in the last days of his life were probably Pss 6, 32, 38, and 51.

16. Alter, "Psalms," 247–48.

17. Pss 5:11–12; 13:5–6; 51:19; 61:8; 79:13; 140:12–13.

to render this praise to God is due to the psalmists' certainty that no one who has died can continue to praise God.[18]

While the lament psalms often end with a statement of trust, they are still asking the "How long, O Lord?" question and eloquently expressing distress. Walter Brueggemann calls the laments "psalms of disorientation" and notes how they express the "disequilibrium, incoherence, and unrelieved asymmetry" we experience in our own time.[19] Whether one is reading the Psalms or any other part of the Bible, the signs of disorientation reflected in the text invite readers to pray Scripture. In the end, only God can address our disorientation and set everything right. So the focus of the laments is God, even when the psalmist is praying about situations that could occupy all our attention. For example, in one of the two psalms that directly mention the destruction of the temple, the first focus is on God.[20] A lament such as Psalm 74 is good for calling us away from tangible blessings that we have taken for granted and redirecting our attention to God, the reality underneath all the blessings of the physical world.[21]

Among the laments in the book of Psalms are the seven penitential psalms: 6, 32, 38, 51, 102, 130, and 143. Unlike many other laments in the Psalter, the speaker in these psalms readily admits guilt and does not accuse God of abandonment. The penitential psalms pulse with an intense need for God's forgiveness and the reconciled state that follows.[22] These psalms provide an inviting point of entry for someone ready to try the prayers model of reading Scripture. Their viewpoint might be different from a postmodern sensibility, however. These psalms view God as the ultimate person with whom we have to deal, and guilt as an actual problem that must be acknowledged and forgiven.[23]

Other psalms allow us to pray in ways that can question God's justice and that can complain of others' intrusion into our lives, including God's own role in our troubles. The Psalms therefore help us to pray even when injustice seems dominant, or when God seems implicated in the troubles afflicting us. The Psalms resist a worldview of the earth as at rest, with peace and justice firmly established. Rather, they show a worldview in which God's people are

---

18. Alter, *Book of Psalms*, xx. On the need to praise God before one falls forever silent in death, see Pss 6:5; 115:17.

19. Brueggemann, *Message of the Psalms*, 51.

20. Brueggemann, *Message of the Psalms*, 69, on Ps 74:1–2.

21. Brueggemann, *Message of the Psalms*, 71.

22. Brueggemann, *Message of the Psalms*, 95.

23. Brueggemann, *Message of the Psalms*, 97, on Ps 32. The same ideas are found in Pss 6:1–4; 38:1–4, 9, 15–22; 51:1–12; 130:3–8.

vulnerable to oppression and injustice. They empower prayers that ask God for answers and intervention.[24] It is especially the lament psalms that seem cut from the same cloth as the divine preference for Job's honest discourse over his friends' forced and idealistic explanations (Job 42:7).

It is common to wonder how one can profitably read or meaningfully pray certain psalms, when their subject matter and voice seem so distant from our situations. It is here that we can return to Athanasius's description of the Psalms as a mirror, described above, and say that while some of the psalms might function as a mirror for us, others function as windows that allow us to see other people's stance before God. If a psalm evokes a recognition that the psalmist's cry is our cry, then we can use the psalm as a mirror and pray it back to God for ourselves. If another psalm does not reflect our situation, we can read it as a window, remembering that there are others in our world today who are experiencing the challenges and questions that the psalm is raising. Our prayer can then flow out of such a psalm, as a prayer for those who can be seen through the window of the psalm that is strange to us.

The book of Psalms contain some prayers that are difficult for us to pray. For example, the communal lament we know as Psalm 44 celebrates the Israel-ites' dispossession of other peoples in a way that does not seem just.[25] And the imprecatory psalms call down curses on the psalmist's enemies. The implied authors of these psalms assume God's forgiveness of their own sins while ask-ing that God not forgive the sins of enemies. We will discuss this difficulty in the New Testament section below.

Any Jewish prayer book will give ample evidence of complete immersion in the Psalms.[26] Our Christian practice of using our Scriptures, especially the book of Psalms, in our own prayers is completely indebted to Jewish practice. The prayers model is valuable for Christians in that it prompts the Scripture reader to enter fully into the discourse of the Psalms, praying them back to God. This is a far cry from the tendency that began in the eighteenth century to regard the Psalms primarily as examples of good poetry.[27]

While the book of Psalms is the primary source of prayers in the Bible, there are prayers contained in other parts of the Bible. Moshe Greenberg calls these "prayers embedded in the narratives of the Bible," admitting he is using "narratives" to denote anything outside the Psalms. He notes that, within the

---

24. Brueggemann, *Message of the Psalms*, 176.
25. L'Engle, *Stone for a Pillow*, 40–41.
26. See, e.g., Davis, *Metsudah Siddur*.
27. Legaspi, *Death of Scripture*, 127–28.

Old Testament, such prayers are especially found in Jeremiah.[28] The narrative prayers highlight how anyone may pray, whether one is a rowdy person like Samson or a pagan like the sailors on Jonah's ship.[29] The type of prayer that God is most likely to hear is the prayer of the desperate person.[30]

New Testament Texts Often Read as Prayers

The Hebrew Bible's interest in names for God is continued in the Christian canon. Jesus famously encourages his followers to address God as "Father" in the Lord's Prayer. Jesus himself calls God "Abba," a respectful but intimate epithet for a father.[31] The care taken not to use God's name in vain that is evident in the Masoretes' decision not to vocalize the proper name of the God of Israel is also evident in some parts of the New Testament. In the trial scene in Mark 14, the religious authorities use "the Blessed" to communicate the term "God" without saying "God": "Are you the Christ, the Son of the Blessed?" Jesus continues with this same care to avoid taking God's name in vain, for in his answer he uses "the Power" to refer to God (Mark 14:61–62 RSV). The Letter of James uses "Father of lights" to refer to God, in an expression that connotes God's place as creator and sustainer of the stars fixed in the heavens (1:17). The book of Revelation uses names like "Lord God," "Lord God Almighty," and "Alpha and Omega" for God the Father.[32] The names for Jesus in Revelation include "faithful witness," "firstborn of the dead," and "ruler of the kings of the earth," titles that depict Jesus as an exemplary leader for his followers on earth.[33] The frequent title "lamb" connotes Jesus's function as a sacrifice for humanity.[34] All of these titles for divine address get added to the believer's thesaurus for his or her own prayers.

Some connotations for God's names certainly are lost in translation, as Hebrew names for God were translated into Greek in the Septuagint and in

28. Greenberg, *Biblical Prose Prayer*, 7.

29. Greenberg, *Biblical Prose Prayer*, 17.

30. Kugel, *God of Old*, 109–36; Greenberg, *Biblical Prose Prayer*, 17.

31. Barr, "'Abbā Isn't 'Daddy.'"

32. "Lord God" (*kyrios theos*) occurs in Rev 1:8; 4:11; 18:8; 22:5, 6. "Lord God the Almighty" occurs in Rev 4:8; 11:17; 15:3; 16:7; 19:6; 21:22. "Alpha and Omega" is used of God the Father in Rev 1:8; 21:6.

33. "Faithful witness" (*ho martys ho pistos*) occurs in Rev 1:5; 3:14. "Firstborn of the dead" (*prōtotokos tōn nekrōn*) and "ruler of the kings of the earth" (*ho archōn tōn basileōn tēs gēs*) are also found in Rev 1:5.

34. "Lamb" (*arnion*) is used of Jesus in Rev 5:6, 8, 12, 13; 6:1, 16; 7:9, 10, 14, 17; 12:11; 13:8; 14:1, 4, 10; 15:3; 17:14; 19:7, 9; 21:9, 14, 22, 23, 27; 22:1, 3.

the New Testament. Thus the Hebrew name El-Shaddai, which connotes not only power but also the nourishing, familial care of a tribal deity, is lost in the "God Almighty" or "Lord" of many Old Testament translations into modern languages, which follow the terms the Septuagint's translators used.[35] The book of Revelation uses the Septuagint's "Almighty" term for El-Shaddai (21:22), and thus readers will understand it as connoting a nourishing provider only if they allow the context to inform their reading (21:22–22:5).

Nonetheless, the power of divine names was acknowledged outside Judaism and Christianity. The Hebrew term *adonai* passed into pagan magical spells and prompted other forms of the name as well, such as Adonaêl and Adonaios. Other forms of divine names from the Hebrew Bible that were valued in pagan spells are Iaô and Sabaoth.[36]

Because of this potential for the widespread invocation and repetition of a divine name, Orthodox author John Breck considers it necessary to retain the titles for God that are found in Scripture rather than the functional titles of "Creator," "Redeemer," and "Sanctifier." Breck asserts that these latter titles could lead to heresy, since they can distort the character of a given person of the Trinity as revealed in Scripture. He notes how Gregory of Nazianzus maintained that the persons of the Trinity can be differentiated only in regard to origin, so that it is incorrect to use the functional titles above as the definitive titles for the Trinity's persons.[37] Thus, to call only the Father "Creator" is to ignore scriptural witness to the roles of the Son and Holy Spirit in creation.

The Gospels are a good source of prayer discourse for Christians because we find ourselves reliving others' experiences with Jesus. It therefore becomes easy for us to place ourselves into the encounters people had with Jesus (e.g., Mark 9:24) or to pray Jesus's words of prayer—for example, his high priestly prayer (John 17:1–26) or his prayer in Gethsemane before his arrest (Matt 26:39 // Mark 14:36 // Luke 22:42).

The Gospel of Luke contains pictures of Jesus praying in scenes that the other Synoptic Gospels do not mention, such as at Jesus's baptism, selection of apostles, and transfiguration.[38] In addition, it contains parables about prayer

35. For the significance of El-Shaddai in the Hebrew Bible, see Janzen, *At the Scent of Water*, 26–29.

36. Gager, *Curse Tablets*, 265, 268–69.

37. Breck, *Scripture in Tradition*, 219.

38. Luke 3:21 (cf. Matt 3:16; Mark 1:9–10); Luke 6:12–13 (cf. Matt 10:1; Mark 3:13–14); Luke 9:28–29 (cf. Matt 17:1–2; Mark 9:2). Note that it is redaction criticism, a strategy associated with the documents model of Scripture, that allows us to see this emphasis on prayer in Luke.

not found in other gospels (18:1–14). One of its special emphases is on persistence in prayer (11:5–8; 18:1–8).

Among the letters of Paul, the Psalms figure prominently in his Letter to the Romans.[39] The book of Ephesians, also in the Pauline corpus broadly conceived, is particularly filled with prayers and encouragement toward prayer.[40]

The book of Revelation is also brimming with prayer language. There are many prayers of praise.[41] There is a cry for justice (6:10) as well as a description of people's prayers reaching God (8:3–4).

We have seen in the Old Testament section above that some psalms are difficult to pray. Certain lament psalms are famous for the way that they ask God to curse others. The moral problem in these psalms is not difficult to see. How can a psalmist ask God to forgive one's own sins and save one's own life while also asking God not to forgive or save another person? John Collins answers this question by saying that the Psalms express emotion and are not intended to give moral instruction.[42] The problem here is that emotional release may have been an initial motive for the composition of some psalms, but as soon as they were copied, prayed by others, and eventually canonized, their purpose also became moral instruction. This is because people read Scripture to receive instruction (Rom 15:4; 2 Tim 3:16–17). So Collins's answer is not sufficient to dispel the moral problem that these psalms raise in our canon. Other writings in the Old Testament, especially those in the wisdom genre, temper the imprecatory psalms. For wisdom literature presents the humble person who tends her or his own life and leaves vengeance to God as living an exemplary life.

The New Testament offers a christological response. It records traditional teachings of Jesus against cursing others (Matt 5:44; Rom 12:14). Imagery from the imprecatory psalms is used in the Gospels' crucifixion scenes, but Jesus does not curse those crucifying or taunting him, and some manuscripts of Luke's Gospel even include Jesus's prayer for forgiveness of his tormenters (Luke 23:34). It thus seems as though there is a canonical progression on the question of whether one can ask God to curse others.

Paul specifically historicizes the actual curse of a lament psalm, identifying it as something David said (Rom 11:9–10; Ps 69:22–23). But then he views an

---

39. Among the Psalms texts in Romans, see 1:23 (Ps 106:20); 2:6 (Ps 62:12); 3:13c (Ps 140:3); 8:36 (Ps 44:22); 11:9–10 (Ps 69:22–23); 15:3 (Ps 69:9); 15:9 (Ps 18:49); 15:11 (Ps 117:1).

40. Prayers in Ephesians come at 1:3–4, 15–23; 3:14–21. Encouragement to pray occurs at Eph 5:19–20 (paralleled in Col 3:16–17); 6:18–20.

41. Rev 4:8, 11; 5:9–10, 12; 15:3–4; 16:5–7; 19:1–4, 6–8.

42. Collins, *Short Introduction*, 301–2.

actual complaint from the same lament psalm as something that Jesus spoke at his crucifixion (Rom 15:3; Ps 69:9). It is possible that Paul is thus modeling how a Christ-follower can pray the lament psalms. The curses remind us of David's trust in God in times of difficulty, and the laments call us to remember Jesus's death.[43] It is possible also that in Paul's statement that no one who is under the influence of God's Spirit can pray *"Anathema Iēsous"* (1 Cor 12:3), the phrase does not mean "Jesus be accursed," as most translations offer, but rather "a Jesus curse." That is, Paul could very well be countering the pagan practice, seen especially in lead tablets recovered from the Temple of Demeter in Corinth, of asking the deity one worships to curse another person. Paul is then in effect saying that the one who calls on Jesus does not ask Jesus to curse others.[44]

An argument against my presentation of Paul's teachings against cursing others is that Paul himself models curse-like behavior in his letters. In 1 Corinthians 5 he asks his church to deliver someone to Satan. But this is done with the ultimate goal of the subject's salvation (5:4–5). At the end of the letter he pronounces a curse on those who do not love the Lord (16:22). And in Galatians 1:8–9 he repeats a curse on anyone who brings to the Galatians a gospel different from what they have received. While these might seem inconsistent with Paul's discourse against cursing that I noted above in the discussion of how Paul uses a lament psalm, Paul has never been one for consistency.

The Lord's Prayer has plenty of parallels with Jewish prayers. But its emphasis on forgiveness—"forgive us our sins, as we forgive those who sin against us"—is not found in the Old Testament. This emphasis on forgiveness is associated by the Gospels with the teaching of Jesus.[45]

The essence of prayer is to call on a deity. The New Testament introduces the discourse of calling on Jesus. Controversially, there is at least one place in which an Old Testament text that mentions the worship of YHWH is repurposed to describe the worship of Jesus (Isa 45:23; Phil 2:9–11).

Other traditional forms of prayer from the Old Testament continue to appear in the New Testament, such as praise of God the creator. Revelation 4:8 employs language from Isaiah 6:2–3 in its picture of praise to God the creator. This is followed by another picture of prayer directed to Jesus, the Lamb (Rev 5:9–10, 13).

---

43. Reasoner, "Paul's Use of Lament Psalms," 214–16.
44. Winter, *After Paul Left Corinth*, 174–79.
45. Cassian, *Conferences* 14.13–14, as summarized in Murphy, *Experiencing Our Biblical Heritage*, 127.

Key Issues in the Prayers Model

It is easy at times to consider engaging with Scripture and praying as entirely different activities. However, Scripture is filled with the language of prayer, and people frequently find Scripture to be very useful when seeking to pray. Each of the key issues below describes ways in which our reading or enacting of Scripture and our praying are intimately related.

Praying in Others' Words and Singing a New Song

Scripture itself indicates, by direct statement and by example, that others' prayers are useful. The evangelists Matthew, Mark, and Luke and the apostle Paul all employ the prayers model of Scripture when they use prayer language from their Scriptures—usually a selection from the Septuagint's version of the Psalms—as a basis for prayers that they insert into their own compositions. Paul writes that God's Spirit intercedes for us, since we do not know how we should pray (Rom 8:26). Soon after that, Paul quotes from a lament psalm, applying its words to his people Israel, who were then oppressed by the Roman Empire, or to the church (Rom 8:36, quoting Ps 44:22). Matthew, Mark, and Luke employ the prayers model of Scripture when they quote prayer discourse from their Scripture within the direct discourse of characters in their gospels.[46] In addition to direct discourse that is drawn from the Psalms, the evangelists also employ the prayer language of Scripture to describe the crucifixion itself.[47] The author of Hebrews relies heavily on the Psalms in presenting Jesus as greater than other revered figures in Judaism and in supporting calls for obedient living.[48]

Besides actual prayers in Scripture, whether found in the Psalms or elsewhere, there are those who view certain parts of Scripture as uniquely written for prayer. For example, the Gospel of Mark can be read as designed to

---

46. Matt 26:30 and Mark 14:26 (Jesus and the apostles sing a hymn, which would have been a psalm); Matt 27:46 and Mark 15:34 (quoting Ps 22:1); Luke 1:46–55 (Mary's Magnificat is based on 1 Sam 2:1–10); Luke 23:46 (quoting Ps 31:5); John 19:28 (quoting Ps 69:21).

47. Matt 27:35; Mark 15:24; Luke 23:34b; John 19:23–25a (enemies divide victim's clothing by casting lots, Ps 22:18); Matt 27:34; Mark 15:23; Luke 23:36; John 19:29–30 (enemies give spiked wine or vinegar, Ps 69:21).

48. Heb 1:5 (Ps 2:7); 1:7 (Ps 104:4); 1:8–9 (Ps 45:6–7); 1:10–12 (Ps 102:25–27); 1:13 (Ps 110:1); 2:6–8 (Ps 8:4–6); 2:12 (Ps 22:22); 3:7–11 (Ps 95:7–11); 3:15 (Ps 95:7); 4:3 (Ps 95:11); 4:7 (Ps 95:7–8); 5:5 (Ps 2:7); 5:6 (Ps 110:4); 7:21 (Ps 110:4); 10:5–9 (Ps 40:6–8); 13:6 (Ps 118:6).

help Jewish followers of Jesus to welcome gentile believers at the table of the Eucharist.[49] And the Gospel of John has been outlined according to the readings of the triennial synagogue lectionary. According to this approach, John included his summaries of Jesus's synagogue sermons and teachings that comment on the weekly readings of the lectionary of first-century Judaism. Even some of the events John narrates contain details that show how Jesus's ministry fulfills the readings of the week.[50]

But beyond the use of prayer language from the Bible, there are ample instances of people praying on the basis of Scripture's narratives. St. Ignatius of Loyola challenged Christians to enter into events in the life of Christ and imagine what it would be like to experience such events. Ignatius popularized contemplative prayer. He challenged people to imagine themselves within a setting described in Scripture or as being in God's presence. While imagining that one is in a place with others who knew God or in God's presence itself, one is opening oneself up to hearing God speak. One can go through the five senses by imagining what anyone in that setting would see, hear, touch, smell, and taste. When exploring the scene in this way, one might readily learn something about what it means to follow God or live in Jesus's presence.[51]

In an analogous way, the Rosary provides a way for people to pray events in the lives of Jesus and Mary. When one prays a given decade of the Rosary's mysteries, one enters into and prays on the basis of the event highlighted in each mystery. Scripture's narratives thus provide a program for prayer. This brings the prayers model of Scripture into sharpest focus. For in these prayers we find ourselves reliving events narrated in Scripture by praying them back to God, as if we are uniting our lives with those people described in Scripture. Our prayers that are based on the Psalms could be understood simply as repeating another's prayer for want of finding a better prayer. But when we pray words out of a narrative, such as the words to Jesus spoken by the centurion or the repentant thief, we are praying our way into someone's life-changing relationship with Jesus. The words of Simeon, the centurion, or the repentant thief are now our words. Their trust is now our trust. And our prayer acknowledges their Lord as our Lord.

Perhaps even a more intimate connection between a believer and our

49. Bobertz, *Gospel of Mark*, 55–102.
50. Guilding, *Fourth Gospel and Jewish Worship*, 1–5, 45–57, 212–33.
51. Martin, *Jesuit Guide to (Almost) Everything*, 145–52.

Lord can occur when one prays the Stations of the Cross. This application of the prayers model calls the believer to follow Jesus to the cross. We therefore are praying through Jesus's walk to the cross, entering into his own passion, or carrying our cross after him, as he commanded (Matt 16:24; Luke 9:23).

This use of Scripture as a thesaurus for our prayer life is seen even within Scripture, in the way that the book of Revelation adapts other parts of Scripture, including the Psalms, in its descriptions of the liturgy of heaven. Thus the language of the four living beings in God's presence is taken from Isaiah's account of the words of the seraphim (Rev 4:8, quoting Isa 6:3). Language of worship before the lamb in Revelation 5:12 is taken from 1 Chronicles 29:11–12. The hymn of Moses and of the lamb in Revelation 15:3–4 quotes phrases from Deuteronomy 32:4 and Psalms 86:9; 111:2; 139:14; 145:17.

The idea of praying the Scriptures back to God is thus a special use of Scripture within the prayers model. What is behind this use of the Bible as a script for people's prayers today? There is perhaps an implicit understanding that Scripture records people's genuine encounters with God. Since God is to be feared, there is a strong attraction to speak with God in words others have already spoken. Since others in Scripture have effectively communicated with God, there is also a practical motivation to use Scripture in prayer. The one who prays with the words of Scripture wants her or his prayer to be heard by God, and what better way to guarantee that God will hear a prayer than to use a prayer that others close to God have prayed?

At the same time, it is clear that no tradition within Judaism or Christianity restricts its prayer language only to what is already found in their respective Scriptures. The "sing a new song" idea in the Psalms, as well as the circumstantial prayers embedded in narrative, poetic, and legal genres of the Bible, provides strong incentive to believers to adapt and compose new prayers.[52] The particular features of prayers embedded within narratives show us that prayer does not have to be spoken according to a fixed formula. The prayer discourse contributes to the plot of given narratives and can provide some character development when we observe how different people respond to God in prayer.[53]

---

52. The "new song" idea occurs in Pss 33:3; 40:3; 96:1; 98:1; 144:9; 149:1. Prayers occur within genres of narrative (Gen 24:12–14; Isa 37:15–20), poetry (Jer 20:7–18), and law (Num 6:22–27; Deut 31:30–32:43).

53. Greenberg, *Biblical Prose Prayer*, 17–18.

Yet even with the "sing a new song" language occasionally appearing in the Psalms, some people find security in praying "old" prayers, repeating others' prayers in their daily lives. The person who reads Scripture with the prayers model is probably more comfortable repeating prayers than someone who tends to use other models.

What does this model of Scripture assume about the nature of the human being? Besides the Psalms, other sections of the Christian canon indicate that the main activity of the human person who is fully alive and in contact with the Creator is that of a *Homo orans*, a praying animal.[54] Those responsible for writing the primeval history record a time when our ancestors began to call on YHWH (Gen 4:26). When Abram gets to the land that God shows him, he builds altars and calls on God's name. His son Isaac follows suit. Isaac's son Jacob does not build altars but sets up stone memorials as his signs of trust in God. Jacob invokes a blessing on his sons. Joseph is not depicted as building altars or memorials, but he catches glimpses of the divine mind, to an extent beyond his contemporaries, through dreams.

It is completely appropriate to conclude this section by summarizing as follows: "Scripture provides the most basic content of Prayer, whereas Prayer articulates the deepest meaning of Scripture."[55] The last half of the sentence provides the basis for what I insist on in the classroom section below. For students studying Scripture because they regard it as Scripture, the prayers model is the one model they must continually practice.

The Mindset behind the Prayers Model

Another aspect of the prayers model, besides using the language of the Bible as one's script for prayer, is to read the Bible while seeking God's will. Because prayer is a conversation with God, the one who employs the prayers model while reading Scripture will often be expecting a specific message from God, through the vehicle of Scripture. Thomas Joseph White includes "abandonment to divine providence" as a mature level in a Christian's prayer life. He defines this abandonment as "receptive availability to the initiatives of God in our life, and the desire to find God in all things."[56] So besides looking for actual prayers or other discourse units that one can pray back to God, one can

---

54. Jenson, *Systematic Theology*, 2:58–59; Jenson, "Praying Animal."
55. Breck, *Scripture in Tradition*, 228.
56. White, *Light of Christ*, 293.

also activate the prayers model by looking for a message from God through the text of Scripture, a message applicable to one's own situation.

This mindset can at times overlap with the oracles model, in which a reader is seeking a sentence that represents God's word for the day. A difference is that the one reading with the prayers model will not limit the goal of Scripture reading to a sound bite for the day, as is often the case with the oracles model. The person with the prayers model may read long sections of Scripture, all the while asking God for specific truths and reflecting on the applicability of them in her or his own life.

Talking to Oneself in Prayer

In Psalms 42 and 43 the psalmist repeatedly asks, "Why are you depressed, O my soul?" and then gives the direction to "hope in God."[57] This illustrates what we see in Psalm 77 as well, where the psalmist asks himself pointed questions about God's rejection (77:2–11) and then responds to the questions with remembrance of how God has worked in the past (77:12–21). Psalm 131 also comes close to being an example of prayer-like discourse to oneself, though this psalm begins with an address to the Lord (131:1). J. Gerald Janzen notes that the Hebrew expression for Hannah's prayer at the tabernacle in 1 Samuel 1:13 actually connotes talking to herself. He thinks that the text portrays Hannah as verbalizing inner distress and then comforting herself with accounts of others whom God has helped. Janzen even wonders if Hannah's discourse to herself is a "plaintive yet hopeful participation in the groaning and travail of the whole creation," as seen in Romans 8:22–23.[58] One could also say that talking to oneself in prayer might be joining oneself to the searching and interceding of the Holy Spirit, as this Spirit searches and prays for us, as pictured in Romans 8:26–27 and 1 Corinthians 2:10–11. Another example of prayer as talking to oneself comes in John 12:27–28, where Jesus is portrayed as asking himself what he will pray.

One way in which the prayers model of Scripture is especially useful is in its function as a thesaurus of blessings. People have an innate desire to ascribe worth to the transcendent. We want to say how great something or someone is that is beyond us. The Psalms in Scripture do this when they declare how awesome God's name is in all the earth.

57. Pss 42:6, 12; 43:5.
58. Janzen, *When Prayer Takes Place*, 72–76, quotation from 76.

People Blessing Other People

Another way we bless is that we wish to extend favor or goodness on others. The prayers model of Scripture is especially keen to find and speak these blessings on others. The blessing found in Numbers 6:24–26 is performative speech. When it is spoken, it accomplishes something. In context, it is a statement meant to be said at the place where God lives, the tabernacle. It accomplishes, by invoking God's name, what God does as recorded in Genesis 1: it helps bring about a new creation out of chaos. This is done by an allusion to God's creative act of bringing "light" into the world (Gen 1:3). The word "shine" in Numbers 6:25 is cognate with "light." Also "LORD" in Numbers 6:24–26 is cognate with "Let there be" in Genesis 1:3. For those with faith who receive the priestly blessing find their outer world now organized around God's presence that shines light onto our world, and they find their inner world calmed of chaos and resting in the spirit that God can renew within them.[59]

Praying for God's Blessing

In the middle of a genealogy, a prayer is inserted as the prayer that one member of the genealogy used to pray (1 Chr 4:10). This was developed into a best-selling book.[60] Some have looked on this prayer as a formula by which one can mechanistically call down God's favor. That attitude is partially to account for why a book on this prayer sold so well. But the prayer and even the book on it demonstrate our need to receive favor and help in our lives.

In our capacities as praying animals, it has been the tendency for those writing, editing, and copying Scripture to complete or add prayers at places where they notice gaps in the prayer record of Scripture. Because 2 Chronicles 33:13, 18–19 mention a prayer of repentance that Manasseh prayed, some collections of the deuterocanonical books contain the Prayer of Manasseh, probably composed to fill in a gap in the narrative about him. The Septuagint's version of Esther adds prayers at 13:9–17 (C:1–10; Mordecai) and 14:3–19 (C:12–30; Esther). The Septuagint's version of Daniel tells us how the three men pray immediately after falling into the fiery furnace (3:24–45). Then it records a long hymn of praise that the three men sing from within the furnace (3:52–90). Because the Tanak in its Hebrew form never records repentant prayers of the exiles in Babylon, the Septuagint provides them in Baruch 1:15–3:8 and in

59. Janzen, *When Prayer Takes Place*, 38, 44–46, 48–49.
60. Wilkinson, *Prayer of Jabez*.

Daniel 3:24–45. Because someone found Psalm 150 inadequate as a conclusion to the Psalter, Psalm 151 was composed and appears in many collections of deuterocanonical literature. Indeed, perhaps partially because the Psalms contain repeated calls to sing a new song to the Lord, those who pray from this book have been empowered to write their own psalms, whether the Hodayot of the Dead Sea Scrolls or other collections of psalms such as the Odes and the Psalms of Solomon.[61]

Aside from filling in gaps in narratives with the direct discourse of prayer, Scripture also displays a tendency to include or add prayers at section endings. Thus, each of the first four books of Psalms ends with a prayer of blessing (41:13; 72:18–19; 89:52; 106:48). In the New Testament, the letters typically end with a blessing. Even the shorter forms of the Letter to the Romans end with blessings. The tendency for copyists to add blessings can be found in the textual variants that add Romans 16:25–27.

Many letters in the first century CE ended with a date, identifying the year of the emperor's reign. This convention may have prompted some New Testament authors to conclude with statements that show ultimate loyalty to God, and often refer to God's eternal reign (1 Thess 5:23; Heb 13:20–21). Endings such as these counter the dominant worldview that the emperor was the world's most prodigal benefactor. The preceding context in some of these letters also signals that the author has a critical view of the Roman principate in light of the lordship of Christ (Rom 16:20; 1 Thess 5:3; Heb 13:14).

It is this model of Scripture that most drives the practice of employing Scripture in the worship life of those reading it as God's word. Robert Jenson emphasizes this with the following guidelines: "The first and foremost doctrine *de scriptura* is therefore not a proposition about Scripture at all. It is rather the liturgical and devotional instruction: Let the Scripture be read, at every opportunity and with care for its actual address to hearers, even if these are only the reader. The churches most faithful to Scripture are not those that legislate the most honorific propositions about Scripture but those that most often and thoughtfully read and hear it."[62]

The prayers model is the one model that most follows Jenson's point. This model considers Scripture in its entirety to be God's word that needs to be heard and prayed. Some monasteries in the past practiced the continuous reading of Scripture; that is, the monks took turns continuously reading aloud

---

61. Old Testament references to singing a new song to the Lord can be found in Pss 33:3; 96:1; 98:1; 144:9; 149:1; Isa 42:10; Jdt 16:1, 13.

62. Jenson, *Systematic Theology*, 2:273.

from the Bible, cover to cover. This was done because they viewed all of Scripture as God's word to them and did not presume to make their own selections of what they thought would be most relevant.[63]

I observed Jenson's point about frequent or continual reading of Scripture when I attended Easter Vigil Mass at a Slavonic Orthodox Church. For at least fifteen minutes before the Mass began, a lector was reading Scripture aloud. It impressed me as a good way to begin any service of worship.

The prayers model of Scripture is the model that most energizes the practice of *lectio divina*. We will review the steps of *lectio divina* in chapter 12, but here it is worthwhile to note how the practice of *lectio divina* regards Scripture, since this will also inform us of how the prayers model views Scripture. *Lectio divina* views Scripture not first of all as documents or stories that can provide knowledge but rather as a medium for God's presence. While involved in this prayerful reading and meditation of Scripture, one finds potential scripts to use in prayer that open one up to God's presence.[64]

Prayer as described in Scripture and experienced within the church is often a social activity in which several or more people join together in lifting their minds and spirits toward God. This correlates as well with the prayers model for reading Scripture. We often engage Scripture with the prayers model in community with others, whether in a Sunday worship service, in a Bible study with friends, or in praying the Liturgy of the Hours with others.

The prayers model considers Scripture to be valuable for softening the human heart. When asked about how to focus on one purpose in life, a desert father named Poemen replied, "The nature of water is soft, that of stone is hard; but if a bottle is hung above the stone, allowing the water to fall drop by drop, it wears away the stone. So it is with the word of God; it is soft and our heart is hard, but the [one] who hears the word of God often, opens his heart to the fear of God."[65] In what ways, according to this model, does Scripture soften the heart? It softens it by teaching us about God and about the salvation that comes through Christ.[66]

This model, with the sense of belonging or appropriate discourse that people experience when praying Scripture, has led theologians to conform their discourse about Scripture to it. When he was thirty years old, Karl Barth gave a talk called "The Strange New World of the Bible," in which he argued that

63. Casey, *Sacred Reading*, 6–7.

64. White, *Light of Christ*, 296–97.

65. Casey, *Sacred Reading*, 10, citing Ward, *Sayings of the Desert Fathers*, 162, 183.

66. These are the anticipated results of *lectio divina* as described in the Pontifical Biblical Commission, *Interpretation of the Bible in the Church*, IV.C.2.

the Bible is not primarily a book of narratives or a book of laws but a world in which God is the dominant presence. It is fitting that he ended the talk as follows: "And now hear: 'A certain man made a great supper, and bade many; and sent his servant at supper-time to say to them that were bidden, Come, for all things are now ready!'"[67] Barth's conclusion calls people into the biblical world. In asking us to respond to the invitation to the supper, Barth is seeking to make us speak in response to God, using Scripture's categories as the basis for our prayer.

STRENGTHS OF THE PRAYERS MODEL

This is the model most suited for helping people engage with God, because it prioritizes prayer texts within Scripture and treats every part of Scripture as a potential prayer.

Augustine, influenced by his reading of Platonic philosophy, understood one's memory to be a significant component of the human soul and a window on the divine. In a sense, Augustine views the memory as a residue of the divine image in each person. Though the truths of God cannot be fully apprehended by our memory, he still teaches that the memory is a doorway through which one encounters God.[68] He therefore recommends that as we prayerfully read Scripture, we ask God to awaken in our memories God's own presence in time's past, whether in our own experience or in the experience of others.

Those who regard the Bible as Scripture, as in some sense God's word to humanity, must include the prayers model among the models with which they approach Scripture. This model allows us today to pray with Jeremiah, "Your words were found and I ate them" (15:16). For all those who seek to follow the counsel that John Cassian passes on from Abbot Nesteros that one should read Scripture with a pure heart and with all the attention one would give one's academic studies, the prayers model must be operative.[69] Even if one is studying the Scriptures academically as documents, for example, the prayers model must also be activated in order to keep one's heart pure. For as long as we humans sense a need to pray to the transcendent, we will be employing the prayers model as we read Scripture.

---

67. Barth, *Word of God*, 50.
68. Casey, *Sacred Reading*, 120–21.
69. Murphy, *Experiencing Our Biblical Heritage*, 127, citing John Cassian, *Conferences* 14.13–14.

LIMITATIONS OF THE PRAYERS MODEL

In a way that is analogous to the oracles model, one who uses the prayers model for one's own life will have difficulty talking about the Bible with an academic who is using the documents model. For the prayers model cannot treat Scripture simply as a collection of artifacts from another culture. It is instead an anthology of musical scores that God has given humanity, music that is meant to be played and sung. A reader relying exclusively on the prayers model will have difficulty following an academic's distinctions between the purposes of each of the Gospels; it won't matter that Luke-Acts seeks to exonerate the Romans in its depiction of the death of Jesus and Paul's mission activity. All that matters is that we find a way to pray Luke-Acts. The focus on prayer keeps one using this model from fully meeting others' questions about historicity that might arise in the documents or stories models. It keeps one from deeply wrestling with the ethical questions that arise in the laws and stories models. It limits one's participation in the communal use of Scripture mostly to prayer times with those who can pray with Scripture in a similar way.

THE PRAYERS MODEL IN THE CLASSROOM

In the aftermath of the attempts to reconfigure Scripture in modernity and postmodernity, academic discourse does not use the prayers model. In order to have common points of discourse, such models as documents or stories usefully provide a common language to talk about Scripture with academics and with people of different branches of the Christian family. But when one is in any biblical studies or theology class, whether in an undergraduate, seminary, or graduate-school setting, the prayers model is indispensable for keeping one's mind and spirit in tune with God. What benefit will it be if you master Hebrew and Greek but lose the contact you once had with the soul of Scripture? If you gain all knowledge about the Gospel of Luke, so that you can immediately recognize which pericopes come from Q, which come from Mark, and which are distinctly Lukan in origin, but lose your love for this gospel that so treasures God's word, has your knowledge really raised your standing before God?

So no matter how stressed you are about papers, projects, and tests in school, it is always good to continue to read Scripture at times with the prayers model. Find a psalm that you can pray out loud. Find texts that raise your perspective to eternity, and pray them back to God. The book of Psalms in our Bible is an underrated treasure. Take every course on Psalms that you can. Learn the distinct characteristics of each of the five books of Psalms. If you are praying the Liturgy of the Hours, pay attention to the psalms that you are praying. Pray a psalm whenever you can.

Remember that the point of reading and studying Scripture is to learn about Christ and deepen our relationship with him. Maximus the Confessor viewed Scripture as part of the world that God designed for our learning. A person progresses through learning the law of nature from the physical world on to learning the law of Scripture, which points to Christ. Christ's death and resurrection represent a third law that brings these earlier laws to an end, allowing one to inherit the Lord.[70] Though Maximus uses "law" to describe Scripture, his description of Scripture as given by God in order to point to Christ is a good example of the portrait of Scripture that the prayers model provides.

If you are a biblical studies or theology student taking classes because you want to get closer to God or grow in your faith, this model of Scripture cannot be neglected. As Christians have acknowledged and repeated for centuries, *lex orandi lex credendi*—the law of praying is the law of believing. Of the five models in this book, this is the model that we followers of Jesus must continually practice. To ignore it is to risk becoming lukewarm and abandoning our Lord.

THE PRAYERS MODEL IN MINISTRY

In ministry, the pastor is frequently called on to offer public prayer. Whenever possible, it is good to incorporate Scripture into such public prayers. Even if the Scripture is not as specifically relevant as you might wish it to be, it is probably better to pray in the words of Scripture than with our own words. This is because people will be more ready to listen to Scripture than to listen to your own words, which some might consider too biased toward one perspective. They will also more likely join in the spirit of your prayer if you pray with Scripture. General, familiar words allow people to make the connections appropriate to their own situations.

It is good also to try to provide examples for how to pray with Scripture. So when called on to pray at confirmations, graduations, and other milestone events in the lives of youth, you could structure your prayers around texts like

70. Balthasar, *Cosmic Liturgy*, 303–12.

Matthew 18:1–5 or Luke 2:52. When called on to pray at weddings, if the liturgy requires you to compose your own prayer at certain points, you could structure your prayers around such texts as Genesis 2:24 or Ephesians 5:25–33.

Beyond the professional instinct to keep people engaged in your ministerial life by crafting scintillating sermons or maneuvering the church's resources or schedule to keep people with you, the one thing needful is your own interior life. If you live out the prayers model in personal and public reading of Scripture, your people will begin to pray with Scripture as well. Once your congregation embraces the prayers model of reading Scripture, they will actively engage in congregational life, for reading Scripture and praying Scripture in both Jewish and Christian circles are essentially community activities.

LAWS

All over the world, . . . there are innumerable people who have abandoned their ancestral laws and their recognized gods and have submitted themselves to the observance of the law of Moses and to the discipleship and worship of Christ.

—ORIGEN[1]

In the years 1527–1534, the most pressing political question in England was how to interpret Mosaic law in relation to the quest by Henry VIII to have his marriage with Catherine of Aragon annulled. Those who supported Henry's quest cited Leviticus 18:16, an apodictic prohibition against uncovering the nakedness of one's brother's wife, and Leviticus 20:21, which labels marrying one's brother's wife as an "impurity" and predicts that those in such a union will be childless.[2] Since Catherine of Aragon had been married to Henry's older brother Arthur before he died, these texts were considered highly relevant to the situation of Henry and Catherine. Before Henry and Catherine's marriage in 1509, Pope Julius II had granted a dispensation for the marriage, allowing it despite Catherine's previous marriage to Henry's brother. When Henry and those biblical scholars supporting him sought an annulment for Henry and Catherine's marriage, they sought to show that the texts in Leviticus made such marriages a violation of natural law and were thus wrong in themselves, even if a papal dispensation had permitted the union.[3]

A second challenge that Henry and his supporters had to overcome was that another provision in Mosaic law actually seemed to command the sort of marriage in the situation of Henry and Catherine. Deuteronomy 25:5 com-

---

1. Origen, *On First Principles* 4.1.1 (Butterworth, 335–36).
2. These two texts were probably in mind when John the Baptist and others criticized the marriage of Herod Antipas to Herodias, who had been his brother's wife (Matt 14:3–4; Mark 6:17–18).
3. Scarisbrick, *Henry VIII*, 163.

mands that in the case of a childless widow, the brother of her deceased husband should marry the woman. This is the levirate law and is the principle behind Naomi's stratagem to secure a husband for her widowed daughter-in-law Ruth who is related to Ruth's deceased husband (Ruth 1:11–13; 3:9–13; 4:3–12). In the years 1529–1530 an international debate was in full swing. Both Christian and Jewish scholars' counsel was sought. For the rigorous interpretation of the Leviticus texts that Henry needed to get out of his marriage to Catherine, scholars cited the church fathers Basil, Tertullian, Augustine, and Gregory the Great and the medieval scholars Bonaventure, Aquinas, Duns Scotus, and Anthony of Florence. And for a nonbinding reading of the Deuteronomy text, Henry's scholars found support in the figurative exegesis of Origen, Ambrose, and Augustine, who interpreted the dead husband as Christ, and the brother who was to marry the childless widow as those who preached the gospel of Christ, raising up spiritual descendants for Christ. An alternative strategy for deconstructing the command in Deuteronomy 25:5 was to note that though the Vulgate uses the same word for brother in the Leviticus and Deuteronomy texts, in the Leviticus texts it means *frater germanus*, a biological brother, while in the Deuteronomy text it means a *cognatus*, a relative (such as Boaz was to Ruth's first husband), and not strictly speaking a brother.[4]

For our purposes, it is useful to understand that the questions raised by Henry VIII's situation were not new. Scholars had worked them over for centuries, trying to explain the apparent conflict between the Leviticus prohibition against intimacy with a brother's wife and the Deuteronomy command to marry a brother's wife. As J. J. Scarisbrick says, Henry's case "had a chance not because it was a novelty but because it was a chestnut."[5] All this is to say that Christians were reading Scripture as law for themselves. Christians, mostly gentiles, were reading the laws that are given specifically to mark Israel as distinct from the nations, and seeking to ascertain these laws' authoritative rulings for marriages within the church. Everyone in the debate regarding Henry's marriage to Catherine understood Scripture to be law that was binding in questions of Christian marital ethics.

As the description above indicates, the laws model is an approach to Scripture that views it primarily as laws that readers need to obey. For one reading Scripture with the laws model, the primary question is "What is this text telling me to do?" But there are still two ways of applying the laws model, determined by how much of Scripture a reader considers to be law.

---

4. Scarisbrick, *Henry VIII*, 164–65.
5. Scarisbrick, *Henry VIII*, 168.

DEFINITION AND CHARACTERISTICS OF THE LAWS MODEL

The laws model views Scripture as essentially a set of laws or rules for people to follow. This model's default setting when reading any literary genre within Scripture, even the stories within the Bible, is to look for a moral, a conclusion that tells the reader how to live.

You know that someone is using the laws model . . .

. . . when they refer to or regard the whole Bible as "law" or "commands." The book *The Year of Living Biblically*, though attempting to be a humorous book, regards the Bible essentially as law. Its author, A. J. Jacobs, lived "biblically" by keeping a law from the Bible every day for a year.

. . . when they announce "the moral of the story" after reading a narrative from the Bible. This phrase may not be used, but if a discussion of a biblical text leads toward what people should or should not do, there is a good possibility that the laws model is being used.

. . . when they refer to a bad result or punishment that occurs in response to a behavior. Armchair ethicists who pronounce on what someone should or should not have done within a biblical narrative, such as analysis of Paul's mistakes in his mission travels as narrated in Acts, are probably employing this model.

. . . when they make an easy transition, whether explicitly or implicitly, from Mosaic law to the implied readers' lives. It may be as easy a transition as applying one of the Ten Commandments to people today, or a higher-threshold transition, such as telling non-Jewish Christians they should observe the Feast of Tabernacles, but in either case the model at work is the laws model. *None of These Diseases: The Bible's Health Secrets for the 21st Century* exemplifies the laws model by the way it assumes that the culture-embedded Mosaic covenant fits readily with current findings of modern medicine.[6]

The official books of the Torah are the first five books of the Bible, Genesis through Deuteronomy. But, of course, not everything in these books fits the genre of law. Genesis is composed of narratives, poetry, and genealogies. The

6. McMillen and Stern, *None of These Diseases*.

laws officially begin in Exodus 20, with the first account of the Ten Commandments, though laws regarding the observance of Passover appear within the exodus narrative in Exodus 12. Different groups of laws are presented in succession, introduced within the narrative of the Israelites' journey toward the promised land: the Ten Commandments, the priestly code, instructions for the tabernacle, the laws of sacrifice in Leviticus, and finally the Holiness Code. As its name implies, Deuteronomy is a second account of the law. Like any repetition of text, interpretive decisions are at work in the selection of laws that are repeated and in their explanations. Thus, for example, Deuteronomy's version of the Ten Commandments gives a different emphasis and explanation for the Sabbath command, and rephrases the prohibition of coveting in a way that is more respectful to women. In this chapter we are focusing on how some Bible readers consider Scripture to be essentially law. An analogy here will help. There are different reasons for reading and ways of reading a nation's constitution. If someone were reading a nation's constitution with the laws model, she would most likely be doing so in order to find out whether she could or should act in specific ways.

Specific Applications of the Laws Model

Those reading Scripture according to the laws model will no doubt focus on certain imperatives found in the Old and New Testaments, but they will find imperatives to live by even in nonlegal genres of Scripture, such as narrative, poetry, and apocalyptic. The model is especially attractive to those looking for guidance on how to live their lives. Compared to those employing the documents model, those engaged in the laws model will not always consider the cultural and political divide between their life situation and that of a biblical text's first audience.

All of Scripture Is Law

Within the Christian family, Protestants from the Reformed tradition might be especially ready to find law in any part of the canon. This is because with Calvin they read Scripture as a unified whole. They see the gospel even within parts of the Old Testament and will be looking for God's guidance everywhere in Scripture. Even though they acknowledge that the Mosaic law was given specifically to Israel, Reformed readers will read Mosaic law for guidelines in how to live the Christian life. This is what is called the third use or didactic use of the law. An example of this, as seen in the first of the biblical examples below, is how Reformed theologians view a covenant of creation to be embedded in the creation narratives of Genesis 1–3.[7]

Catholic and Orthodox readers as well might be ready to find law anywhere in the canon and approach any genre of discourse within their Bibles as law. This is because they do not participate in the Lutheran approach to Scripture, which divides it up into law and gospel.

Only Part of Scripture Is Law

Luther famously explained Scripture as containing laws that highlight a person's sinfulness and point the person to Christ. This is called the second use, Lutheran use, or the pedagogical use of the law. The latter term is used because it is cognate with the word *paidagōgos* (a tutor or guardian for children) that Paul uses for law in Galatians 3:24–25. In this application of the laws model, only certain parts of Scripture are considered to be law. Certainly the law codes that begin in Exodus 20 are considered law. But Lutherans will even look at some texts in the New Testament, such as the Sermon on the Mount or ethical commands in Paul's letters, and consider them "law," and then identify something in the following context as "gospel." Lutherans continue to follow Luther's idea that within Scripture the law accuses and judges, whereas the gospel comforts and saves.[8] So those who are apt to label only certain parts of Scripture as law are participating in a Lutheran application of the laws model.

The Bible continued to be regarded in Europe into the seventeenth century as a significant treasury of laws, as the following anecdote illustrates. Jack Fisher, who taught economic history for decades at the London School of Economics, specialized in the economic history of England during the time of the Tudors and the early Stuarts. When a student asked him what to read for sixteenth- and seventeenth-century economics, his answer was simply to read the Bible, since it was viewed as the text that outlined how to secure the economic, political, and social elements of society.[9]

OLD TESTAMENT TEXTS OFTEN READ AS LAW

The narratives in Genesis 1–3 are generally read as two creation stories. People, created on day six in the first story, are told to be fruitful and exercise do-

---

7. Berkhof, *Systematic Theology*, 211–18; Robertson, *Christ of the Covenants*, 67–87.
8. *LW* 35:242–44.
9. McGrath, *In the Beginning*, 2–3.

minion on the earth. The story ends with a description of God resting on the seventh day, which makes best sense in the context of the Mosaic covenant's command to keep the Sabbath. In the second story, Adam and Eve are told they can eat from all trees in the garden except from the tree of the knowledge of good and evil. I list these commands just to point out that the imperatives do not amount to major parts of either story. One could object by pointing out that the commands to people on day six in Genesis 1 come near the end of the story, in what could be read as a climactic position. But still, most of the first creation story is a seven-day narrative that answers the Babylonian Enuma Elish with a more positive view of the human being. And while the prohibition of eating from the tree of the knowledge of good and evil is significant enough that its infraction changes the whole plot of Genesis 2–3, most Jewish readers do not consider this prohibition as evidence for a binding command on all humanity today.

It is noteworthy, therefore, that Christian readers influenced by the Reformed tradition tend to view these first three chapters as containing a creation covenant. They view these chapters as providing a legal framework into which every human is born, which is definitely an example of the laws model. O. Palmer Robertson thus presents the Sabbath, marriage, and labor as general decrees of the covenant of creation. He also finds a specific demand of obedience placed on humans as part of this covenant, exemplified in the prohibition of eating from the tree of the knowledge of good and evil.[10] After this covenant of creation, Robertson identifies a covenant of commencement in Genesis 3:14–19. This latter covenant distinguishes the seed of the serpent from the seed of the woman, which Robertson understands as indicating a distinction between the elect and those God has not elected.[11]

Christian scholar Gordon Wenham has explored how Old Testament narratives can be read for their ethical import. He explains why narrative can be more instructive toward virtue than can law. "What legislators and judges tolerate may not be what they approve. Laws generally set a floor for behaviour within society, they do not prescribe an ethical ceiling. Thus a study of the legal codes within the Bible is unlikely to disclose the ideals of the law-givers, but only the limits of their tolerance: if you do such and such, you will be punished. The laws thus tend to express the limits of socially acceptable behaviour: they do not describe ideal behaviour."[12]

---

10. Robertson, *Christ of the Covenants*, 67–87.
11. Robertson, *Christ of the Covenants*, 93–107.
12. Wenham, *Story as Torah*, 80.

Narrative scenes or patterns expressing ideal behavior include the portrait of intimacy between God and humankind in Eden, which is seen again in divine communication to Abraham, Jacob, and Joseph. The patriarchs' generosity, such as is seen in the willingness of Abraham and Isaac to give up land, and reconciliation between the estranged brothers Jacob and Esau are other moral ideals expressed in ways that the legal genre within Scripture does not communicate.[13]

Even the narratives that do not describe ideal behavior can offer moral instruction. Though other scholars have argued over whom the implied author of Genesis 34 is most blaming in the story of the rape of Dinah and subsequent massacre, Wenham concludes that neither the Israelite nor the Canaanite side meets the ideals of the God of Israel. In the conclusion of the story, Simeon and Levi, as well as the entire family of Jacob, get off lightly. Wenham suggests that the story ends this way in order to show how faithful God is to his own promises.[14] It is evident in the survey of different interpretations of this narrative that the lawlike import of the story lies in the discussion and introspection regarding ethical behavior that it facilitates.

For those reading with the laws model, there is lawlike potential even in the poetry of Psalms. Since praying or singing the Psalms is a performative speech act by which one gives one's emotions and will to God and commits to following God, these texts engage the worshiper in God's will in ways that legal texts cannot do.[15]

The Psalms also celebrate what God's judgment means. It is easy for us to consider God's judgment as naming sinners as guilty and rendering punishment, but the essence of judgment in the Old Testament is to exonerate and uphold the ones who are marginalized and abused. The Psalms address the exploitation by praying or describing how evil people will experience the evil they inflict on others (18:25–26; 28:4; 37:14–15). God's attention to the poor and marginalized is a recurrent theme (10:14, 17; 69:33; 104:41; 109:31; 113:7; 132:15). And the citizen or king who pays attention to the poor is considered blessed (41:1–2; 72:12–14).[16] One can even read the five books of the Psalter through the lens of the poor. The first book describes the poor as those the wicked abuse. The second book ends with the poor hoping for a messiah who will rescue them (72:12–14). The third book concludes with the messiah as one of the poor (89:39–46). The fourth book links what happens with the poor to

13. Wenham, *Story as Torah*, 81–82, 92, 97.
14. Wenham, *Story as Torah*, 110–19.
15. Wenham, *Psalms as Torah*, 67–76.
16. Wenham, *Psalms as Torah*, 113–17.

what happens to God's people and Jerusalem (102:14; 106:42). And the fifth book celebrates the liberation and divine vindication that the poor experience (126; 149:4).[17] Discrete texts and the general flow of the Psalms thus emphasize that God attends to the cry of the poor and blesses those who care for them.

The Psalms also contain narrative summaries that promote righteous living. The summary of creation in Psalm 104 is offered in a way to prompt committed worship and love for God.[18] Wenham employs the laws model when reading Psalm 106. He understands its summary of Israel's disobedience in the wilderness, followed by God's attention and steadfast love for the people, as an encouragement to confess sin and live on the basis of God's mercy.[19] Paul reads the same psalm through the laws model in order to motivate his audience to avoid any commerce with idolatry.[20]

The virtuous behaviors of fearing God and confessing sin are emphasized in the Psalms. At the same time, the Psalms portray sinful people as guilty because of their speech, often deceitful or rebellious because they speak out of pride.[21]

New Testament Texts Often Read as Law

All who read Scripture as law find special significance in Jesus's Sermon on the Mount (Matt 5–7). Reformed readers will emphasize Jesus's words on the permanence and significance of the law (Matt 5:17–20), pointing out that there is every evidence that this sermon is included in this gospel so that believers literally will keep its commands. The Sermon on the Mount, including Jesus's affirmation of the Mosaic law, would be considered as evidence for the third use of the law, a distinct emphasis among Reformed readers of Scripture (also favored by Melanchthon, but not Luther). As we will see in more depth in the metanarratives chapter, the Reformed do have an echo of the Lutheran law-gospel distinction in their explanation of a covenant of works that precedes the covenant of grace. Reformed theologian Louis Berkhof notes that those Reformed scholars who considered law and gospel to be complete opposites—denying that any action was required from the human side in God's relationship with the Christian believer—were reacting to the Arminians who emphasized obedience to God as a necessary component of salvation. Berkhof

17. Wenham, *Psalms as Torah*, 118, citing Vesco, *Le psautier de David*, 154.

18. Wenham, *Psalms as Torah*, 129–32.

19. Wenham, *Psalms as Torah*, 126–27.

20. Israel's experiences that Paul describes match Ps 106 better than the Corinthian problems recoverable from the letter. And Paul's "our fathers" in 1 Cor 10:1 matches the phrase in Ps 106:6–7.

21. Wenham, *Psalms as Torah*, 147–55.

thinks it better to see gracious promises within the law and expectations for obedient behavior, or discipleship, within the gospel.[22]

Somewhat similarly to Reformed readers' idea of the third use of the law, the Anabaptists read the Sermon on the Mount as a central teaching of Jesus, at the core of Jesus's gospel. In their quest to keep the Sermon on the Mount literally, they emphasize living in peace with others and turning the other cheek to abuse or wrong (Matt 5:9, 38–42). Luther objects to the Anabaptist view of the Sermon on the Mount, advocating a "two kingdoms" approach—for example, not resisting evil as a servant of Christ (Matt 5:39–42) but serving in the military as a servant of the state.[23]

In the dispensationalism that developed from the teachings of J. N. Darby, the Sermon on the Mount came to be viewed as spoken by Jesus to Israel. Traditional dispensationalists view this sermon as Jesus's offer of the kingdom to Israel. They understand Israel to have rejected this offer, and therefore do not consider it relevant for the church. In contrast, Luther regards the Sermon on the Mount as the fruit expected of those who are justified by faith. It is not just for the monastery. Traditional dispensationalists state that the Sermon on the Mount will be relevant again when Israel turns to Christ in the millennial age. Though some progressive dispensationalists view the Sermon on the Mount as becoming fully relevant when Christ returns and establishes his kingdom on earth, they break with the traditional dispensationalists and regard it as an ideal to be followed today, as the church lives to fulfill the ideal pictured in the sermon, so that Christ's teachings will permeate society at large.

In church history, those influenced by Luther's law-gospel distinction have often read Paul as negative toward law, especially when relying on his letters to the Galatians and the Romans as central to Christian theology. But Luther was no antinomian. He gave a prominent place to the law and offered probing explanations on the Decalogue in both his *Small* and *Large Catechisms*.[24] And there have recently been some voices calling for more recognition of Paul's positive respect for the law. Thus, Lutheran scholar Kari Kuula surprisingly writes, "Paul's own soteriology is quite legalistic and it lays much weight on human works."[25]

Paul does affirm that the law is a good thing (Rom 7:12, 14; Luther would agree), and some strands of Christianity continue to hold the law as found in the Pentateuch in high regard. Paul, who says that Christ is the end of the law for those who believe (Rom 10:4), still writes as though one would naturally

22. Berkhof, *Systematic Theology*, 612–13.
23. He cites Titus 3:1 on this point in *LW* 46:99.
24. See also *LW* 44:23–27.
25. Kuula, *The Law, the Covenant and God's Plan*, 2:5.

want to observe the law's commandments (Rom 13:8–10; Gal 5:13–14). The tension in Christianity's understanding of God's law is partially due to Paul's situation as apostle to the nations (Rom 11:25; 16:25–26). Since he seeks to spread his gospel of salvation through Christ *to the gentiles* without requiring them to keep the Mosaic law, he downplays and criticizes gentiles who would want to keep this law (Gal 2:21; 5:2). But as a native Hebrew, he also respects the gift of God's law and at times seems instinctively to assume that people will want to keep it (Rom 3:31). This tension surfaces in Paul's description of his own life vis-à-vis law, for he claims to live as though under Mosaic law when he is with others who follow the law, though he does not consider himself to be under Mosaic law (1 Cor 9:20). Part of the tension is also due to a lack of specific vocabulary. While not considering himself under Mosaic law, Paul still considers himself under some kind of natural law and under "the law of Christ" (Rom 1:32; 2:14–15; 1 Cor 9:21; Gal 6:2). So Paul's diction can leave one at times wondering how it is that Paul can criticize and endorse Mosaic law. Though Paul is thus ambiguous on Mosaic law, his positive statements about the law (Rom 7:12) combine with the pro-Torah portrait of Jesus in Matthew (5:17–20) to keep Christians actively engaged in the laws model of reading Scripture.

James is the one letter that is most explicitly positive toward law and thus likely to be quoted by someone using the laws model. James refers to the Mosaic law as a "royal law" and a "law of freedom" (2:8, 12). Values of the Mosaic law, such as mercy and justice for the poor, are emphasized in this letter (2:1–7, 13; 5:1–6).[26]

Key Issues in the Laws Model

Discourse in some sectors of Christianity commonly includes assertions that the New Testament teaches that Christians are no longer under Mosaic law, that justification by faith frees Christians from needing to keep this law. Yet the Bible—including the New Testament—engages deeply and often with Mosaic law, and theologians from all sectors of Christianity spend considerable energy describing how Christians should relate to this law and how some parts of the law might apply to us. The key issues below cover the general contours of how Christians in the past two millennia have been using and categorizing laws in the Bible.

26. Although he admitted that James has "many excellent passages," Luther in 1522 considered it problematic and called it "an epistle full of straw, because it contains nothing evangelical" (*LW* 35:395–97).

Our Conflicted Engagement with the Bible's Laws

Christians who have been reading Scripture with the laws model throughout the last millennia have struggled to comprehend and decide how to respond to the significant number of laws it contains (613 in the Torah, according to Maimonides). These are challenges arising out of the text of Scripture, challenges faced and negotiated by Judaism as well.

In general, the Hebrew Bible has a positive regard for law. Law or torah (in the sense of instruction) is the foundation of Scripture. The books of Moses, known as the Torah, come first in the canon. Then, at the seams of the Hebrew Bible, there are connections back to the Torah that seek to present the Prophets and the Writings as extensions of the Torah. At the beginning of the Prophets section, God commands Joshua to perform all of his law and meditate on it always (Josh 1:7–8). And in the antepenultimate verse of the Prophets section, the reader is commanded to remember the law that God give Moses at Horeb (Mal 3:22/4:4). There is the anomalous text in Ezekiel 20:25, "I even gave them decrees that were not good and commandments in which they did not live." It is translated in Christian Bibles with the idea that the divinely given laws were inappropriate or unable to be life-giving: "So I gave them other statutes that were not good and laws through which they could not live" (NIV) or "Therefore I gave them statutes that were not good, and ordinances through which they could not have life" (NABRE). The Hebrew text does not necessarily demand that the final phrase of the verse connotes inadequacy in the commandments; it could simply be read as a description of the people's disobedience to the commandments. In any event, despite the singular, potentially negative description of the law at Ezekiel 20:25, the predominant voice in the Prophets section is overwhelming positive toward law.

The third section of the Hebrew Bible, the Writings, begins with Psalms. Roland Murphy has remarked on how Psalm 1 is not a prayer to God, such as most of the psalms. Instead, it portrays an exemplary pattern of behavior—meditating on God's law day and night—behavior commanded in the beginning of the Prophets section as well (Josh 1:7–8). Psalm 1 is also missing a superscription, perhaps because Psalm 1 as a whole serves as a superscription for the whole book of Psalms. If so, with its vivid portrait of the one who meditates on the Torah day and night, its placement at the beginning of the Psalter represents a quest to transform the collection of prayers to God so that they become imperatives from God.[27] The Torah poem of Psalm 19 seeks to

27. Murphy, *Experiencing Our Biblical Heritage*, 13–14.

picture the Torah given to Moses and the witness of God in nature as a single Torah. And then the longest chapter in the Bible, the Torah poem of Psalm 119, includes a term for God's law in every verse, focusing the attention of the one praying this psalm on the functions of this law and the joy it brings.[28]

Though the laws of the Mosaic covenant are positively regarded in most sectors of Judaism today, it is impossible to observe all the Mosaic laws found in Scripture because of differences in the situations in which the Torah was written and in which it is read today (e.g., casuistic law). Even Orthodox Jews do not keep all 613 laws of the Mosaic covenant. Those who live outside the land do not keep the laws that apply to life in the promised land. Those who live in Israel may keep some of the laws applying to life in the land, but they cannot keep those that apply to worship in the temple. Still, Judaism displays a much more positive regard for Scripture's legal material than does Christianity. In that regard, the laws model is a more dominant model for Jews reading the Hebrew Bible than it is for Christians reading the Old and New Testaments.

The rhetorical situations of certain New Testament texts, such as the narrative of a church council's decision not to apply Mosaic law to gentiles, James's warnings against showing favoritism, and Paul's description of a person who cannot perform what he knows to be right (Acts 15:10; Jas 2:8–11; Rom 7:12–25), have supplied various Christian exegetes with discourse that prompts them to emphasize that the law is impossible to keep.[29] The impossibility of keeping divine law is emphasized in Christianity in ways not found in Judaism. And yet the law remains a significant category that various sectors of Christianity cannot discard or ignore.

Origen describes Christians as those who follow the laws of Moses and the teachings of Christ.[30] Still, he excises certain laws that he considers nonsense or impossible to keep. The prohibition against eating vultures is senseless, since no one would want to eat vultures. The ruling that any male descendant of Abraham who is not circumcised on the eighth day will be cut off from his people cannot be meant to be literally followed, since, if it were, the father or guardians of the child would be the ones to be punished.[31] Moses's command that the Jews should offer the goat-stag as a sacrificial offering is similarly not meant for literal fulfillment since that animal does not exist. The prohibition against consumption of the griffin also cannot be literally fulfilled since that

---

28. Murphy, *Experiencing Our Biblical Heritage*, 14–15.
29. Calvin, *Inst.* 2.7.5.
30. Origen, *On First Principles* 4.1.1 (Butterworth, 335–36).
31. Origen, *On First Principles* 4.3.2 (Butterworth, 386–87); Gen 17:14.

animal also does not exist. Other commands that are irrational, according to Origen, are the command to stay seated in the same place on the Sabbath and the prohibition against carrying loads on the Sabbath. The former command cannot be taken literally since it would not be possible to stay seated in the same position for the whole day.[32] Origen asserts that the prohibition against carrying loads on the Sabbath is impossible, but the only support he offers for this assertion is his caricature of involved rabbinic debates on carrying loads over one (prohibited) or two shoulders (allowed) and on which type of shoes can be worn on the Sabbath.[33] Origen does not limit his deconstructive activity to Old Testament laws. He also considers Jesus's command to turn the other cheek when hit on the right to be intentionally figurative, because he thinks it highly unlikely that anyone would ever be struck first on the right cheek. If a right-hander struck another person on the face, the blow would land on the left cheek.[34] Similarly, Origen regards Jesus's command to his disciples not to greet others along the way as simply incredible.[35] For Origen the impossibility for these laws' literal interpretation and application is not simply a way of dismissing them. The inherent impossibility perceived in them signals for Origen that the laws must be interpreted on a spiritual level.

Tyconius, a biblical scholar who flourished in 370–90 CE, wrote in his manual for reading the Bible, *The Book of Rules*, that God did not give his law to those who he knew "would persevere in the image of God." He states that God's law is only given to unrighteous people.[36] It seems that his strong endorsement of predestination lowers his respect for the law.

Biblical law in Christian theology took another hit in the sixteenth century, when Luther drew a parallel between the Hebrew nation, which seeks to keep Mosaic law, and Catholics, who seek to live virtuously and cooperate in their salvation. With this parallel drawn, Luther considered both the Jewish people and Catholics as off the rails in their relationships with God. Luther went on to emphasize a way of reading Scripture that we have already noted in this chapter, the bifurcation of it into law and gospel. The law sections of Scripture, according to Luther, are not valuable in themselves. They are only valuable in a secondary sense, as pointing to the gospel, which promises salvation not by

---

32. Origen, *On First Principles* 4.3.2 (Butterworth, 387); goat-stag (in two manuscripts of LXX at Deut 14:5); griffin (Lev 11:13; Deut 14:12); stability on the Sabbath (Exod 16:29c).

33. Origen, *On First Principles* 4.3.2 (Butterworth, 389); Jer 17:21.

34. Origen, *On First Principles* 4.3.3 (Butterworth, 389–90); Matt 5:39.

35. Origen, *On First Principles* 4.3.3 (Butterworth, 389–90); Luke 10:4.

36. Tyconius, *Book of Rules*, 43 (quotation), 44.

human performance but by grace. Yet both Jews and many Christians experience God's grace even within the laws of Scripture.

Later, during the time when Western civilization was shifting its portrait of the Bible from Scripture to a collection of documents from the ancient Near East, Johann David Michaelis (1717–1791) studied and presented the law as though it made no sense outside its ancient Near Eastern context. This was accompanied in his presentation by the insistence that the law as found in the Pentateuch "has no claims to moral or religious normativity."[37] While one might at first glance accept Michaelis's claim that the law makes no sense outside its cultural context, the track record of the Old Testament's Jewish and Christian readers indicates an opposite reception. Diaspora Jews throughout the Mediterranean world were making sense of the Torah and living by it, *mutatis mutandis*, in their differing cultural situations. While Michaelis's assertions played a key role in turning Scripture study in universities into the secular discipline of biblical studies, Christians still employed the laws model in their engagement with the Scripture. For example, one aspect of this engagement, arising out of texts like the Sermon on the Mount or Jesus's words to the rich young ruler, is whether Jesus has added to the laws of Moses.

Jesus's intensification of the Mosaic law in texts like Matthew 5:21–48 has led both Catholic and Lutheran theologians to say that the gospel adds laws to the Mosaic law. Thus, Aquinas describes how Christ has brought a new law that addresses the internal lives of God's people, a more demanding law for which the Mosaic law made preparation.[38] The four types of law, according to Aquinas, are the eternal, the natural, the human, and the divine.[39]

Melanchthon's distinctions regarding law are not too different. He writes that the three parts of the Mosaic law are laws concerning virtues, which he calls the moral or eternal law; the ceremonial law, which he calls the laws concerning the church; and the judicial law, which he says are laws concerning the civil government. Melanchthon says that the Ten Commandments form the most significant part of the moral or eternal law. In contrast to this law that will always exist, Melanchthon teaches that ceremonial law was instituted for a limited time within Judaism.[40] This division usually aims at emphasizing how the moral law is still in effect, while the ceremonial law is no longer in effect. We Christians disagree among ourselves regarding what are identified as civil

---

37. Legaspi, *Death of Scripture*, 141.
38. *ST* I-II.91.5.
39. *ST* I-II.94.
40. Melanchthon, *Loci Communes*, chap. 7 (Manschreck, 83–85).

laws. In what follows, we consider the three uses and the three divisions that Christians have made when considering Mosaic law.

The Three Uses of the Law in Christian Theology

Calvin notes how the law functions to restrain evil in society in general.[41] This is the civil use of the law (*usus politicus*) and is called today the first use of the law. One can see how Calvin understood this function of the law by reading the records of the consistory (town council) of Geneva.[42] For Calvin and his spiritual descendants, Christians can participate in the law courts of society; this is unlike the Anabaptist tradition, which originally considered civil law courts as useful only for nonbelievers.[43]

Calvin does not consider Jesus's additions to specific laws from the Mosaic law code to be examples of a "new law," as did Aquinas and Melanchthon. Rather, he considers Christ to be drawing out a moral sense that was always in the laws as given by Moses. Calvin explains by saying that the Mosaic laws, whether positive commands or prohibitions, contain a deeper sense than the words indicate.[44] This moral sense drives us to Christ, since we cannot keep the law's moral demands adequately. This function of the moral sense of the law is often referred to today as the second use of the law, or the pedagogical use, since Paul likens the law in this function to a *paidagōgos*, or tutor, who would escort children to school (Gal 3:24–25). Luther emphasized these two uses of the law. For him, the two significant purposes of the law were to restrain the wicked in society and to command, accuse, and judge the human conscience before God. These are the political and pedagogical uses of the law.[45]

But for Calvin, what is most significant in the moral sense of the law for believers in Christ is the way that the law serves as a guide for our own morality.[46] This is what is called the third use of the law. It is in this context that Calvin condemns Christians who say that there is no sense in which the Mosaic law applies to believers today.[47]

---

41. Calvin, *Inst.* 2.7.10–11. Luther also has a high regard for this use of the law; see *LW* 26:308.

42. Kingdon, Lambert, and Watt, *Registers of the Consistory of Geneva*, 1:5–61.

43. Calvin, *Inst.* 4.20.17–19.

44. Luther emphasizes this—e.g., *LW* 26:315. See also Calvin, *Inst.* 2.8.7–8.

45. *LW* 26:308–9.

46. Calvin, *Inst.* 2.7.12.

47. Calvin, *Inst.* 2.7.13.

Calvin taught that the ceremonial laws, such as the laws of sacrifice and ritual purity, are not binding on Christians. He writes that Christ has honored them by becoming the sacrifice to which they point, but that they are no longer to be kept.[48]

In summary, Calvin uses all of Scripture when discussing how the laws of Scripture should be applied to society in general in order to restrain evil, how the laws of Scripture drive some to faith in Christ, how Scripture provides moral guidance for believers, and how the ceremonial law is honored but no longer observed. He is definitely using the laws model when reading Scripture for providing an ethical basis for his political and moral theologies. Calvin's discussion of how God's law as found in Scripture is to be used provides a general background for Christian theologians' division of biblical law into moral, civil, and ceremonial laws.

Divisions of Mosaic Law According to Christian Theology

Christians' need for selective observance of Scripture's laws is evident in the division of these laws into moral, civil, and ceremonial laws, as mentioned above. But the strategy is foreign to the Old Testament, which contains various forms of laws intermingled with one another (e.g., casuistic and apodictic), as part of its authors' idea that all the Israelites' lives are to be lived in the presence of God. Jon Levenson's discussion of how both casuistic and apodictic laws are juxtaposed and intermingled makes this point well:

> All law in Israel, whether casuistic or apodictic in form, has been embedded within the context of covenant. In so doing, the tradition has endowed laws with the status of covenant stipulations, whether the individual ordinances show a formal connection to stipulations or not. . . . There were in ancient Israel more ways of conceiving the laws than simply that of the covenant theology. But by ascribing all normative law to Moses, the canonical Pentateuch has made laws into personal commandments, and it has made the secular into a matter of the greatest sacral concern.[49]

---

48. Calvin, *Inst.* 2.7.16.

49. Levenson, *Sinai and Zion*, 49–50. And E. P. Sanders, in *Paul and Palestinian Judaism*, reminds us that obeying the covenant commandments is what is expected in the Israelite response to God's initial acts of grace (Exod 20:2).

The Christian distinction between ceremonial, moral, and civil laws, then, is foreign to the Pentateuch, though some ground for it can be found in the New Testament.

Though Christians divide up what is presented as law in the Pentateuch, effectively jettisoning some of it, there are still some who can refer to all of Scripture as law. The tendency to name a variety of genres in Scripture as law is not merely an issue of nomenclature. In some cases, at least, naming Scripture as law reflects the model that considers the essence of Scripture to be God's commands and standards for humanity. Origen seems to operate with the laws model when he writes that simple people are instructed by the flesh or shell of Scripture. He goes on to say that while those who are partially mature are instructed by the soul of Scripture, those who are completely mature engage with the "spiritual law" in it.[50] Augustine works within this model when he argues against those who consider Abraham, Isaac, Jacob, Moses, and David to be guilty of sin for behaviors that differ from the readers' cultures:

> True inward righteousness takes as its criterion not custom but the most righteous law of almighty God, by which the morality of countries and times was formed as appropriate to those countries and times, while God's law itself has remained unchanged everywhere and always, not one thing in one place and something different elsewhere. . . . Equally foolish are people who grow indignant on hearing that some practice was allowed to righteous people in earlier ages which is forbidden to the righteous in our own day, and that God laid down one rule for the former and a different one for the latter, as the difference between the two periods of time demands; whereas in fact both sets of people have been subject to the same norm of righteousness.[51]

Even when distinguishing between types of law and noting cultural differences in fulfilling God's law, both Jews and Christians have also sought to keep the "Scripture as law" model relevant by allegorizing its laws so that they provide ethical norms that are meaningful in new situations, whether these allegories are based on legal or other genres within Scripture.[52] A late first- or

---

50. Origen, *On First Principles* 4.2.4 (Butterworth, 363–64).

51. Augustine, *Confessions* 3.7.13 (Boulding, 84–85).

52. For Jewish allegories of laws, see Philo, *On the Decalogue* and *Allegorical Interpretation* 1, 2, 3.

early second-century Christian wrote that the food laws God included within Mosaic law teach Christians what sorts of people and vices to avoid.[53] Mervin Monroe Deems would criticize the Epistle of Barnabas for how it allegorizes law in the same way that he rejects Augustine's allegorization: "The use of allegory by Augustine was not only a means of making Scripture say something, it was also a technique for bringing Scripture down to date, by forcing ancient words to minister, through prophecy, to the weaving of present patterns of behavior or through the summoning to higher ideals. But it was also dangerous for it came close to making Scripture say what he wanted it to say (through multiplicity of allegories of identical Scripture), and it prepared the way for Catholic or Protestant, later, to find in Scripture what he would."[54] Deems's negative assessment of allegorization seems at least partially based on his discomfort with a plurality of interpretations from the same text, according to his parenthetical aside. But this is a narrow assessment, for it ignores how many Scripture readers remain completely comfortable with multiple meanings from the same text. In fact, the exegesis of the Torah's food laws informed by modern medicine that explains them as providing for the Israelites' physical health is just as much an allegory as what the Epistle of Barnabas offers.[55] So although Christian theology has divided up Mosaic law and often states that one or more divisions are not relevant for Christians, there remain deeply seated attractions to explain even these irrelevant laws in ways that connect them to Christian experience. These connections are done by means of allegory. Allegory should not be rejected outright, since it is necessary for helping us read Scripture as a unified and relevant whole. Not all allegories are equally helpful or legitimate. But allegory, kept in check by a text's literal sense, remains a useful way of reading Scripture.

STRENGTHS OF THE LAWS MODEL

The strength of the laws model is that it facilitates the transformative potential of God's word. When people come to the Bible with the assumption that it is telling them how to live, they are more likely to change their lives than if they are simply reading with the documents or stories models. Here is how the laws model benefited me and my wife.

As a gentile Christian, I am not obligated to keep all of Mosaic law. But

---

53. Barn. 10:1–12 (Holmes, *Apostolic Fathers*, 373 [date of letter], 410–15).
54. Deems, "Augustine's Use of Scripture," 200.
55. This exegesis can be seen in McMillen and Stern, *None of These Diseases*.

I decided with my wife, on the basis of Deuteronomy 24:5, not to commit to any extra work during the first year of our marriage. That text mandates that in their first year of marriage, Israelite men are not to serve in the military or be tasked with other civic duties, in order that they may bring joy to their wives. Though my wife and I were in a much different context than the implied audience of Deuteronomy, we read the text with the laws model and followed it as appropriate in our new life together.

LIMITATIONS OF THE LAWS MODEL

We have already seen that it is difficult to make a definite application today of everything in the Bible that is explicitly law (e.g., the Mosaic law). It is even more of a logical challenge to read other parts of the Bible, such as its narratives or letters, as law.

People need stories and prayers in order to understand their lives and relate to God. So it is asking too much to read the whole of Scripture as law. The Bible's narrative and prayer discourse must be fully respected and integrated into one's life to take advantage of what it has to offer. But these models must be balanced with the laws model, for the laws model helps us recognize the dependence we have on God and the obedience we owe to him.

Jews are more able to read their Scripture, the Hebrew Bible, with the laws model, because they have a more holistic view of law than Christians do. Many Christians, because of generations of reading that treats law as sin-identifying and grace as the answer to law, find the laws model to be limited in its capacity to inspire them in their relationship with God.

THE LAWS MODEL IN THE CLASSROOM

Undergraduate theology majors and seminary students will encounter the laws model in ethics classes that cite the Bible to support a given response to moral questions. As in any application of the Bible to current life, care must be taken to ensure that the legal material in the Bible not be taken out of context.

Sometimes the laws model is adopted as a matter of course to awaken or influence people toward new concerns. For example, the ecologically minded theologians will read material from various genres in Scripture with the laws model in order to help people see the significance of caring for our planet. We can heartily agree with the ecological concerns represented, but still should be ready to admit when such concerns may be imported into the exegesis of a biblical text.

THE LAWS MODEL IN MINISTRY

In ministry there is no shortage of disagreements among parishioners regarding what is obligatory behavior for a Christian. The laws model is often assumed when arguments over Christian behavior arise.

The first response for anyone in ministry to show toward those who come advocating a certain practice on the basis of Scripture is to respect their regard for Scripture. Don't say, "Oh, you're locked into the laws model. You should balance this with a regard for the stories model." Instead say, "It is great that you are reading the Bible and taking it seriously. Please show me the texts that are influencing you to regard this as something Christians should do." Then take the time to listen to the people read the texts and explain to you how they are understanding them.

A recognition of the original context of any scriptural text is often a good way to de-escalate an argument. For example, someone may come quoting 1 Corinthians 11:5–10 when advocating that all women cover their heads when gathered with others in worship. It is useful, and does not involve taking a side in the argument, to point out that this paragraph arose in a letter to a disorderly church in Corinth around the years 50–55 CE. Most people do not consider women with braided hair or gold jewelry to have sinned by these adornments, though they are prohibited in 1 Peter 3:3. So some effort at bridging the cultural gap and explaining why 1 Corinthians 11:5–10 matters for today would be a good step in clarifying the arguments about head coverings for women in church. The same general strategy is a good way to respect others' sensitivities to Scripture while not automatically endorsing every application of Scripture into law that a parishioner may wish to make: search together to see if other Scriptures also speak on a given question and discuss how the principle behind a law in Scripture applies in a given culture today.

ORACLES

*A monk once came to Basil of Caesarea and said, "Speak a word, Father";
and Basil replied "Thou shalt love the Lord thy God with all thy heart";
and the monk went away at once. Twenty years later he came back, and
said, "Father, I have struggled to keep your word; now speak another word
to me"; and he said "Thou shalt love thy neighbor as thyself," and the monk
returned in obedience to his cell to keep that also.*

—BENEDICTA WARD[1]

Augustine portrays in his *Confessions* how, after hearing Ambrose expound the
Scriptures and coming to understand the truths of the faith, he still struggled
with lust in his life. While praying in agony for deliverance from his sins, he
heard a child's voice chanting "Pick it up and read." The rest is best told in his
own words.

> I stemmed the flood of tears and rose to my feet, believing that this could be
> nothing other than a divine command to open the Book and read the first
> passage I chanced upon; for I had heard the story of how Antony had been
> instructed by a gospel text. He happened to arrive while the gospel was be-
> ing read, and took the words to be addressed to himself when he heard, *Go
> and sell all you possess and give the money to the poor: you will have treasure
> in heaven. Then come, follow me.* So he was promptly converted to you by
> this plainly divine message. Stung into action, I returned to the place where
> Alypius was sitting, for on leaving it I had put down there the book of the
> apostle's letters. I snatched it up, opened it and read in silence the passage
> on which my eyes first lighted: *Not in dissipation and drunkenness, nor in
> debauchery and lewdness, nor in arguing and jealousy; but put on the Lord
> Jesus Christ, and make no provision for the flesh or the gratification of your*

1. Ward, *Sayings of the Desert Fathers*, xxii.

desires. I had no wish to read further, nor was there need. No sooner had I reached the end of the verse than the light of certainty flooded my heart and all dark shades of doubt fled away.[2]

Both the account of Antony's hearing of Jesus's words to the rich young ruler and Augustine's own account of reading what first he saw when opening a book of Paul's letters illustrate the oracles model of Scripture. A short passage of Scripture is read and treated as a breakthrough text that can provide direct, divine guidance for a life.

The oracles model is also on display in Martin Luther's reminiscence of his "tower experience," which involved an encounter with another text from the Letter to the Romans. In the 1545 edition of his Latin writings, Luther recounts how he read "the just shall live by faith" in Romans 1:17 and thought that heaven had just opened, since that text prompted his new understanding of "the righteousness of God." He had earlier called Romans 1:16–17 the whole conclusion of the letter. Luther's use of the oracles model in this experience is somewhat different from St. Antony's in that Luther claimed that his new insight into God's righteousness from those two verses unlocked all of Scripture for him.[3] Luther came to view Romans 1:16–17 as the very top of a pyramid of all Scripture, the most meaningful text in all of Scripture. He rated other texts in relation to how they fit with the perspective of Romans 1:16–17. Thus, the Letter to the Galatians came very near the top of Luther's pyramid arrangement for Scripture as well. Old Testament texts were lower in the pyramid.[4]

Definition and Characteristics of the Oracles Model

An oracle is a revelatory word, presented as a divinely originating command, diagnosis, or prediction that is spoken to guide people's attitudes and behavior in their own lifetimes. The oracles model approaches Scripture as a potential treasure house of short, maxim-like sayings that can have revolutionary effect when fully understood and actualized in a life.

---

2. Augustine, *Confessions* 8.12.29 (Boulding, 206–7). The gospel text that Antony heard is Matt 19:21. The text from Paul's letters that spoke so powerfully to Augustine is Rom 13:13–14.

3. For his fullest autobiographical reflection on the "tower experience" with Rom 1:17, see *WA* 54.185–86; ET in Bainton, *Here I Stand*, 49–50. Luther also refers to his tower experience several times in his table talk (*WA TR* 2:177 §1681; 3:228 §3232a, b, c; *LW* 54:193–94, 308–9, 442–43). For identification of Rom 1:17 as "whole conclusion" of the letter, see *WA* 3.174.13–16; *LW* 29:188.

4. See Pelikan, *Luther the Expositor*, and Ebeling, "Church History."

The quest for a divine word that can speak directly to one's situation seems deeply seated in the human psyche, since we can see evidence of it in the popularity of the Delphic oracle, the Sibyl of Cumae, and people's quest for a word from a desert father. People who read with the oracles model have such a regard for the power of the divine word focused on their situation that they expect it to come in a short discourse unit, such as a single sentence.

Because Scripture is God-breathed (2 Tim 3:16), it is a short step for readers to view each encounter with it as potentially a revelatory moment when God will speak a word directly to the reader. The "fit" of a given reading at a given moment of difficulty or uncertainty confirms for some their sense that the Bible is a thesaurus of oracles, which, when consulted properly, will give God's word to them. The oracles model therefore is a way of reading Scripture that treats it as a compendium of discrete, insightful commands, diagnoses, or predictions that are infinitely reapplicable across the spectrum of human experience throughout generations.

You know that the oracles model is operating . . .

. . . when you hear people say they opened the Bible at random to a text that spoke exactly to their situation. The practice of interpreting as direct guidance whatever one first reads when opening a text is known as sortilege. People have been doing this for millennia, at times using other texts besides the Christian Scriptures.

. . . when you hear or write a homily/sermon based on a single phrase or sentence of Scripture. People need slogans or mottos to live by, and the message from a single phrase or verse can be memorable and life-changing when developed in a homily or sermon.

. . . when you read the Bible for an encouraging word, typically a single verse that you can remember through the whole day. People often read Scripture in order to be spiritually nourished. Scripture readers so motivated often look for a verse that will encourage, motivate, or warn them in ways that seem very relevant to them.

. . . when you see a verse from the Bible tattooed, printed on a T-shirt, or otherwise prominently displayed. One day while in a senior seminar for undergraduates in biblical studies, one student removed his shirt at the beginning of class to reveal what was newly tattooed across his back: ὁ δὲ δίκαιος ἐκ πίστεώς μου ζήσεται. This represents Habakkuk 2:4b LXX—"the

just one shall live by my faith"—a sentence that our textbook that semester was emphasizing as very influential among New Testament writers.[5] As all class sessions on Scripture should be, that day was an exciting one. My student's desire to brand himself with that text represented his deep appreciation for that single sentence of Scripture. He understood that text as a meaningful, guiding text for his life. This is the oracles model.

Specific Applications of the Oracles Model

The most significant application of the oracles model is the christological-apocalyptic application, evident among the New Testament and patristic writers. Others apply the oracles model by identifying doctrinal, ethical, or spiritual principles from short sections of the text.

Christological-Apocalyptic Application of the Oracles Model

In Revelation 5:1–10, only the slain lamb, John's image of Jesus, is found worthy to open the sealed scroll. The scene's sealed scroll is perhaps taken from Daniel 12, where Daniel is commanded to seal up what he has recorded so that the scroll remains unread until the end of time (12:4–9). The vision in Revelation 5, then, shows how Jesus is the one who is worthy of opening the record of what will happen at the end, and this fits with the christological-apocalyptic way of reading Scripture, which views Christ as the key for all of Scripture, both Old and New Testaments.

In this application of the oracles model, Christ is the ultimate content or focus of all of Scripture. Thus Jesus says in John 5:39, "You examine the Scriptures, because you think in them you have eternal life, and they are what bears witness concerning me." Jesus is therefore correcting the mindset that Scripture is valuable in itself with the different portrait of Scripture as a witness to him. Such a witness is seen in Acts 8. After the eunuch asks Philip if Isaiah the prophet is speaking about himself or someone else in his fourth servant song, Philip describes how the song is really about Christ (Acts 8:26–40, quoting Isa 53:7–8).

The christological-apocalyptic application of this model does not simply view Christ as the *Sache* or main content of all Scripture. It also views Christ as the best interpreter of Scripture. Thus, in Luke 24:27 we read a description of the resurrected Christ interpreting what is written about him "in all the Scriptures." The Gospels' depictions of Jesus citing Scripture when tempted

---

5. Watson, *Paul and the Hermeneutics of Faith*.

and interpreting Scripture in his home synagogue or when asked questions by others are all presenting him as the ultimate interpreter of Scripture, who can take a sentence from the Old Testament and show exactly what it means.[6]

This application of the oracles model is evident in the church fathers' understanding of Scripture. John Behr favorably cites Origen's description of the Gospels:

> In their Gospels the evangelists proclaimed Christ by drawing upon the language of the Scriptures, investing or clothing him with these words, as the flesh by which he is made known, seen, and understood. However, these narratives are thus also a veil, which, while essential for communicating the gospel, must also be "unveiled" for the gospel to be received as a proclamation rather than a report about past events. Origen, in the first sustained reflection on what is meant by the term "gospel," argues that it does not primarily mean "the narrative of the deeds, sufferings, and words of Jesus," but rather designates an "exhortatory address," and as such it includes all the writings which "present the sojourn [ἐπιδημία] of Christ and prepare for his coming [παρουσία] and produce it in the souls of those who are willing to receive the Word of God, who stands at the door and knocks and wishes to enter their souls."[7]

Augustine similarly encounters Christ in Scripture after he understands Christ to be both the beginning through whom God created and the Word eternally spoken by God.[8] With this understanding, Augustine can read sentences from Scripture as oracles that communicate Christ. This application of the model influences his early exegetical works.[9]

Doctrinal Application of the Oracles Model

In the early fourth century, when the Arian controversy was in full swing, the Arians applied Proverbs 8:22 in an oracular way to the question of the pre-existence of the Son. Since personified wisdom claims in that verse to be God's creation, the Arians pressed this phrase into their argument for the creation of the Son. Orthodox theologians, led by Athanasius, argued from the general

---

6. Matt 4:1–11; Mark 1:12–13; Luke 4:1–13 (temptation); Luke 4:16–21 (interpreting Isaiah in Nazareth synagogue); Matt 19:3–9; Mark 10:1–12 (interpreting Scripture regarding divorce).

7. Behr, *John the Theologian*, 112, citing Origen, *Commentary on the Gospel of John* 1.18–26.

8. Augustine, *Confessions* 11.7.9–11.9.11 (Boulding, 290–92).

9. Cameron, *Christ Meets Me Everywhere*.

sense of other Scriptures against the emphatic application of single verses that could be co-opted by the Arians.[10]

Today as well, people may in cases press a given verse in Scripture to argue for how a person must be saved, be filled with the Holy Spirit, or display their faith. John 3:16 is often cited to say that a person must believe in Jesus, and in general the church affirms that this is so for people who have opportunity to do so. The oracles model would press this verse into saying that it is a necessary and sufficient condition for salvation. Those operating with a stories model might cite other texts in the Bible that seem to envision salvation for people irrespective of a conscious identification with Jesus, and say that John 3:16 represents only a sufficient condition for salvation.

Passages in Acts that describe people filled with the Holy Spirit after the apostles lay hands on them and baptize them can be adopted by the oracles model as the necessary signs of true conversion.[11] This illustrates one vulnerable point of the oracles model. There are times when a given verse, cited as an oracle that has universal applicability for all people, cannot bear that semantic or theological load, given other texts in the Scriptures that offer different perspectives.

Ethical Application of the Oracles Model

Moral theologians and ethicists may be tempted to latch onto single texts that seem to speak to ethical questions in our day. The "do justice" phrase in Micah 6:8 is particularly adaptable and useful in this regard. One can apply it to whatever situation that appears unjust and argue that Micah 6:8 means that the situation should be changed according to one's preconceived ideas of justice.

In the nineteenth-century United States, those with a conservative view of Scripture considered that it endorsed slavery, since a text like "Slaves, obey your masters" was taken as an oracle that spoke into the country's situation. The abolitionists, who argued from the general emphasis of mercy in the Bible and the seemingly more unrelated command "Love your neighbor as yourself," were considered to have a more liberal view of Scripture. Slaveholders and slaves cited different verses to support their positions on slavery. As a general rule, slaveholders did not want their slaves reading the whole Bible, since they

10. O'Keefe and Reno, *Sanctified Vision*, 56–61. Athanasius sought for a context from throughout the Bible rather than for an isolated oracle: "For Athanasius, what is prior is the urgency of a unified, coherent reading of scripture, a reading that maximizes the number of unstrained interpretations of individual words, verses, and episodes. Doctrine 'follows' from that priority" (61).

11. Acts 8:14–17; 10:44–48; 19:1–7.

knew that the slaves would find verses to counterbalance the "Slaves, obey your masters" perspective.[12]

A similar drama also played out in the late twentieth century in regard to the death penalty. Death is prescribed for murderers in the Old Testament. Yet in the ongoing reflection of the Catholic Church, the death penalty is now considered to be a fundamental crime against humanity made in God's image. So both in regard to slavery and the death penalty, oracle-like statements in the Bible that seem to condone the practices seem now to be read in the broader context of the whole canon. This contextual reading is winning over the oracles of specific verses that accept the realities of slavery and death to murderers in the ancient Near East.[13]

Spiritual Application of the Oracles Model

The spiritual application of the oracles model may be the one that is most easily recognizable. This is the display of Scripture texts in order to remind one or others of their significance. At times these texts appear to function as a sort of talisman, a charm that will bring success. Thus, someone might write Philippians 4:13 (either the verse itself or simply the reference) across a textbook cover or at the top of a test, as if to say that, with this verse in mind, he or she will succeed in their class or test. Bible covers and journals that feature this verse are also popular.

OLD TESTAMENT TEXTS OFTEN READ AS ORACLES

Our Scriptures certainly employ oracles as keys to given narratives. For generations, people have read God's messages at the end of the second creation account, directed respectively to serpent, woman, and man, each as programmatic statements for the following battle between good and evil, woman's experience, and man's work (Gen 3:14–19). For those who read with the oracles model, these statements function as oracles that outline what the future will hold.

The man of God's words to Eli, early in 1 Samuel (2:35), provide a key to the rest of the narratives in 1 Samuel–2 Kings. That one sentence functions as an oracle that encapsulates the rivalry between the houses of Zadok and Abiathar

---

12. Noll, "Biblical Nation," 48–50. The "Slaves, obey your masters" text is Eph 6:5–6. "Love your neighbor as yourself" is Lev 19:18. Favorite texts of slaves included Mal 2:10; Acts 10:34; 17:26.

13. The extreme limits placed on use of the death penalty are evident in *CCC* §2267, which ends by citing John Paul II, *Evangelium vitae* §§56, 68 on how cases where the death penalty should be used "are very rare, if not practically non-existent."

for the office of high priest, and the rise of the anointed king whom they serve. And the man of God's word about the house of Eli also is regarded as an oracle that comes true when Eli and his sons die and their descendant Abiathar is expelled from office (1 Sam 2:33–34; 4:11, 18; 1 Kgs 2:27). The conclusion of Nathan's announcement of the Davidic covenant functions as an oracle for how God will treat Solomon (2 Sam 7:14–15; 1 Kgs 11:11–13, 32, 34–36). Not long after this in the narrative, Nathan's words to David after his affair with Bathsheba and murder of Uriah function as another oracle that points ahead to later narratives in the book (2 Sam 12:9–12; 13:28–29; 16:21–22; 18:14–15). Later in the Deuteronomistic History, the words of another man of God are treated as an oracle that points to a Davidic king, Josiah, who will come to reign three centuries after the oracle is spoken (1 Kgs 13:1–2; 2 Kgs 23:15–16). The oracles in the Deuteronomistic History thus evoke confidence in the power of God's word and serve as stitches that hold the narrative together.

Single verses in the Psalms may be identified and repeated as promises that can come true in one's life. Ideas like the Lord's shepherding care for a life or God's generous giving of good things have a strong appeal for those who read and repeat these descriptions to themselves (Pss 23:1; 84:11). And people can value maxims from wisdom literature as oracles that, when "claimed" or repeated, guarantee success for them in life (Prov 10:22; 22:6).[14]

Within the Prophets, a favorite verse of readers employing the oracular approach is Jeremiah 29:11: "For I know the plans I have for you, says the LORD, plans for welfare and not for harm, to give you a future and a hope." The context clearly places this as a word to Judah at the time of its impending exile to Babylon. But readers today grasp it as God's word of hope for them, even though they are in very different situations from Judah in the sixth century BCE.

New Testament Texts Often Read as Oracles

When reading the Gospels' genealogies, the reader with an oracles model of Scripture will intuitively seek a main point or a single ancestor that the genealogy is highlighting. Thus, the oracles model will rightly see that the Matthew genealogy is emphasizing Jesus as the ultimate descendant of David and Abraham (Matt 1:1, 6, 17) and that the Luke genealogy is emphasizing that Jesus is the ultimate human (Luke 3:38).

Luke-Acts, which seems to imitate the oracular strategy of the Deuteronomistic History by providing programmatic statements through the direct

---

14. Copeland, *Blessing of the Lord*, is a book that treats Prov 10:22 as an oracle that can come true in anyone's life.

discourse of its characters, certainly contains some oracle-like sayings. The words that the angel Gabriel, Elizabeth, and Simeon speak to Mary all function as oracles in the text—that is, iconic statements that encapsulate Jesus's role on earth.[15] The hymns of praise spoken by Mary, Zechariah, and the angels also function in an oracular way, situating the incarnation in the God of Israel's immanent disposition toward Israel and humanity as a whole, humbling the proud and exalting the lowly.[16] The author of Luke-Acts, so aware of the rhetorical potential of the debut scene, makes certain to give us oracular statements in the first sermons of his main characters.[17] The author of John's Gospel similarly can use oracular statements within direct discourse, and also provides the "I am" sayings of Jesus to emphasize Jesus's divine status.[18]

The association of God's word with the future, so evident in prophetic texts of the Old Testament, is also found within the epistolary genre of the New Testament. The one text in the New Testament that explicitly describes Scripture as divinely inspired comes at the end of a chapter that begins with discussing the evils of the last days (2 Tim 3:1–5, 16–17). The clarifying paragraph on the "day of the Lord" in 2 Thessalonians is bracketed by references to letters that the Thessalonians have received (2:1–15). And Paul's words that are primarily meant to give comfort to church members who have lost loved ones include an oracular description of the parousia or return of Jesus to earth (1 Thess 4:13–18). The letters within the Pauline corpus function as written oracles to mediate the presence of Paul to his churches and churches of later generations.

Key Issues in the Oracles Model

If you are in a Scripture or biblical studies class right now, or are engaged in ministry and teaching from Scripture, it may be easy for you to dismiss the oracles model as superstitious. You may consider it an unwarranted appropriation of Scripture without attention to context. In the key issues below, we consider some of the dangers of this model. At the same time, this model offers distinct possibilities for hearing and incorporating God's word in one's life in ways that the other models do not provide. We consider these positive possibilities within the oracles model as well.

---

15. Luke 1:32–33, 35, 42–45; 2:29–32, 34–35.

16. Luke 1:46–55, 68–79; 2:14.

17. Luke 4:17–27; Acts 2:14–40; 13:16–47.

18. Oracular statements within conversations: John 1:49, 51; 2:5, 19; 19:26–27. "I am" statements: John 8:12, 58; 10:7, 11, 14; 11:25; 15:1, 5.

Hidden Meanings of Scripture

Because Scripture contains revelatory sentences that function as moments of illumination in their own right, its sentences require careful and loving exegesis. Exegesis means a close and respectful reading of the text to unpack its meaning. It can be done by those who read the Bible only in their native language. It does not require that one know the Bible's original languages, though that can help. Eugene Peterson makes these points and drives them home better than I can.

> Exegesis is the furthest thing from pedantry; exegesis is an act of love. It loves the one who speaks the words enough to use every means we have to get the words right. Exegesis is loving God enough to stop and listen carefully to what he says. It follows that we bring the leisure and attentiveness of lovers to this text, cherishing every comma and semicolon, relishing the oddness of this preposition, delighting in the surprising placement of this noun. Lovers don't take a quick look, get a "message" or a "meaning," and then run off and talk endlessly with their friends about how they feel.[19]

A more extreme approach to exegesis looks for hidden meanings behind almost everything in the text. Origen comes close to this when he writes that all Scripture contains a spiritual meaning, while not all of it contains a physical or literal meaning, since sometimes the literal meaning represents impossible conditions.[20] He describes the Holy Spirit as hiding spiritual truths far beneath the narratives of Scripture. Origen understands Jesus's parable of the treasure hidden in the field to represent how spiritual truths are buried underneath the literal sense of the text of Scripture. For Origen it is not simply prophecies in the Bible that have a spiritual sense; it is Scripture's narratives as well. Divine assistance is required to break through the gates behind which these spiritual truths are concealed.[21]

The oracles model has the potential therefore to motivate readers to come to the text carefully and lovingly, listening to its nuances. Part of this motivation is no doubt due to the window on the transcendent that the text provides.

19. Peterson, *Eat This Book*, 55.
20. Origen, *On First Principles* 4.3.5 (Butterworth, 396).
21. Origen, *On First Principles* 4.3.11 (Butterworth, 406–8). The parable of the treasure hidden in the field is in Matt. 13:44.

Encounter with the Transcendent

Because the oracles model expects a word that will speak right to the heart of a reader's life situation, this model places high expectations on the encounter with the text, whether by reading or hearing. Among English-language editions of the Bible, *The Serendipity Bible* especially exemplifies the oracles model. On its jacket cover it defines "serendipity" as what the Holy Spirit does unexpectedly when several believers gather together. The implied scenario is of several believers gathered for Bible study and coming to a new insight or experience of the Holy Spirit that will change their lives.[22] Both the prayers and the oracles models consider reading Scripture to be an activity that connects with the transcendent. But the oracles model, more than the other models in this book, considers inspiration to occur not only at the time of composition but also at the time when the text is read. This model thus inspires readers to take immediate action when they receive an oracle.

At the same time, the high expectations can lead to self-delusion, since the audience receiving the oracle from an encounter with Scripture often views the oracle as especially applicable to themselves. In Scripture, most of the prophets who received oracles from God do not invite their audience to seek oracles in their own right. Everyone—whether prophet/prophetess or audience—recognizes the reception of an oracle to be unique.[23] Because a message from God is often understood within the oracles model to be specifically directed to a particular life situation, there is not always a way to compare the received oracle with what others have received. When commanded to marry a prostitute, the prophet did not say, "Lord, you have not commanded others to marry prostitutes!" He obeyed, because the oracle was specifically to him (Hos 1:2–3). So also today; if someone is convinced that a given verse of Scripture is God's way of telling them to do something, there is little room for argument. The singular nature of an oracle makes it unfalsifiable in the short term for its recipient.

The whole process of seeking a divine word by oracle is therefore open to abuse, as biblical texts dealing with the assessment of prophecies amply demonstrate (Deut 18:20–22; 1 Kgs 13:11–25; 22:24–28). People can persuade themselves or be persuaded by spirits that God is speaking a special word,

---

22. Coleman, *Serendipity Bible*.

23. Von Rad, *Message of the Prophets*, 42. Exceptions von Rad cites are Joel's prediction of God's Spirit coming on all flesh (Joel 2:28–29 in most translations; 3:1–2 in LXX, MT, and NABRE) and Moses's wish that all Israelites would prophesy (Num 11:29).

when perhaps God is not (1 Kgs 22:19–23). The inspired believer who receives a word from the Lord has often been someone other believers don't know how to handle, whether one considers the Montanists in the second through fourth centuries, John of Leiden in sixteenth-century Münster, Hong Xiuquan in nineteenth-century Taiping, or David Koresh in twentieth-century Waco.

Yes, God does speak to people through the gift of prophecy (1 Cor 12:28–29; 14:1–5). And God does speak to people through an oracle-focused reading of Scripture. But we humans are fallible and easily distracted. So the oracles model can never be the only model one uses in reading Scripture. When one comes close to receiving an oracle from Scripture, it is always a good idea to check its "fit" with a consideration of the Scripture passage's context, accessible by reading the text through the lens of the stories model.

Consumer Mentality

Scripture employs the figure of consuming God's written word, a positive image of fully engaging with divine revelation (Jer 15:16; Ezek 2:8–3:3; Rev 10:8–11). But the oracles model is often the default setting for us when we read the Bible with a specific, self-oriented question in mind, a question needing an immediate answer. In those situations, we are not approaching the text to hear whatever God wishes to tell us. Instead, we are reading the text as consumers, with our own agenda determining how we read. We read to receive an answer to the question we have framed, or to receive confirmation for the decision we want to make. This is not a functional way to read Scripture, for a regard for the Bible as Scripture includes an openness to hearing what God speaks to us, even when it does not seem to fit our question. For example, just as the captain of the Lord's armies does not answer Joshua's question with a response presupposed by Joshua (Josh 5:13–15), so we need to read Scripture in a more open frame of mind than simply looking for what we think we need to find in it. Since the oracles model so readily matches this self-oriented frame of mind, it should always be used alongside one or more other models.

The consumer-oriented attitude evoked by the oracles model can be seen in the organization and study questions of *The Serendipity Bible*. This edition of the Bible is accompanied by various study plans for different books of the Bible. On the opening page of Genesis, the following questions are offered: "How aware are you of the created world in your everyday life? What aspect of the created world is most inspiring to you? Why? How does it affect your understanding of God? What does it mean to you to be created in God's image?

How does knowing this affect how you feel about yourself?"[24] These questions illustrate the consumer-oriented approach that the oracles model brings to the text. The model expects immediate answers to one's own questions, just as a consumer expects instant details such as the price and full description of any commodity when considering a purchase. Since the oracles model readily contributes to a consumer mindset when reading Scripture, it also raises some readers' expectations of an immediate word for them when the Scriptures are randomly opened. This longstanding practice is known as sortilege.

Sortilege

In the introduction to this chapter, we saw how Augustine encountered two life-changing verses in Romans when he opened a copy of Paul's letters to wherever it would open. As Augustine relates the scene, the text identified by his sortilege shone a light of certainty into his heart and scattered his doubts; he treats this as a key turning point in his journey toward Christ and into the church.[25]

What is sortilege? It is a large class of activities, also known as "divination by lot" or "cleromancy," we humans have engaged in for millennia, in which objects like lots, dice, or even written texts are used to provide guidance in decision-making or general knowledge. Sortilege entails the assumption that there are equal chances for a variety of outcomes when we engage in it, so that the outcome we receive is thus viewed as supernaturally given.[26] Besides throwing dice, many readers will be familiar with tossing a coin when facing a decision.

Our tendency at times to open a book or other source of information at random and take the first sentence we encounter as the word we are to follow is the type of sortilege used in an oracles approach to Scripture. Sortilege with a written text was practiced in ancient times by opening Homer's *Odyssey* or *Iliad*, Vergil's *Aeneid*, or the Bible and taking whatever sentence one's finger first fell on as indicative of divine guidance. Those who use sortilege in this way are usually very familiar with the text being consulted, and they typically hold a strong conviction that the text they are using has a meaning deeper

---

24. Coleman, *Serendipity Bible*, 40.
25. Augustine, *Confessions* 8.12.29–30 (Boulding, 206–8).
26. Luijendijk and Klingshirn, *My Lots Are in Thy Hands*, 1.

than the life situation described in the world of the text.[27] Sometimes called "cutting the Bible" or "bibliomancy," sortilege with a Bible is simply opening the Bible randomly and beginning to read. This practice can be motivated by a desire to let God be responsible for what one reads. But because one begins reading wherever one's eye falls on the page to which one has been randomly (or divinely?) moved, one will almost inevitably read the text in the context of one's own life situation. This can be problematic in that it is a step toward denying that there is determinate meaning in the text.[28]

The Atomization of Scripture

Because the oracles model expects a divine word in a compressed format, such as a single sentence or a poetic couplet, the model tends to consume Scripture in small bites. The oracles model thus is often associated with Scripture in an atomized format. Because the oracles model regards Scripture as a collection of profound announcements from God, each verse can be considered an oracle—a revelatory statement with its own unique message—in its own right.

We have already observed how the oracles model is readily adopted by a consumer mentality, in which one reads Scripture to fulfill one's personal agenda. As consumers, we take what we like from Scripture and domesticate it. As we see in bookstores or online catalogs, plaques, posters, and other decorative objects are readily available with Bible verses on them. We might label some such item as "Christian kitsch" in another's home and actually treasure something very similar in our own.

The atomization of Scripture that happens with this model is a factor that makes it easy to read Scripture as a consumer. When one focuses only on a given phrase or sentence—a bite-sized Scripture oracle—then one is freer to interpret that phrase or sentence as one wishes, since less attention is paid to the context around the oracle. (Don't worry; I won't be asking you to throw out your parents' Bible-themed coffee mugs! But I do challenge myself and others to read the chapters around our favorite verses.)

This atomization of the text is evident in the format of the first edition of the King James Version. When the King James Version was first published in 1611, the text was not divided into paragraphs. Each verse was typeset as its

---

27. Luijendijk and Klingshirn, "Literature of Lot Divination," 49.
28. Casey, *Sacred Reading*, 12.

own discrete unit of text.[29] This format lends itself to reading the text as if each verse is its own message—almost as if each verse is the fortune on the slip of paper in Chinese fortune cookies. Expectations that one will find in a single verse God's word to the reader can run high when encountering the text in this way. And this reflection on the King James Version also helps us become conscious of a mode of reading that often accompanies the oracles model of Scripture: the quest for the single, golden verse.

Key Verse

The oracles model is the model with most potential for awakening in a reader a hunger for a single phrase or verse that will provide guidance for one's life or open all of Scripture. The gospel text that St. Antony heard one day in worship was Matthew 19:21, in which Jesus tells the rich man that the one thing he needs to do is to sell all that he has, give the proceeds to the poor, and follow Jesus. St. Antony received that gospel text as though it were an oracle spoken specifically to him, and on that day gave away the land that his father had owned and sold the possessions he had inherited.[30]

The quest for a key verse is sometimes found in practices of daily devotions. Booklets that seek to facilitate a quiet time with God will offer a single "verse of the day" with a meditation on that verse. In my own spiritual journey, a friend once showed me how he carried around with him, on a small piece of paper, a Bible verse that he had found in his daily devotions. I continued the practice by sometimes writing down a key verse for the day in a journal. This quest for a key verse is not limited simply to one's spiritual experience for a day. It even extends to the quest for a verse that encapsulates the good news.

We already observed how the doctrinal application of the oracles model readily applies John 3:16 when considering one's entry into the Christian faith. Many Christians' regard today for John 3:16 as the one verse in all the Bible that one needs to know to get close to God is an actualization of the oracles model that is analogous to Luther's experience and subsequent dependence on Romans 1:16–17. These Christians might consider John 3:16 to be the ultimate litmus test for one's faith. If one has a due appreciation for it, then one is regarded as orthodox. I witnessed this firsthand after I was received into the Catholic Church. A college friend wanted to see me after this change in my life.

29. McGrath, *In the Beginning*, 202.
30. Athanasius, *Life of Antony* 2.

While sharing a meal in a restaurant near my home, he said, "It's fine with me that you are Catholic, since Catholics now believe in John 3:16 and grace."

The oracles model does not look to the paragraph, chapter, or book as the basic unit of meaning in Scripture's discourse. Instead, it reads to discover a single truth, often from a single verse, which can provide meaning, encouragement, or a divine perspective that the reader can carry for the day, the week, or longer. Those who advocate finding a "life verse" from the Bible participate in this mode of reading that is especially based on an oracles model.

The Second Lives of Scripture's Oracles

The extended usefulness of oracles is evident in how postexilic prophets and editors recycled material from writings of earlier prophets. For example, the very time-specific, preexilic prophecies of Amos to the northern kingdom of Israel were given new life when editors added two oracles to the end of Amos in order to update the whole book and thus package it for continued effectiveness as a compilation of oracles.[31] The Nahum *pesher* among the Dead Sea Scrolls is also a good example of how verses from a biblical text can be treated as oracles that speak to generations long removed from a first audience.[32]

Another way that oracles are given new lives within Scripture is that they are quoted and given a new emphasis or application. Texts in the final ten chapters of Isaiah, considered by many to be later than those from Isaiah 40–55, thus recycle some of the language of return from exile in chapters 40–55 and apply them to the need for justice and the celebration of the salvation that God will bring.[33] A more radical reapplication of a prophetic oracle comes in the reversal that Joel 3:10 makes to the "swords into ploughshares" phrase of Isaiah 2:4. Similar recycling of prophetic oracles can be found in New Testament quotations of the prophets. For example, the prophecy of a birth in Isaiah 7:14 makes sense only if it were fulfilled in the years immediately following the prophecy. When Matthew quotes it as fulfilled in Jesus's birth, he is applying it to Jesus as though the prophecy were receiving a second fulfillment.[34] Similarly, when Matthew quotes Hosea's pronouncement "Out of Egypt I have called my son" as fulfilled in the Holy Family's sojourn in Egypt, he is reap-

---

31. Schuller, *Post-exilic Prophets*, 112–13, citing Amos 9:11, 13.

32. *Pesher* means "commentary." See Berrin, *Pesher Nahum Scroll*.

33. Schuller, *Post-exilic Prophets*, 114, citing how Isa 57:14 recycles 40:3 or how Isa 58:8 recycles language from 52:12. See also Sommer, *Prophet Reads Scripture*.

34. See Matt 1:23, quoting Isa 7:14. See discussion in Collins, *Short Introduction*, 206–7, and Roberts, "Isaiah and His Children."

plying an oracle that Hosea speaks about Israel's exodus from Egypt under Moses.[35] The oracular model of Scripture views single sentences in Scripture as enduring speech acts that continue to speak through the centuries. Thus, even a line in a Passover recipe can be considered fulfilled in the death of Jesus, when the recipe itself is viewed as an oracle from God.[36]

The oracles reader will approach the book of Revelation as prophecy that must still be fulfilled, citing the "prophecy" descriptions of the text in Revelation 1:3; 10:11; 22:6–7, 10, 18–19. Other texts as well, whether they are from law or narrative sections of Scripture, will be viewed as texts that are still open for fulfillment.

The oracles reader will not be immediately receptive to reading the eagle vision in 2 Esdras 11–12 in order to understand Revelation 13, or reading other apocalyptic texts in order to understand Revelation. Someone reading with the documents or stories model would be more ready to read analogous extrabiblical texts in order to understand a biblical text. But for one committed to an exclusive use of the oracles model, the text of Scripture is a direct word from God, and to read extrabiblical literature in order to understand Scripture better could be viewed as keeping the oracle at arm's length. A second reason that one reading with the oracles model would not readily look to other texts for understanding is that this model operates primarily out of the reader's own context. The reader needs a divine word and consults the oracles of Scripture to find one that fits her situation. The motivation for reading Scripture in this way also is likely to prompt the person who reads a text when in oracles mode to seize on any sentence or phrase of Scripture that seems to capture a course of action that one is ready to pursue.

The benefits of an oracles approach to Scripture is that it allows one to engage deeply with the text, since one regards it as containing a direct word from God. The disadvantage of an oracles approach to Scripture is that one might lose sight of others involved in the composition, editing, and transmission of the text of Scripture, for whom a given verse might mean much more than what the oracular reader finds in it.

STRENGTHS OF THE ORACLES MODEL

One strength of the oracles model is that by definition it requires the reader to engage with the text. This model arises out of a reader's felt need to hear a

35. Matt 2:15, quoting Hos 11:1.
36. See John 19:36, quoting Exod 12:10, 46.

divine word that addresses the reader's own life. This model is not as vulnerable to the attitudes of disengagement or even skepticism that can arise in some applications of the documents or stories models.

A second strength of the oracles model immediately follows. Because this model takes seriously the church's conviction that God speaks to us through Scripture, there is a high probability that when one is reading Scripture by means of the oracles model, one will follow through with what Scripture says. As mentioned above, Antony followed through on the gospel texts he heard by immediately divesting himself of the family property and by giving his belongings to the poor.[37] Augustine also acted on his hearing of Romans 13:13–14. After experiencing "the light of certainty flood[ing his] heart," he set in place a plan to retire sooner rather than later from teaching rhetoric.[38]

A third strength of the oracles model is its convenience. It often allows one to read Scripture for less time than do the stories and prayers models. Once one has found a gem from the text that speaks to one's situation, one can then close the Bible and resume one's other activities. This is therefore a low threshold model. It allows a way for people to engage with Scripture without reading large sections of text.

LIMITATIONS OF THE ORACLES MODEL

Sometimes people read through the lens of the oracles model when seeking their own agenda. The Bible is a lengthy text, and people can abuse the oracles model by seeking only confirmation of their own agenda rather than reading for all that the Bible might have to say about a given question. Augustine, who seems to have used the oracles model when he opened a book of Paul's letters and applied the first passage his eyes landed on to his own situation, actually writes elsewhere that people should not regard Scripture as giving oracular counsel for "worldly business and the vanity of this life": "Regarding those who draw lots from the pages of the Gospel, although it could be wished that they would do this rather than run about consulting demons, I do not like this custom of wishing to turn the divine oracles to worldly business and the vanity of this life, when their object is another life."[39] This quotation illustrates a potential weakness of the oracles model. Because the oracles model regards Scripture as a direct medium for God to speak to one's immediate situation, it

---

37. Athanasius, *Life of Antony* 2–3.

38. Augustine, *Confessions* 8.12.29 (quotation; Boulding, 207), 9.2.2 (retirement plan; Boulding, 210).

39. Childers, "Hermeneutics and Divination," 129, citing Augustine, *Ep.* 55.37.

is easy for people using this model to come to Scripture looking for confirmation of their own agenda. They might not ask themselves whether the question they are bringing to the text of Scripture is actually framed in a way that allows for God's will to be accomplished in their lives. For example, the interpretation provided in one manuscript that corresponds with John 6:26–27 reads, "If you believe, you will have a good fortune."[40] People might misunderstand this sort of interpretation to expect that God owes them health or prosperity because they claim to trust God.

A dangerous instance of how the oracles model can be abused to confirm only what one wants to see in Scripture is in the open path it has provided at times for Christians to ignore or exclude Israel from a Christian summary of how God works with humanity. An early precedent for this use of the oracular model in this damaging way is Justin Martyr's exegesis of God's blessing to Abraham, at the end of the binding of Isaac narrative, as a blessing on Christians and a curse on Jews. Justin interprets the positive simile of "sand on the seashore" as a curse indicating the sterility of Israel.[41]

In an ostensibly less antagonistic mode, Origen considers Paul's references to a heavenly Jerusalem as an interpretive key indicating that the biblical prophets' references to Jerusalem and other cities in Judea are actually referring to gentiles from around the world who will follow Jesus Christ. From there he goes on to offer the oracular interpretation of the geography behind even the Bible's narratives: those in Israel and Judea refer to those mature souls who live in various places of heaven with God, and descriptions of Israel's and Judah's exiles or captivities in other nations signify the descent of these souls to lower places, further from God.[42] This is a case where Origen's consideration of literal and spiritual senses of Scripture operates in a manner that is too exclusively binary. He drops a regard for the literal sense of references to Israel and Judah once he has found the text's spiritual sense. Our own mistakes of ignoring Israel that allowed the unspeakable horrors of the twentieth century illustrate what can go wrong when Christians abandon the literal sense of Israel in Scripture. Church teachings from that century have responded to correct this so that we never abandon the literal sense of Scripture's narratives and prophecies regarding the people of Israel.[43]

40. Wilkinson, "*Hermēneiai*," 109.
41. Justin Martyr, *Dialogue with Trypho* 120.2 on Gen 22:17. See discussion in Bokser, "Justin Martyr and the Jews," 208–9.
42. Origen, *On First Principles* 4.3.6–10 (Butterworth, 396–407).
43. *Nostra Aetate* §4; Pontifical Biblical Commission, *Jewish People and Their Sacred Scriptures* §§36, 58–59, 65c.

Another weakness of the oracles model is that one can invest all one's attention on one text from Scripture in a way that ignores other relevant texts. For example, one might seize Ephesians 2:8–9 as one's motto for how God saves humanity, and ignore the "good works" mentioned in Ephesians 2:10 or the many texts that highlight how all people will be judged according to their works.

The oracles model predisposes its adherents to equate the truth of any Scripture text with its comprehensiveness. But truth and comprehensiveness are different. Just because a single verse of Scripture is true does not mean that it encapsulates the whole story. For example, a reader might regard John 3:16 as a comprehensive statement for how God in Christ saves humanity. In doing so, the reader may ignore all the New Testament texts that speak of a judgment according to works, and instead focus on convincing himself that he really believes. In so doing, the reader may be missing how God saves humanity.[44]

Various sectors of Christianity tend to select different texts as their oracles by which to live. As we seek to understand one another, we will do well if we identify what texts other groups take as their guiding words, and seek to understand why they have selected the text or texts they most emphasize.

A limitation of the oracular use of a key verse is that there is now lower Scripture literacy in most sectors of Western culture, so that fewer people understand scriptural allusions. So using a Bible verse as a theme verse for one's outreach or organization is not as effective as it was in previous generations, and may even be more open to misunderstanding. After a racially insulting epithet was scrawled on a door of a dormitory in a Christian college, well-meaning students put up posters on campus with a quotation of Galatians 5:6: "For in Christ Jesus neither circumcision nor uncircumcision counts for anything; the only thing that counts is faith working through love." For those who know the story behind Paul's Letter to the Galatians, this verse is an understandable response to racially charged graffiti on campus. But to those unfamiliar with the New Testament book of Galatians, this verse might confuse more than inspire.

When considering using a Bible verse as a motto or tagline for one's business or ministry, it is always a good idea to consider one's audience. Will those seeing the verse on the logo of your business or ministry understand how it connects to your work or outreach? If not, it might be good to consider a more

---

44. My example here is influenced by a pre-Catholic sermon of Newman, "Self-Contemplation."

understandable verse, or even a phrase of your own making that captures what your venture does.

The oracles model can be mistakenly applied. Christians might fixate on a text as the indication for God's leading. But the application of that text to the situation might prove to be misguided. A teacher of mine who had lived in California told of a time when parks in California were closed because of a health alert. People were being told not to enter parks to camp. My teacher saw some people cheerfully packing their vehicle and tying down some of their camping gear on the top of the vehicle. He learned they were leaving to camp at one of the affected parks and asked what was motivating them to do this. The response he received was that since the Bible says "There shall no evil befall thee, neither shall any plague come nigh thy dwelling" (Ps 91:10 KJV), it would be safe for them to go. My teacher commented that it would never have entered his mind to read that verse as guaranteeing that one could stay unscathed in a park with dangerous bacteria, but that these people seemed to be completely assured of their interpretation. Since all Scripture is inspired, we might ask those going camping in the compromised area also to consider Deuteronomy 6:16, "You shall not test/tempt the LORD your God."

THE ORACLES MODEL IN THE CLASSROOM

As a biblical studies, pre-seminary, or theology student, you will inevitably encounter cases where a single verse of Scripture is cited in support of a given theological or ethical position. This can sometimes be an incomplete way of accounting for a given position. It is always good to acknowledge the variety within the Bible. As Robert Jenson writes, "The Bible is not theologically homogeneous even within itself; nor is point-for-point unanimity the mode of any community's diachronic consensus."[45] When your professor presents an oracular nugget to prove a given position, you will do well to consider how that reading fits with how the church has traditionally read the text and how that oracle of Scripture fits with the rest of Scripture. Thus, for example, to use a text from the Bible's wisdom literature to support a proposed strategy of gaining wealth in a way that harms a neighbor would never be an appropriate use of the oracles model, since such behavior violates the command to love one's neighbor as oneself.[46]

---

45. Jenson, *Systematic Theology*, 2:281.

46. This is my practical formulation of Robert Jenson's statement, "Historical honesty requires the church to interpret Scripture in the light of her dogmas" (*Systematic Theology*, 2:281).

A practical strategy for using the oracles model in a way that avoids confirming only what one wants to hear is to read longer segments of biblical text than one considers necessary and to seek and read biblical texts that speak against what one wants to hear. For example, suppose one finds Paul's words on the advantages of the single life for serving God (1 Cor 7:32–35, 38) to be speaking into one's life. When considering the single life as a life to be intentionally pursued, one should read all of 1 Corinthians 7 and then go on to read biblical chapters that affirm the value of marriage—for example, Genesis 2, Proverbs 18 and 31, Tobit 7–8, and Ephesians 5. It is in the prayerful reading of all these texts, both those that affirm the single life and those that affirm married life, that one should make one's decision. Thomas Aquinas illustrates this procedure in the way that he cites Scripture both for and against certain choices made in his theological reasoning.

The Oracles Model in Ministry

Homilies or sermons arising out of the oracles model tend to focus on a single phrase or sentence from Scripture. The homilist preaching out of the oracles model typically presents the phrase or statement as though it encapsulates the whole sermon. For example, in a late eighteenth-century sermon preached to an artillery company at the time when it was voting on its officers, Peter Thacher's text was Judges 18:7, which describes an isolated community of Israelites in Laish, with no leaders instituted over them. Thacher explained this text as a negative example in order to motivate his audience to continue in their role of defending their community and to elect leaders who would maintain their readiness.[47]

It is perfectly legitimate to deliver homilies or sermons that are based on a single verse or phrase. But when you do so, always refer at least in passing to how the context of the verse supports the points you are making. And it is best to vary the scope of Scripture used in a homily or sermon. So on some days it is fine to go with a single verse or phrase as your text. On other days it would be good to talk about both the paragraph from the gospel and the Old Testament text or the New Testament's epistolary text for the day, explaining how they fit together.

When a congregant tells you what their life verse or favorite verse of Scripture is, it is best not to criticize their choice or bluntly suggest another one. Treat another person's life verse or favorite verse as an aspect of their identity, like place of birth and early childhood, or position in the birth order of

47. Thacher, "Sermon Preached before the Artillery Company."

their family. It is possible, however, that you may question how appropriate someone's self-selected life verse is. For example, if someone has bought into the prosperity gospel and tells you that their life verse is John 16:24, in which Jesus tells his listeners that they will receive what they ask for in his name, so that their joy might be full, your first reaction might be to argue with them about that verse. You have a higher chance of persuading them to broaden their perspective not by direct criticism but by respectfully suggesting other texts that might help them see places in the Bible where God's chosen ones are called to experience loss or persecution.

The tendency some of your congregants will have to seek for a Bible verse as a verse for the day, week, or month or for their whole life is a good tendency, since it involves an opening for God to speak into a person's life. Never tell your parishioners that they are simplistic or Bible-thumpers for choosing a key verse. At least they are reading and paying attention to Scripture! But since our Christian Scriptures are a collection of sixty-six or more books, we can experience a more balanced engagement with these Scriptures if we vary our theme verses. In a way analogous to changing one's password for access to a network, gently encourage congregants who tell you what their life or favorite verse is to look for another one once in a while. And just as most networks will not let a person return to a previously used password, so it is best for us, when looking to change our special verse, to find a new verse that approaches a spiritual condition in a different way. So if I have gone one month with Philippians 4:13 ("I can do all things through the one who strengthens me") as my motto, I might switch the next month to Galatians 2:20 ("I have been crucified with Christ. It is no longer I who live, but Christ who lives in me").

Scripture offers so much more than a phrase or sentence that speaks to a particular situation. So we should encourage parishioners and all those who share with us their favorite verse to make a conscious effort to read Scripture not simply for a "sound bite" that can function as an inspiring oracle but with other models as well. For example, if reading for a word that will speak to one's situation, one would do well also to read a narrative simply to enjoy the narrative (stories model) or to learn about history (documents model).

And yet the oracles model will always be a popular model among Christians. All of us need an oracle at some time or other to break through the fog in our lives. As the prophets gave an "oracle of the LORD" in ancient Israel, so God can speak to us with an oracle from Scripture today.

part three

DEVELOPMENTS *in* SCRIPTURE READING

LITERAL AND SPIRITUAL SENSES

What wonderful profundity there is in your utterances! The surface mean-
ing lies open before us and charms beginners. Yet the depth is amazing, my
God, the depth is amazing. To concentrate on it is to experience awe—the
awe of adoration before its transcendence and the trembling of love.

—AUGUSTINE[1]

The exclamation above from Augustine comes in the context of his meditation
on Genesis 1. The depth of Scripture he describes means that he understands
there is more to Scripture than first meets the eye. Since God is our ultimate
example of transcendence, the transcendence he experiences when reading Scripture indicates that he experiences God encountering him through
Scripture. He also experiences love—"the trembling of love"—as he considers
the text.

Augustine's response to the text is exemplary for us—students and faculty—
who study it in school. Too often in school, whether because of attitudes within
us or circumstances outside us, Scripture becomes a dry textbook. But here
is Augustine, the busy bishop of the North African diocese of Hippo, ecstatic
over what he experiences in Scripture. How did Augustine develop this attitude toward Scripture? He understood its depth, the multiplicity of meanings
that it holds. This chapter will begin to help us see the same depth of Scripture
that so impressed Augustine.

MULTIPLE SENSES SIGNALED IN SCRIPTURE

We may think that everything is straightforward in the Bible, with every sentence communicating one and only one meaning. But there are plenty of examples in Scripture of the same narrative or statement carrying more than one
sense—that is, more than one meaning. To begin at the beginning, Augustine

1. Augustine, *Confessions* 12.14.17 (Chadwick, 254).

finds in the divine word "Let there be light" of the first day (Gen 1:3a) the illumination of the spiritual creation, a grant of blessing to the spiritual beings God had already made, and the Holy Spirit's call to them for repentance.[2]

In John 11:49–50 we read what the high priest said about addressing Jesus's notoriety in light of the Jews' precarious position under the Romans. But John goes on to say that there is more to the high priest's statement than he realized when he spoke it, explaining that there is a theological value to Jesus's death beyond simply the political expediency of it (11:51–52). So the words in John 11:49–50 have more than one meaning.

Similarly, 1 Peter 1:10–12 indicates that the prophets did not fully understand all that they were prophesying. A fuller understanding has come to those who have heard the gospel proclaimed in the power of the Holy Spirit. With this text in 1 Peter in mind, we can see how a text like Isaiah 7:14 might well refer in its literal sense to a child who will be born in the lifetime of King Ahaz of Judah and how Matthew can understand it to be fulfilled also in the birth of Jesus.

Paul illustrates readings of the Old Testament in ways other than the literal sense. In 1 Corinthians 10:11, after referring to certain events in the Israelites' wilderness experience, Paul writes, "These things happened typologically for them, but they were written down for our instruction." This explains why Paul earlier in the chapter referred to one baptism that both the Israelites and the members of the Corinthian church experienced, one spiritual food (the manna and the body of Jesus), and one spiritual drink (water from the rock and the blood of Jesus) (10:1–4). Paul is thus modeling a way to read the Old Testament narratives of Israel in the wilderness. Instead of simply reading in the literal sense, as though the text is only a record of how a group of freed slaves made it across the Sinai desert, Paul is showing that he reads the wilderness narratives in Exodus–Numbers as prefiguring what followers of Jesus experience. In terms of the three spiritual senses of Scripture practiced by medieval Scripture exegetes, Paul's reading of the wilderness narrative would be the anagogical sense.

Paul also identifies the saying in Genesis 2:24 regarding a man leaving parents, cleaving to his wife, and becoming one flesh with her as actually concerning Christ and the church (Eph 5:31–32). This is a case again where Paul goes beyond the literal sense and looks for a deeper, christologically informed, theological meaning in the Old Testament text.

---

2. Augustine, *Confessions* 13.3.4–13.4.5, 13.12.13 (Boulding, 344–45, 350–51).

IDENTIFICATION OF SCRIPTURE'S SENSES

As most of the examples above show, there is a basis from within the New Testament for reading Scripture in different senses. The church fathers followed Paul's lead and would read the text in either the literal or the spiritual sense. Origen famously found in Scripture a threefold sense based on his understanding of the human person. The body of the text represents its "common and historical understanding"; this is the sense that will instruct and build up even those with the most simple understanding of Scripture. The soul of the text is a meaning based "in broader terms," able to build up those who are somewhat more mature. Finally, the spirit of the text speaks to those who are mature, who can penetrate into the hidden wisdom of the text.[3] There are real similarities between Origen's exegesis of a text and the exegesis practiced by Philo, a Jewish scholar from Alexandria. In his quest to make Judaism acceptable in the Greco-Roman world, Philo presented deeper meanings to the laws within the Mosaic covenant. He was attempting to show that the laws within the Mosaic covenant were not arbitrarily constructed but signified deeper levels of morality and virtue.

Augustine, who was an accomplished professor of rhetoric, was turned off when hearing or reading the Old Testament, since it seemed very primitive at points in its subject matter. It was after hearing the bishop of Milan, Ambrose, give sermons that explained the Old Testament in a spiritual sense that Augustine came to accept and value the Old Testament.[4] Augustine's experience with the Old Testament thus matches the advice that Origen gave two centuries before: one should begin with the literal sense, if there is one in the text; then one should move on to the more figurative senses.[5] Centuries later, Thomas Aquinas would similarly describe the literal sense as the foundation of the other senses of Scripture.[6] Near the end of his *Confessions*, Augustine interprets the creation account of Genesis 1 mostly in a spiritual sense. Different modes or specific senses within the spiritual sense came to be relatively standardized in the medieval period.

Medieval exegetes recognized the literal sense as the directly referenced, historically indicated meaning. This is the best definition of it, though someone

---

3. De Lubac, *Medieval Exegesis*, 1:143, explaining Origen, citing Rufinus's translation of Origen's *On First Principles* 4.2.4.

4. Augustine, *Confessions* 3.5.9; 6.3.4–6.5.8 (Boulding, 80, 138–42).

5. Origen, *On First Principles* 4.2.4–5 (Butterworth, 363–67).

6. *ST* I.1.10, ad. 1.

like Nicholas of Lyra (ca. 1270–1349) is known in places for finding two literal senses for the same text. Then, on the other hand, there was the spiritual sense, which contained three options: allegorical, moral, and anagogical readings.

The allegorical reading typically finds another web of reference for two or more entities in the text. Thus, Augustine's interpretation of the parable of the good Samaritan, in which the Lord Jesus (the good Samaritan) takes Adam (the robbers' victim) to the church (the inn) and asks the innkeeper (the apostle Paul) to take care of him, is an allegorical interpretation.[7]

The moral sense can also be called the tropological sense. When one reads the laws for ceremonial or ritual purity in the Old Testament as pointing beyond themselves to spiritual virtues, one is reading in this sense.[8]

The anagogical sense can also be called the eschatological sense. It is a reading that sees the meaning in the end times, after the judgment, when the saved lived in God's presence and the rest are separated from God. Augustine's summary of the creation narrative in Genesis 1 is in the anagogical mode of the spiritual sense: "This order of creation is God's house, neither terrestrial nor some massive celestial building, but a spiritual structure which shares your eternity, and is unstained forever. You have established it to last for ever, and your ordinance will not pass away."[9] Another example of the anagogical sense comes from Origen's explanation of the conquest of Jericho. He understands the narrative of the fall of Jericho's walls to signify the end of this world. Rahab's house and the scarlet rope hanging from its window signify the church, which is saved by the blood of Christ.[10]

Allegorical reading is actually a natural way to read religious texts and was endorsed as a fruitful way of reading the Bible by Vatican II.[11] The *Catechism of the Catholic Church* affirms the traditional division of Scripture's senses between literal and spiritual, explaining the spiritual as composed more specifically of the allegorical, moral, and anagogical senses.[12] While there is a specific allegorical sense within the spiritual sense of Scripture, "allegory" among church fathers like Augustine and even into the Middle Ages is at times used for a number of nonliteral ways of reading the text. In this general sense,

---

7. Augustine, *Questions on the Gospels* 2.19.

8. 1 Cor 5:6–8; Barn. 10:1–11.

9. Augustine, *Confessions* 12.15.19 (Boulding, 322).

10. See Josh. 2:1–24; 6:1–25; and Origen, *Homilies on Joshua* 6.4 (PG 12:855–56).

11. Huizenga, "Christian Allegory."

12. CCC §§115–19.

the term is sometimes used for any of the three spiritual senses for reading the Bible, whether moral, anagogical, or the specifically allegorical.[13]

The Senses of Scripture in Church History

A general stereotype of exegetes who interpreted Scripture often divides between literal and spiritual senses of Scripture.[14] Antioch and places near it, such as Constantinople, are known for reading Scripture according to its literal sense. Alexandria in Egypt is known for fostering the allegorical approach to Scripture that looks for a spiritual sense beneath the surface level of the text. Both schools sought to understand the spiritual or interior meaning of Scripture. Their methods differed because the schools differed in their understanding of the way in which history contained spiritual meaning.[15] This stereotype is now viewed as inaccurate. An easy counterexample to the stereotype is the Alexandrian exegete Origen, who attended very closely to the literal sense of the text and also employed allegorical exegesis.

The difference between Antiochene and Alexandrian exegesis is better understood according to the focus of the exegete. Exegetes in Antioch were more focused on the text as a whole; they looked at large sections of text, viewing the text as an icon or mirror that would provide understanding. In contrast, exegetes based in Alexandria viewed the text as a collection of smaller pieces that present a code needing to be deciphered.[16] Theodore of Mopsuestia (350–428), Diodore of Tarsus (ca. 330–390), and his student John Chrysostom (347–407) are known as exegetes in the Antiochene school. Origen (ca. 184–253), Augustine (354–430), and Cyril of Alexandria (ca. 376–444) are exegetes of the Alexandrian school.

In books 12–13 of his *Confessions*, Augustine prayerfully reads Genesis 1. He understands its first description of God's creation, "In the beginning God created the heavens and the earth," to signify that God made a spiritual house that, once created, will last with God eternally.[17] The earth signifies the physical creation of our planet. Augustine enters into a dialogue with those who read

13. Huizenga, "Christian Allegory," 79.

14. This section is a limited survey of how the senses of Scripture were regarded in church history. For a more detailed survey, see Grant and Tracy, *Short History*, or McKim, *Dictionary of Major Biblical Interpreters*.

15. Florovsky, *Eastern Fathers*, 261–62.

16. Pentiuc, *Old Testament*, 189–90, citing Young, *Biblical Exegesis*, 164.

17. Augustine, *Confessions* 12.15.19 (Boulding, 322).

"the heavens and the earth" only in a literal sense to signify the atmospheric and terrestrial dimensions of our planet, as well as with those who hold other views, such as that "heaven and earth" refers simply to the undifferentiated matter that was originally "formless and void." In the end, he affirms that the Scripture is true, even with a multiplicity of human approaches to it.[18]

Augustine goes on to offer an allegorical interpretation of the seven days in the first creation account. At least three assumptions that he makes predispose him to do this. The first assumption is a metaphysical one: Augustine is convinced that there is a spiritual reality as well as a physical reality indicated in the first verse of Genesis.

> It was on account of these two realities—the one formed from the very first and the other formless through and through, the one a heaven, but a heaven above our heavens, the other an earth, but an earth invisible and unorganized—on account of these two it was that your scripture states, without mentioning days, In the beginning God made heaven and earth; for it immediately adds a line to show what "earth" it means. And by recording that on the second day a vault was established and called "heaven" or "sky," it indicates of what heaven it had been speaking before it began to count the days.[19]

If our world is composed of a spiritual and a physical reality, then one is predisposed to expect that the word these worlds' creator has left to humanity will sometimes refer to the spiritual reality and sometimes refer to the physical reality, or at other times refer to both realities in different senses.

The second assumption is a textual one: Augustine is convinced that some truths are deeply hidden in the Scriptures. "I have believed your scriptures, but those words are full of hidden meaning."[20] If some truths are deeply hidden, then there must be meanings of the text that are deeper than or different from the surface-level, literal sense of the text. A deeply hidden meaning of a text is sometimes called the *sensus plenior*, "deeper sense."

The third assumption is also textual in nature: Augustine is convinced that God has invested certain passages of Scripture with meanings of which that Scripture's human author was unaware.

18. Augustine, *Confessions* 12.14.17–12.32.43 (Boulding, 321–41).
19. Augustine, *Confessions* 12.13.16 (Boulding, 320–21).
20. Augustine, *Confessions* 12.10.10 (Boulding, 318).

Lord, what if human vision is incomplete? Does that mean that anything you intended to reveal by these words to later generations of readers—you who are God, not flesh and blood—was hidden from your good Spirit, who will, I pray, lead me into the right land? Is this not the case even if the man through whom you spoke to us had perhaps only one of the true meanings in mind? If he did, by all means let that one which he intended be taken as paramount. But as for us, Lord, we beg you to point out to us either that sense which he intended or any other true meaning which you choose, so that whether you take occasion of these words to make plain to us the same thing that you showed him, or something different, you still may feed us and no error dupe us.[21]

This quotation is significant because it has an expansive view of how texts communicate meaning. It directly contradicts those who regard the text's meaning to be limited to what its author intended, a view we will consider later in this survey.

The church fathers who advocate reading the Bible through the lens of multiple senses usually remark on the difficulty of understanding some parts of Scripture. Jerome says that it is hard to discern where the sealed well and walled garden in Scripture are located.[22] This regard for the difficulty of the exegesis of Scripture continued to be common among Catholic authors through the Middle Ages.

Throughout the Middle Ages, the literal sense and the threefold spiritual sense (see the previous section, "Identification of Scripture's Senses," above) continued to be the dominant understanding of how Scripture communicates meaning. Though not always recognized today, medieval exegetes were brilliant in their insights and left much of enduring value.

At the end of the Middle Ages, while Martin Luther (1483–1546) was lecturing on the Psalms, he changed the distinction between the letter and the spirit of Scripture from one separating Old and New Testaments to one within the Old Testament itself. Luther claims to have seen within the Old Testament a distinction between the "law of Moses" and the "law of the Lord."[23] He comes to understand Israel in the Old Testament as a figure for the church. The church represents the real people of God, even though it can only hope for the

21. Augustine, *Confessions* 12.32.43 (Boulding, 341).
22. Jerome, *Ep.* 15 (1:46), cited by de Lubac, *Medieval Exegesis*, 1:28.
23. Preus, *From Shadow to Promise*, 200.

completed, perfect character it will have in the eschaton.[24] The moral sense of Scripture had traditionally been understood as indicating what the believer needs to do to fulfill the obedience owed to God. Thus, the moral sense of the parable of the good Samaritan would be that we should love our neighbors as the Samaritan loved the man who fell among thieves. But for Luther the moral sense became what God does in conforming believers to the image of the Son.[25] This fits Luther's emphasis that a person does not need to do anything to be saved. James Samuel Preus explains that this adjustment in the moral sense arises out of Luther's insistence that Christ is the literal subject of the Psalms.[26] In Luther's mind, if Christ is the subject of the Psalms in a literal sense, then any moral activity indicated by the text should be understood as already completed by Christ, whose merits alone can count in the process of salvation.

The fluidity of Scripture's senses for Luther can be seen in his glosses on the Vulgate's Psalm 118 (our Ps 119). Luther states that he will give the prophetic and the moral senses of the psalm. First, he writes that the prophetic sense is a prediction of how those faithful to Christ will be set against people like the Pharisees, which he goes on to say is the struggle between Christians and Jews. Next, he states that the moral sense refers to proud people in general, who neglect what they should do in order to follow their own desires.[27] But then he goes on to write of the same psalm, "In the literal and prophetic sense, this psalm is a *petition* for the advent of Christ, and a commendation of the church of Christ. In the moral and doctrinal sense, it is a petition for the spiritual advent of Christ through grace, and a commendation of his grace."[28]

There are several big ideas to take away from our consideration of Luther's exegesis. First, the literal and spiritual senses of Scripture were subject to redefinition in the sixteenth century. We might think that everyone could agree on what the literal sense of the text was, but this was not the case. People differed on what they understood the literal sense to be. Second, it is noteworthy how Christ-centered Luther is in his exegesis of Psalm 119 and, as can be seen elsewhere, throughout the Old Testament. While there are New Testament stimuli for this sort of reading (Luke 24:25–27, 44–45; Acts 3:18, 24; 10:43), we need to think twice about calling the christological sense of an Old Testament text the literal sense. This is because the people of Israel are the first recipients of more

---

24. Preus, *From Shadow to Promise*, 224.

25. Preus, *From Shadow to Promise*, 227, citing *WA* 3.46.32–33 and 3.468.17–19.

26. Preus, *From Shadow to Promise*, 228.

27. Preus, *From Shadow to Promise*, 177, citing *WA* 4.281.30–32.

28. Preus, *From Shadow to Promise*, 177–78, citing *WA* 4.281.35–37.

than half of our Scriptures, and as they remain God's beloved and the heirs of God's irrevocable gifts and calling (Rom 3:1–2; 9:4–5; 11:28–29), we must affirm as the literal sense the historical situation of Israel when we can see this in the Old Testament text. The French exegete among the second generation of Protestant reformers, John Calvin (1509–1564), wisely tended to look to historical Israel when discerning the literal sense of the Old Testament. We must never lose sight of the text's literal sense, especially when it refers to Israel. At the same time, as we saw in the chapter on the oracles model, Christian reading of Scripture includes in its essential orientation a christological-apocalyptic mode in which one of the text's spiritual senses points toward Christ.

Luther's claim that he could interpret the Bible better than the church he left sparked other reformers to interpret the Bible for themselves. They could not agree among themselves, as the record of the Marburg Colloquy between Luther and Zwingli indicates.[29] The disagreement over what Scripture means eventually led some intellectuals to the philosophical position of skepticism, as Richard Popkin ably demonstrates.[30] Since the Catholic Church was no longer accepted by Protestants as the arbiter for what Scripture means, and a Protestant reformer on his own could say what it meant on a *sola Scriptura* basis, the appeal to certainty moved from the Catholic Church's teaching office and traditions to an insistence on Scripture's single meaning.

In contrast to how the church fathers and medieval exegetes regarded exegesis as difficult, some Protestants in the sixteenth century began insisting that Scripture's single meaning was clear and easy to understand. The quest for a single meaning in the text, so that someone could purportedly prove that his or her interpretation was right and all other interpretations wrong, combined with Enlightenment-based approaches to Scripture that questioned miracles and traditional ascriptions of authorship, led to the rise of historical criticism, which generally seeks for a single meaning of the text, just as Luther and Calvin did. This single meaning, practically speaking, was functionally equivalent to the literal sense of the patristic and medieval periods.

The twentieth century actually was the temporal stage on which two different approaches to Scripture played out among Roman Catholic scholars. There were those who were very invested in the historical-critical method,

29. On October 1–4, 1529, Protestant reformers Martin Luther and Ulrich Zwingli met at the castle in Marburg, in Hesse, Germany. They debated whether Christ was really present in the Eucharist, and parted in disagreement.

30. See the chapter "The Intellectual Crisis of the Reformation" in Popkin, *History of Scepticism*, 3–16.

such as Roland Murphy (1917–2002), Joseph Fitzmyer (1920–2016), and Raymond Brown (1928–1998).[31] When some Catholic exegetes studied the Bible with the historical-critical method, they sought the text's literal sense with a singular focus. One example of this is Murphy's commentary on the Song of Songs. He interprets this poetic book simply as an example of love poetry from the ancient Near East, with little attention paid to the allegorical and anagogical senses St. Bernard saw in the same biblical book.[32]

On the other hand, Henri de Lubac (1896–1991), Jean Daniélou (1905–1974), and Henri Crouzel (1918–2003) sought to call Scripture readers back to the church fathers.[33] In general, the latter group has been successful, and biblical scholars in all branches of the Christian family have come to appreciate what the church fathers have to offer. Though biblical scholars today are not actively explaining Scripture with the literal sense and a threefold spiritual sense as was done in the Middle Ages, they are more open to seeing a spiritual sense, or at least more than one meaning in the text.[34] The writings of Joseph Ratzinger (Pope Benedict XVI, born in 1927) on the Gospels illustrate the confluence of those two approaches. He employs the historical-critical method while also seriously engaging with the exegesis of the church fathers.[35] This is the result of the opening that a papal encyclical of Leo XIII (1810–1903) gave for the historical-critical study of Scripture, and one by Pius XII (1876–1958) that reasserted the need for the historical-critical study of Scripture to balance a singular, uncritical quest for a spiritual sense.[36] The Catholic Church therefore teaches that literal and spiritual senses should be seamlessly integrated in exegesis.[37] While integrating the senses of Scripture, the exegete is to keep in view what all of Scripture teaches, read Scripture within the tradition of the church, and attend to the analogy of faith—that is, the coherence of all that God has revealed.[38]

In a way that is analogous to our assumption that our medical science is now more advanced than in previous times, sometimes biblical scholars will dismiss past ways of reading the Bible. In a textbook of biblical hermeneutics

---

31. See Fitzmyer, *Gospel According to Luke I–IX* and *Gospel According to Luke X–XXIV*; R. E. Brown, *Birth of the Messiah*.

32. Murphy, *Song of Songs*.

33. See de Lubac, *Medieval Exegesis*; Daniélou, *From Shadows to Reality*; Crouzel, *Origen*.

34. See also Reasoner, "*Dei Verbum*."

35. See Ratzinger's three-volume *Jesus of Nazareth*.

36. Leo XIII, *Providentissimus Deus*; Piux XII, *Divino afflante Spiritu*.

37. Benedict XVI, *Verbum Domini* §37; *CCC* §115.

38. The three guidelines in this sentence are found in *CCC* §§112–14, following *Dei Verbum* §12.

of the twentieth century, Protestant author Berkeley Mickelsen takes pains not to dismiss the work of Origen but consistently criticizes allegory as good ideas that come from the interpreter's own mind rather than from the text itself.[39]

The criticism that allegory represents the freewheeling innovation of the interpreter ignores the way that both Origen and Augustine anchored their allegorical readings in specific abnormalities or triggers in the literal sense of the text. In actuality, allegory is a necessary way of reading Scripture, since it helps provide a unified reading to the variety in the Bible. In a chapter called "Return to Allegory," Orthodox scholar Andrew Louth calls for Christians once again to recognize the value of allegorical readings of Scripture.[40]

Coupled with a scorn for allegorical exegesis, there is sometimes an insistence that the text means only what its human author intended. The following two sentences from a popular book on interpreting the Bible exemplify this perspective: "The meaning of a text depends on the specific, conscious intention that the author willed in the past when the text was written (i.e., on his communicative intent when he wrote). It is the biblical author who is the determiner of the text's meaning."[41] Some biblical scholars who limit the meaning of Scripture to the author's intention support their claim by appealing to literary scholar E. D. Hirsch Jr., whose book *Validity in Interpretation* argues for authorial intention as the basis of meaning.

But this argument is highly contested in the literary studies and does not cohere with how the church fathers read Scripture.[42] As we have seen, Augustine held that God may have willed for more meanings to be invested in the text of Scripture than the human authors intended. Since we recognize that Scripture is divinely inspired and that parts of Scripture have been edited in the process of being collected into the canon, we cannot limit the text's meaning to the conscious intention of its human author.

LITERAL AND SPIRITUAL SENSES IN CONTEXT

The continuum running from literal to spiritual senses fits within a more inclusive grid of three axes, or continuums, which track how people engage with

39. Mickelsen, *Interpreting the Bible*, 32–33.

40. Louth, "Return to Allegory."

41. Stein, *Basic Guide*, 31. Stein admits that a text may have implications of which its author was unaware, but he does not budge on the claim that the meaning is determined by the author's intention (32).

42. Cf. E. D. Hirsch, *Validity in Interpretation*. Against Hirsch's exclusive reliance on authorial intention for meaning, see Wimsatt and Beardsley, "Intentional Fallacy."

Scripture. Since these axes help locate any interpretation within the expanding universe of biblical interpretation, I call the grid "BPS," for Bible Positioning System (see the diagram below). The *r* axis (for reference) runs from literal to figurative. This is the axis we have been especially considering in this chapter. Sometimes what one reader claims to be the literal sense of the text may not strike another reader as its literal sense. And different figural readings can be given to a text. Nevertheless, this axis helps us talk about how a text refers to reality.

The vertical *s* axis (for subject matter or *die Sache*) concerns the essential content of Scripture—is it God or is it the human subject? Someone might object that this should not be a continuum, since a text might equally be about God and the human subject. But one may still observe a tendency for readers of Scripture to approach the text's main focus along a continuum extending from the transcendent down to the immanent.

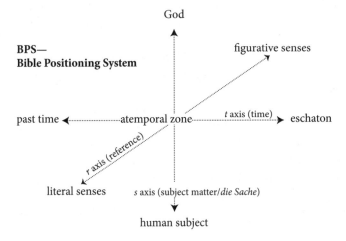

Finally, the *t* axis (for time) extends from historical to eschatological. One way of viewing this continuum is to ask whether the text refers to events in past history, such as a view of the beast in Revelation that explains it as referring to Nero or Domitian, or whether it refers to some leader who is yet to come on the world scene. I have chosen to designate the middle of this axis as an atemporal zone, in which readers regard the text as speaking to time-transcendent values that cannot be fixed on a temporal continuum.

The specific models explored in this book can be located—with BPS coordinates in three-dimensional space, as it were—in relation to the three axes noted. The documents model is mostly located on the literal side of the literal-figurative continuum, the past side of the historical-eschatological continuum, and the human end of the divine-human continuum. Since the laws model typically includes the idea that the Bible represents God's laws for all of humanity, it is similar to the documents model in location on the three axes, except that it might be more toward the divine end of the *s* axis, since it holds that Scripture as law teaches us about God. The oracles model will allow for more figurative readings of Scripture, at least in the apocalyptic sections of Scripture, and it is most comfortable toward the eschatological end of the *t* axis. It can easily move between divine and human ends of the *s* axis, which deals with Scripture's essential subject, though it invests most energy on the human end of this axis. The prayers model lands in the atemporal zone and moves all along the literal-figurative and divine-human axes. The stories model works primarily on the past time end of the *t* axis, the literal end of the *r* axis, and the human side of the *s* axis.

The five models thus represent how specific approaches to Scripture would characterize Scripture. The models are not pure types. That means that no approach would categorize the whole of Scripture as exemplifying the most characteristic object of such an approach. For example, the prayers model does not claim that all of the Bible is prayer discourse. But it will speak of Scripture as including prayers, and it will find grist for prayers even in places outside the book of Psalms and other explicitly liturgical texts.

Literal and Spiritual Senses of Scripture in the Classroom

Whether you are in a Catholic, Orthodox, or Protestant seminary, your Scripture professors will have been trained in the historical-critical interpretation of the Bible, a modern enterprise that has focused on the literal sense to the exclusion of all other senses of the text. Your professors will answer your questions on the historical veracity of the text in different ways. For example, most will say that Peter denied Jesus three times, as all the Gospels indicate. Only a minority will say that he denied Jesus six times, as Harold Lindsell says, in order to harmonize minor differences in the trial accounts.[43] Most will be comfortable saying that the Sermon on the Mount in Matthew's Gospel could well be a compilation of Jesus's teachings from different occasions in his ministry. Only a minority will say that the Sermon on the Mount is a transcript of a single sermon that Jesus gave on one occasion.

We are actually in a good moment in time for interpreting Scripture, for the historical critics' insistence that miracles do not happen and that texts must be treated as artifacts within the documents model of Scripture is widely

---

43. Lindsell, *Battle for the Bible*, 174–76. See discussion in chap. 3 above.

acknowledged as an incomplete and dangerously disengaged way of reading Scripture. In whatever sort of college, university, or seminary you are studying, and whether you read Scripture looking only for a singular, author-intended meaning or are open to both the literal and spiritual senses of the text, I hope that you can begin to appreciate the expansive horizons that Scripture opens for us. Scripture is not a closed universe. There is more in it than first meets the eye. When you have finished and submitted a required exegesis paper on a given paragraph of Scripture, you are not finished with the paragraph. There are more questions regarding it that you have not yet addressed, and more ways for you to engage with it and process its meaning in your own life than your paper allowed. Keep reading your Bible prayerfully every day, even in the days after your Scripture course has ended.

LITERAL AND SPIRITUAL SENSES OF SCRIPTURE IN MINISTRY

When you minister, your job is to encourage people to read Scripture so that by so doing they will encounter Christ. Your job is not to show them how much you know about Scripture, or how skillful you are in the original languages of Scripture—Hebrew, Aramaic, and Greek.

When studying Scripture for your own nourishment and preparing Bible studies and sermons, it is always best to start with the literal sense, if possible. Once you have considered the literal sense, it is useful to go beyond to one of the spiritual senses.[44] If the spiritual sense helps people understand a text that is difficult to understand literally, then it should be used. This is how Ambrose helped Augustine come to accept and read the Old Testament. As long as the literal sense is given full consideration and the passage is read in its context within Scripture, the specifically identified spiritual senses of the text—allegorical, moral, and anagogical—can be fruitfully used.

The joy of discovery can be addictive, and sometimes someone studying Scripture thinks he or she is the first to come to a new, insightful interpretation. In whatever branch of the Christian family you find yourself, please remember that Scripture reading is a communal activity. This means that we always read Scripture with the full knowledge and respect for how others have read it before. Catholic exegetes understand that the church is the final arbiter in questions of interpretation.[45] What this usually means is that the church sets up boundary lines, much as the sidelines are marked out on a soccer field, designating the range of possible interpretations.

44. Benedict XVI, *Verbum Domini* §38.
45. *CCC* §119.

So in whichever branch of the Christian family you are ministering, it is best to make connections with the ways the text has been read before.[46] Your goals in explaining Scripture should be helping people encounter Christ in the text, and helping people love God and love neighbor more as a result of reading Scripture. These goals are more in line with your pastoral identity than any exegesis motivated by a desire to impress your flock with brilliant, entertaining, or innovative readings.

Some of you reading this may be fully on board with the literal and spiritual senses of Scripture. You may even find yourself sitting down with a paragraph from Scripture and trying to write out its literal and threefold spiritual senses. Not every text can be interpreted in all three of the specifically spiritual senses—allegorical, moral, and anagogical. Instead of mechanistically running every paragraph through the four possible senses, it would be better to start with the following questions:

- In what ways does this text help us see Christ encountering us?[47]
- In what ways does this text motivate us to love God with all that we are and have?[48]
- In what ways does this text motivate us to love our neighbor as ourselves?[49]
- In what ways is this text connected with the other Scripture readings for the day? What theme or themes do these connections embody?
- In what ways is this text connected to today in the church calendar?

Of course, these questions do not exhaust what can be done with the text. Similarly, when offering Bible studies, short homilies, or longer sermons on Scripture, never present your exegesis as the complete explanation of the text. Always communicate, along the lines of the quote from Augustine at the beginning of the chapter, that there is more in the text on which your audience can meditate and ruminate than you can offer them.

---

46. See the chapter "The Corporateness of Scriptural Interpretation" in Goldingay, *Models for Interpretation*, 233–50.

47. Luke 24:27, 44–47; John 5:39.

48. Augustine, *On Christian Doctrine* 1.36.40.

49. Augustine, *On Christian Doctrine* 1.36.40.

SOLA SCRIPTURA

Among the doctrines and teachings preserved by the Church, we hold
some from written sources, and we have collected others transmitted in
an inexplicit form (μυστικῶς) from apostolic tradition. They have all the
same value. For if we were to try to put aside the unwritten customs as
having no great force, we should, unknown to ourselves, be weakening
the Gospel in its very essence; furthermore, we should be transforming
the kerygma *into mere words.*

—BASIL OF CAESAREA[1]

I . . . protest against that unrighteous and ungodly pretense of making the
writings of the fathers, the decrees of councils, and synods, or the sense of
the church, the rule and standard of judging of the sense of Scriptures, as
Popish, Anti-Christian, and dangerous to the church of God.

—ELIAS SMITH[2]

This chapter focuses on the claim that began in the sixteenth century, voiced
by Protestant reformers, that all a Christian needs to form doctrine is found
within the Bible. *Sola Scriptura* means "Scripture alone," and it summarizes the
idea that Scripture by itself, apart from tradition, any other revelation, or the
magisterium (teaching office) of the church, is all that one needs for knowing
God and knowing how to live.

The quotations at the top of this chapter illustrate the opposite poles on
this "Scripture alone" idea. Basil of Caesarea represents the position held by
Catholics, Orthodox, and some Protestants that the Bible is a source of "the
same value" as the traditions that have been handed down from the apostles.
Elias Smith represents the Protestant, "Scripture alone" idea. His statement

1. Basil the Great, *On the Holy Spirit* 27 (PG 32:188A; ET *NPNF²* 8:41), quoted in John
Meyendorff, "Doing Theology," 82.
2. Smith, *Life, Conversion, Preaching*, 352–53, quoted in Hatch, *"Sola Scriptura,"* 67.

registers opposition to any attention paid to the church fathers, church councils, or what has traditionally been church teaching for interpreting the Bible. In other words, he is advocating that the Christian should simply read the Bible on her or his own and then believe and live on the basis of how she or he understands the text.

As you read this chapter, two questions will arise repeatedly. The first one is in the genre of chicken or egg questions. Which comes first, the church or Scripture? The second question is for those who accept the *sola Scriptura* principle. Does the *sola Scriptura* principle apply only to the leaders of a given faith community, or does it mean that every individual within a given faith community interprets Scripture for himself or herself?

This chapter may not seem relevant to some of you undergraduate theology majors or seminary students who are reading this book. But sooner or later you will meet someone who differs from you on this question. This chapter offers a selective historical survey of the *sola Scriptura* principle in Christian discourse, and descriptions of the developments of the principle in different branches of the Christian family. After reading this chapter, you will have more resources for informed and respectful conversations with those who differ from you on the question of whether the Bible plays an exclusive role in determining the Christian's belief system and ethics.

Historical Survey of the Tradition and Scripture Question

Tradition was by necessity an early guide for interpreting the Bible, for as early as the second century CE, when gnostics and Montanists were referring to Scripture in support of their positions, the church came to see that appeals to Scripture were not in themselves sufficient evidence for the ideas being disseminated. It was only through the faith of the church that the Scriptures could be accurately read, and thus the church fathers came to emphasize tradition when reading the Bible.[3]

Jerome drives this point home, with the urgency of someone in the throes of doctrinal disputes.

> Marcion and Basilides and other heretics . . . do not possess the gospel of God, since they have no Holy Spirit, without which the gospel preached becomes human. We do not think that gospel consists of the words of Scrip-

---

3. Florovsky, "Function of Tradition," 99–100.

ture but in its meaning, not on the surface but in the marrow, not in the leaves of sermons but in the root of meaning. In this case Scripture is really useful for the hearers when it is not spoken without Christ, nor is presented without the Fathers, and those who are preaching do not introduce it without the Spirit. . . . It is a great danger to speak in the church, lest by a perverse interpretation of the gospel of Christ, a gospel of man is made.[4]

The idea that authoritative guidance for how one believes and worships should come only from Scripture is a relatively recent one, first being articulated in 1518 by a colleague of Martin Luther's at the University of Wittenberg, Andreas Carlstadt (1486–1541). In Luther's *Resolutions Concerning the 95 Theses*, a book completed in May of 1518 and published that August, Luther portrayed himself as faithful to the church's authentic traditions. But in the same month that these *Resolutions* appeared, August 1518, Carlstadt's book was released, in which he claimed that only Scripture was authoritative, not the patristic writings, rulings of popes, or decrees of synods.[5] Carlstadt reordered the chain of authority for Christians' guidance. Whereas traditionally the church is regarded as the body that collected, canonized, and interprets Scripture, Carlstadt initiated a tendency to place Scripture above the church.

Two years later, Luther wrote in a foreword to his colleague Philipp Melanchthon's (1497–1560) explanatory notes on the Letter to the Romans, "You say '*scripture alone* must be read without commentaries.' You say this correctly about the commentaries of Origen, Jerome, and Thomas. They wrote commentaries in which they handed down their own ideas rather than Pauline or Christian ones. Let no one call your annotations a commentary [in that sense] but only an index for reading Scripture and knowing Christ, on account that up to this point no one has offered a commentary which surpasses it."[6] The picture of an individual interpreting Scripture according to his or her own idiosyncratic whims is not what Luther had in mind when applying the principle of *sola Scriptura*. He used reason, creeds from the church, and even writings of the church fathers to help him explain Scripture. So he viewed Scripture as a text to be interpreted with others: "Reading Scripture is a fel-

4. Jerome, *Commentary on Galatians* 1.1.2 (PL 26:386), quoted in Florovsky, "Function of Tradition," 113.

5. Kittelson, *Luther the Reformer*, 113, 115.

6. Luther, "Vorwort zu den *Annotationes Philippi Melanchthonis in epistolas Pauli ad Romanos et Corinthios* (1522)," WA 10.2:310.12–17, quoted in Thompson, "*Sola Scriptura*," 154.

lowship activity in which the voices of those who have read before us need to be heard attentively."[7]

But Luther did not mean what many today think *sola Scriptura* means. He was adamant that common people, untrained in the biblical languages or theological study, could not interpret the Bible for themselves. Thus, the Bible that he published in the vernacular language of Saxony contained commentary to guide the readers' interpretation. Commentary similarly accompanied the text of Calvin's French translation of the Bible, as well as the Geneva Bible.[8]

Luther indeed had more regard for tradition than did the radical reformers after him. While Jaroslav Pelikan was still a Lutheran, he explained that Luther was attacking the traditionalism of the Catholic Church but was not attacking all tradition. Pelikan notes that the early church looked for authoritative guidance in three directions: the Scriptures, the confessions or creeds and traditions associated with them, and the bishops. He maintains that the Orthodox Church, or Eastern Christianity, has emphasized the Scriptures and the bishops as the more potent of these three authorities. He characterizes the Roman Catholic manifestation of Western Christianity, especially after Vatican I when papal infallibility was defined, as emphasizing the bishops over the other two sources of authority.[9] The specific aspects of Roman traditionalism that Luther rejected were its perceived emphases in moral theology on the value of celibacy and the saints as perfect, alongside its attention to Aristotelian philosophy in its systematic theology. Luther drove a wedge between Scripture and tradition, authorities that cannot be separated in the Catholic Church, by insisting that the first church father was Tertullian, who lived over a century after the last New Testament book was written, according to Luther's chronology. He also regarded the New Testament as a proclamation firmly based on the Old Testament, and the church fathers as imperfect and offering ideas derived from the Scriptures in a secondary sense.[10] Still, it would be a mistake to stereotype Luther as against tradition in an unqualified way. As Pelikan writes, "At the Leipzig Debate in 1519 [against papal nuncio John Eck] Luther had to admit that, in the name of the Scriptures as he interpreted them, he was setting the authority of the Scriptures against and above the authority of the tradition of the church. Within less than five years Luther was defending

7. Thompson, "*Sola Scriptura*," 155–56, quotation from 156.
8. Stout, "Word and Order," 22.
9. Pelikan, *Luther the Expositor*, 72–73. I refer to Pelikan as Lutheran since he was Lutheran when he wrote the work cited, about four decades before his entrance into the Orthodox Church.
10. Pelikan, *Luther the Expositor*, 75–85.

the tradition of the church against those who, in the name of the Scriptures as they interpreted them, wanted to set aside the liturgical and ecclesiastical forms developed in that tradition."[11]

What, then, did *sola Scriptura* mean for Luther? It did not mean that anyone could interpret the Bible however he or she wanted. But it did mean that Luther understood Scripture to be a more reliable guide to God's will than tradition. And it meant that in the construction and maintenance of liturgy, only discourse that had its basis firmly in the New Testament could be used.[12]

Melanchthon focused Luther's emphasis on Scripture as the final authority with the idea of a single sense that Scripture contains. Papal nuncio John Eck (1486–1543) critically responded to Melanchthon with his *Excusatio*, published in 1519. Eck called Luther and Melanchthon back to the church's historic position of listening both to tradition and Scripture. Melanchthon promptly offered a rejoinder and clarified how he sought to use the *sola Scriptura* principle as follows:

> First, it is not in my heart to detract from the authority of anyone in any way. I revere and honour all the lights of the church, those illustrious defenders of Christian doctrine. Next, I consider it to be important that the opinions of the holy fathers when they differ, as they do, be judged by Scripture, not vice versa, [which would result in] Scripture suffering violence from [their] diverse judgments. There is a single and simple sense of Scripture, as also the heavenly truth is most simple, which brings together a thread of Scripture and prayer. To this end we are commanded to philosophize in the divine Scriptures, that we might assess the opinions of men and decrees against the touchstone. . . . The Scripture of the heavenly Spirit, which is called canonical, is one, pure and true in all things.[13]

Mainstream reformers such as Luther, Melanchthon, and Calvin at times appealed to the church fathers and early ecumenical creeds for guidance in their biblical interpretation and in the construction of their theologies. In contrast, radical reformers such as Menno Simons (1496–1561) or Conrad Grebel (1498–1526) pushed the *sola Scriptura* principle in such a way that they would pay no attention to the church fathers or creeds and advocated any person's right to interpret Scripture as he or she thought best.[14] Radical

11. Pelikan, *Luther the Expositor*, 71.

12. Pelikan, *Luther the Expositor*, 223.

13. Melanchthon, *Defensio contra Johannem Eckium* (1519), CR 1:113–14, 115, quoted in Thompson, "*Sola Scriptura*," 161–62.

14. Mathison, *Shape of Sola Scriptura*, 126.

reformer Sebastian Franck (1499–1543) expressed himself as follows: "Foolish Ambrose, Augustine, Jerome, Gregory—of whom not one even knew the Lord, so help me God, nor was sent by God to teach. Rather, they were all apostles of Antichrist."[15] With their focus only on Scripture and intentional rejection of tradition, the radical reformers allowed every individual in their communities to exercise their own private judgment in interpretation. Not only did they therefore reject infant baptism, they also rejected foundational truths of historic Christianity like the Trinity and the deity of Christ, since they could not find clear proof of these in Scripture.[16]

Melanchthon did not believe in doctrinal development, as can be seen in his assertion of the following three statements among the twenty-four that he presented before being examined for his baccalaureate degree in Scripture:

> 16. It is not necessary for a Catholic to believe any other articles of faith than those to which Scripture is a witness.
> 17. The authority of councils is below the authority of Scripture.
> 18. Therefore not to believe in the "character indelibilis," transubstantiation, and the like is not open to the charge of heresy.[17]

Notice how Melanchthon's item 16 in the selection above functions as a lever to marginalize tradition. The difficulty with this, as we will see in the next stop on our selective survey, American religious history, is that it can lead to some rather non-Christian positions.

Protestant historian Nathan Hatch is aware of the more guided, less democratized way that *sola Scriptura* was used by the magisterial reformers. He argues, on the basis of primary texts from the eighteenth and nineteenth centuries, that some American religious leaders came to a position of "the individualization of conscience" in regard to how they used their Bibles to guide their beliefs and practices, and summarizes the use of the Bible in those centuries of American history as follows:

---

15. Mathison, *Shape of Sola Scriptura*, 127, citing McGrath, *Reformation Thought*, 145–46, who identifies the statement as written in 1530.

16. Mathison, *Shape of Sola Scriptura*, 126–27, citing McGrath, *Reformation Thought*, 144–45.

17. *Melanchthon: Selected Writings*, 18, quoted in Thompson, "*Sola Scriptura*," 161. "Character indelebilis" is the Catholic idea that the sacraments of baptism, confirmation, and holy orders leave an indelible mark or imprint on the soul, and thus cannot be repeated in the life of the human subject (*CCC* §§698, 1121, 1272–74).

What strikes one in studying the use of the Bible in the early years of the American Republic, is how much weight becomes placed on private judgment and how little on the role of history, theology, and the collective will of the church. In a culture that mounted a frontal assault upon the authority of tradition, of mediating elites, and of organizations that were perpetual rather than volitional, the Bible very easily became as John W. Nevin complained, "a book dropped from the skies for all sorts of men to use in their own way." This shift occurred gradually and without fanfare, concealed, I think, because innovators could exploit arguments as old and as trusted as Protestantism itself. Luther, Calvin, Wesley and Backus had all argued for the principle of *sola Scriptura*; Elias Smith [a founder of the Disciples of Christ/Christian Church], Elhanan Winchester [champion of Universalism], William Smyth Babcock [independent preacher who left the Free-Will Baptists to form a nondenominational church], Lucy Smith [mother of Joseph Smith, who founded the Church of Jesus Christ of Latter-Day Saints], and John Humphrey Noyes [Bible Communism; Oneida Community] all argued that they were merely fulfilling that same mandate. Yet somewhere along the line, I would argue, a revolution had taken place that made private judgment the ultimate tribunal for the exposition of Scripture.[18]

Hatch's description shows that *sola Scriptura* was invoked by founders of new sects, without appreciation for the way that mainstream Protestants like Luther and Calvin claimed to interpret in ways consistent with the tradition.

The sea change in the way that the Bible was used in American Christianity was influenced also by the trend, beginning in the nineteenth century, to view all knowledge as historically and socially conditioned. Timeless truths began to vanish from people's consciousness as they absorbed the perspective that all knowledge—including our knowledge of God as found in Scripture—is culturally and historically embedded and changing with time.[19] One text that illustrates this trend is Karl Mannheim's *Ideology and Utopia*, which argues that all knowledge is culturally conditioned and significantly influenced by the knowing subject.

Both sides in the dialogue between the Roman Catholic and Reformed Protestant groups voice a desire "to listen together to the Word of God," but the difference of opinion on the question of *sola Scriptura* and the locus of

---

18. Hatch, "*Sola Scriptura*," 70–71; he introduces his term "the individualization of conscience" on 66–67. The Nevin quotation is from Nevin, *Catholic and Reformed*, 255.

19. Wacker, "Demise of Biblical Civilization," 125–27.

Scripture's authoritative interpretation will make it difficult for both sides to hear Scripture in the same way.[20]

Contemporary Orthodox theologians consider *sola Scriptura* to be untenable. Theodore Stylianopoulos considers the Protestant Reformation to have helpfully moved readers of Scripture back to a patristic way of reading Scripture as centered on Christ and essential for the church. But he considers the idea of *sola Scriptura* "highly problematic," since in its Protestant outworking it ran roughshod over the unity of the church. He writes that if the "scriptural principle" is not balanced by a church principle, believers' personal interpretations are considered authoritative, and this then prompts such diversity in interpreting Scripture that in the end the *sola Scriptura* principle, against the reformers' intentions, lowers the value of Scripture.[21]

We have already seen how Martin Luther respected some traditions, in contrast to the radical reformers. Lutheran theologian Robert Jenson strongly objects to the use of *sola Scriptura* as denoting any disregard for tradition.

> Most of the books that make up the canon themselves came to pass by lengthy processes of community tradition, first of oral tradition and of glossing, supplementing and editing texts. The documents' selecting and collection into volumes understood as Scripture came similarly to pass. If we have no confidence in tradition under the leading of the Spirit, we can have no confidence in supposedly inspired Scripture. Moreover, there was no New Testament for the first 150 years of the church; thus the rule that the writings there collected are authoritive [*sic*] for the life of the church is itself a pure piece of churchly tradition. . . . The church received the New Testament as a controlling *part of* her tradition, not as a substitute for it.[22]

After thus explaining that *sola Scriptura* cannot meaningfully connote Scripture in place of tradition, Jenson goes on even to question the common Protestant idea that *sola Scriptura* means that Christians look to Scripture instead of a magisterium. He notes that, as a book, Scripture cannot directly assert its authoritative voice. Someone has to be the teacher of Scripture. He observes that the "decentralized magisterium" attempted in Protestant circles has had "discouraging results." He concludes that "to continue with this experiment against the evidence of its results, in the name of 'only Scripture,' is

---

20. The quoted phrase is from *Towards a Common Understanding of the Church*, §164.
21. Stylianopoulos, *New Testament*, 1:156–57.
22. Jenson, *Lutheran Slogans*, 66–67.

surely an abuse," explaining that "use of 'only Scripture' to cover the disasters of Protestantism's lack of a magisterium is an abuse."[23]

These clarifications fit Jenson's introduction to his discussion of *sola Scriptura*, which he considers the "most problematic" of Lutheran slogans: "it cannot finally be salvaged for any significant use."[24] At the end of his section on this principle, however, he favorably cites how the second generation of Lutheran theologians used the term: as an indication that Scripture is the primary source for liturgical, doctrinal, and ethical discourse in church life.[25] Despite this principle's limitations, its entrance into theological discourse in the sixteenth century has produced ripples throughout the Christian family's engagement with Scripture. These developments are worth considering in order to see whether we are reading Scripture as well as we can today.

DEVELOPMENTS OF THE *SOLA SCRIPTURA* PRINCIPLE

Because Scripture concerns faith and practice, the *sola Scriptura* principle has been invoked and extended in ways that do not automatically suggest themselves when one simply hears of living by the authority of "only Scripture." In this section we will explore three developments that *sola Scriptura*'s proponents typically endorse, and then, in the next section, offer one surprising development of the principle.

Scripture Is Its Own Interpreter

A corollary of the *sola Scriptura* principle valued by Luther was that Scripture is the basis for how one should interpret Scripture. Practically, this means that when a given text of Scripture seems difficult to understand, another scripture can be offered to shed light on the best way to interpret the text under consideration.

A positive and practical example of this idea that Scripture is what interprets Scripture can be seen on the question of Israel in Christian theology. One might read much of the New Testament and wonder what happened to God's covenants with the nation of Israel. Christian anti-Semitism or anti-Judaism has found some prooftexts in the New Testament. But when one considers the

---

23. Jenson, *Lutheran Slogans*, 67–68 (final two quotations from 68).
24. Jenson, *Lutheran Slogans*, 63.
25. Jenson, *Lutheran Slogans*, 68–69.

one New Testament text that directly addresses the question of Israel, Romans 9–11, there one finds a different attitude. For after deep engagement with his Scripture on the question of Israel, Paul affirms God's faithfulness to Israel and Israel's ultimate salvation (11:25–32).[26]

The general way in which Luther applied this idea of Scripture interpreting Scripture was that since the New Testament focuses on Jesus Christ, the christological reading of texts from the Old and New Testaments is always to be preferred.[27] This is a time-honored way of reading Scripture, extending back through Augustine to New Testament authors themselves.[28]

But Scripture interpreting Scripture can also be a mantra behind which an interpreter can ideologically prioritize or marginalize sections of Scripture. By prioritizing gospel over law, Luther pioneered *Sachkritik*, a critical reading of Scripture based on a criterion that one values over all others.[29] For example, he placed the Letter of James in an appendix, at the back of his published New Testament, because he thought that it did not cohere with the idea of justification by faith that he found in Paul's letters. So Scripture interpreting Scripture can be a useful approach, but it must be used responsibly and in respectful relationship with tradition and the community of faith.

Scripture Is Clear

Scripture's clarity, comprehensive scope, and self-authenticating nature are related ideas that entered into theological discourse at this time. Radical reformer Ulrich Zwingli (1484–1531) emphasized that it is God's word of Scripture that must teach people, and that when illuminated by the Spirit, Scripture is clear. He wrote on the clarity of Scripture about three years before Luther would write on it.[30]

Clarity is a positive characteristic that is usefully asserted to motivate people to read Scripture. At the same time, assertions of Scripture's clarity can become a means to neutralize others' interpretations of Scripture. As can be inferred from some of the reformers' quotations above, *sola Scriptura* em-

---

26. *Nostra Aetate* §4.

27. Thompson, "*Sola Scriptura*," 159.

28. Luke 24:27, 44–46; Acts 10:43; Rom 1:2.

29. Capetz, "Reformation Heritage," 52–54.

30. Thompson, "*Sola Scriptura*," 166–67, citing Ulrich Zwingli, *Von der gewüsse oder kraft des worts Gottes*, in *Sämtliche Werke*, 1:369–70, 377, and Bromiley, *Zwingli and Bullinger*, 82, 89. The clarity of Scripture is sometimes referred to as its perspicuity.

powered them to say that their interpretation of a given text was right and that another interpretation was wrong. This pattern of argument assumes that there is a single sense to Scripture. Thus, a general result of the principle of *sola Scriptura* and the emphasis on clarity that developed out of it was the view that Scripture's texts have a single meaning rather than the literal and trifold spiritual senses of the patristic and medieval interpreters.

The clarity of Scripture continues to be asserted today. Wayne Grudem uses Moses's command that parents teach children the Torah, the psalmist's joy in how God's law enlightens the simpleminded, and the fact that most New Testament letters were written to congregations that included uneducated gentiles as biblical evidence for the Bible's clarity. He defines his notion of Scripture's clarity by asserting that it "is written in such a way that its teachings are able to be understood by all who will read it seeking God's help and being willing to follow it."[31]

Scripture Is Sufficient

Henry Bullinger (1504–1575), who followed Zwingli as Protestant leader in Zurich, published a set of fifty sermons that not only were read in Switzerland but also became required reading for some Protestant clergy around Canterbury, England. Bullinger insists that Scripture is God's own truthful word, which is complete—providing all that a believer needs. Bullinger argues that each of the New Testament's authors wrote all that is necessary for us to know. He cites John 20:20–31 to support this claim for the Gospel of John. He asserts that Luke left out nothing in his gospel that we need to know, and that since Paul wrote fourteen letters (he includes Hebrews), Scripture is sufficient for giving us what we need. He was arguing against the Catholic Church's recognition of apostolic traditions not written in Scripture.[32]

As we have already seen with Bullinger, John Calvin began to emphasize the sufficiency of Scripture for knowing God in the 1539 edition of *The Institutes*. The authority that Scripture holds is based on the text of Scripture itself and on how the Spirit witnesses to a Scripture-reading believer.[33] Calvin continued to

---

31. Grudem, *Systematic Theology*, 105–6 (citing Deut 6:6–7; Ps 19:7), 108 (quotation).

32. Thompson, "*Sola Scriptura*," 168–71, citing Bullinger, *Sermonum Decades quinque*, 1, 5, 7; *Decades of Henry Bullinger*, 37, 54, 62–63.

33. Thompson, "*Sola Scriptura*," 174, citing Calvin, *Inst.* (1539) 1.21, 24 (CR 29:293, 295).

hold the self-authentication and the work of the Spirit together when writing about Scripture's sufficiency and authority in the years that followed. He wrote that though Scripture needs no proof of its authority, its grand simplicity and the general agreement of the church regarding its authority provide secondary support for its witness.[34] In the 1559 edition, he wrote more on the necessity of Scripture, noting the inadequacy of natural revelation to turn fallen humanity toward God.[35] The necessity of Scripture thus became connected with what is still a characteristic of Reformed theology—its low regard for natural revelation.

Calvin provides us with a Protestant perspective on the difference between Catholic and Protestant views on Scripture. He had written a response to the Council of Trent in 1547, and so in the 1559 edition of his *Institutes*, he clearly is seeking to distinguish the Catholic use of Scripture from his own: "This, then, is the difference. Our opponents locate the authority of the church outside God's Word; but we insist that it be attached to the Word, and do not allow it to be separated from it."[36] Calvin follows up on this idea with a comment on what he perceives are illegitimate developments of doctrine in the Catholic Church.

This . . . is the difference between the apostles and their successors: the former were sure and genuine scribes of the Holy Spirit, and their writings are therefore to be considered oracles of God; but the sole office of others is to teach what is provided and sealed in the Holy Scriptures. We therefore teach that faithful ministers are now not permitted to coin any new doctrine, but that they are simply to cleave to that doctrine to which God has subjected all men without exception. When I say this, I mean to show what is permitted not only to individual men but to the whole church as well.[37]

Calvin thus solidified the ideas of earlier Protestants on the singular authority of Scripture and offered a rationale for the claim that Protestants were following only Scripture, rather than human teachings in addition to Scripture. This helps us see that assertions of the sufficiency of Scripture may be motivated by an aversion to the idea of doctrinal development.[38]

34. Thompson, "*Sola Scriptura*," 175–76, citing Calvin, *Inst.* (1539) 1.33 (CR 29:300).
35. Thompson, "*Sola Scriptura*," 176–77, citing Calvin, *Inst.* (1559) 1.5.11, 1.6.1 (CR 30:49, 53).
36. Thompson, "*Sola Scriptura*," 179, citing Calvin, *Inst.* (1559) 4.8.13 (CR 30:855; Battles 2:1162).
37. Thompson, "*Sola Scriptura*," 179, citing Calvin, *Inst.* (1559) 4.8.9 (CR 30:851–52; Battles 2:1157).
38. Cf. Newman, *Development of Christian Doctrine*.

Calvin's contemporary Thomas Cranmer (1489–1556) extended the idea of the sufficiency of Scripture in what is now known as the sixth of the Thirty-Nine Articles for the Church of England. In this article, Cranmer makes explicit what Calvin had implied, that if anything is not found in Scripture, it cannot be considered a required item of faith.[39] Yet the Church of England enshrines in its articles a qualification that Scripture is sufficient only as interpreted by its authorities, as is clear in article 20.

The sufficiency of Scripture continues to be asserted in some Protestant sectors today. Grudem presents it as the fourth of his four characteristics of Scripture, asserting that "Scripture contained all the words of God he intended his people to have at each stage of redemptive history, and that it now contains all the words of God we need for salvation, for trusting him perfectly, and for obeying him perfectly."[40]

The three developments just surveyed—Scripture's self-interpreting function, clarity, and sufficiency—all emerged in the early decades of the Reformation. Now that five centuries have elapsed, there are Protestants from the *sola Scriptura* camp calling for a return to tradition. We next consider this surprising development.

Protestant Appeals to Tradition

We have already seen in this chapter how Lutheran theologian Robert Jenson finds no way in which *sola Scriptura* can be used to indicate that Scripture instead of tradition is authoritative for the Christian family. In what might seem a counterintuitive turn, other Protestants who still recognize the *sola Scriptura* principle are now emphasizing the need for tradition.

Reformed author Keith Mathison thus adopts Alister McGrath's term "Tradition 1" for the magisterial reformers' respect for the church fathers and for traditional ways of reading Scripture, and McGrath's term "Tradition 0" for the radical reformers' thoroughgoing disavowal of all tradition. It is clear that he favors Tradition 1 as being a more workable approach for exegesis and constructive theology.[41] "The magisterial Reformers never advocated for an individual's right to interpret Scripture as he or she thought best. They saw themselves as moving Christians back toward the corporate mind of the

---

39. Thompson, "*Sola Scriptura*," 181.
40. Grudem, *Systematic Theology*, 127.
41. Mathison, *Shape of Sola Scriptura*, 126–28.

Church as established by the church fathers, before the perceived corruption of the medieval church occurred."[42]

In light of what has since transpired, it is worth pointing out that those Protestants who identify with the magisterial reformers still consider the church to be the only legitimate interpreter of Scripture. For example, Keith Mathison writes,

> Unlike modern Evangelicalism, the classical Protestant Reformers held to a high view of the Church. When the Reformers confessed *extra ecclesiam nulla salus*, which means "there is no salvation outside the Church," they were not referring to the invisible Church of all the elect. Such a statement would be tantamount to saying that outside of salvation there is no salvation. It would be a truism. The Reformers were referring to the visible Church, and this confession of the necessity of the visible Church was incorporated in the great Reformed confessions of faith. . . .
>
> . . . The authority of the Church is real, but it is not to be confused with the authority of God's Word in Scripture. The Church is the pillar and ground, the interpreter, teacher, and proclaimer of God's Word. But it is only the scriptural Word she proclaims that carries supreme authority. Apart from the Word, the Church is mute.[43]

As one can see from the perspective of this quotation, Mathison rejects the idea that each believer can interpret Scripture for himself or herself. One can study Scripture by oneself, but one "should not study Scripture *individualistically*, in isolation from the communion of saints—past and present."[44] This is a significant statement, one that if taken to heart would have spared us the tragedies in Jonestown and Waco.

The Protestant appeal to reading Scripture with tradition and the church draws our attention beyond Scripture to the church. What is the church? Catholics and Orthodox believe that the church is in the first case that visible body on earth that is intentionally following tradition and the apostles, connected to them by the chain of apostolic succession. Protestants such as McGrath and Mathison want to acknowledge historic Christianity, but balk at defining it specifically as Catholic or Orthodox. In order to understand anyone's position on the question of *sola Scriptura*, one therefore has to understand how that person defines "the church."

---

42. Mathison, *Shape of Sola Scriptura*, 127, citing McGrath, *Reformation Thought*, 145–46.
43. Mathison, *Shape of Sola Scriptura*, 268–69.
44. Mathison, *Shape of Sola Scriptura*, 271.

THE TWO QUESTIONS OF *SOLA SCRIPTURA*

Let's return to the two questions raised near the end of this chapter's introduction. It really does matter whether one prioritizes the church or Scripture when taking a stand on *sola Scriptura*.

Those who favor the principle insist on a priority that Scripture has over the church. One could perhaps call this a "doctrinal priority," since *sola Scriptura's* proponents regard Scripture as being a more significant voice than the church for the formation of doctrine. Melanchthon, for example, did not reject all other authorities except Scripture. He placed Scripture above the church and taught that all theological claims need to be compared with Scripture, so that when any claim differed from Scripture, Scripture alone needed to be followed. "Let us . . . hear the church when she teaches and admonishes, but not believe merely because of the authority of the church. For the church does not originate articles of faith; she only teaches and admonishes. But we must believe because of the Word of God when, to be sure, admonished by the church, we understand that a particular opinion has been handed down in the Word of God truly and without sophistry."[45] Luther's view of *sola Scriptura* similarly was that Scripture was the final authority. He cited rulings of the early church when he considered them as supported by Scripture. "I do not want to throw out all those more learned [than I], but *Scripture alone* to reign, and not to interpret it by my own spirit or the spirit of any man, but I want to understand it by itself and its spirit."[46] These statements by Melanchthon and Luther assume that texts have a determinate meaning that can be understood by a reader. Both statements also assume, against the literal and threefold spiritual sense of the text that had been recognized for over a millennium, that the meaning of a given scriptural text is singular—that is, its one meaning must exclude other interpretations.

Catholic and Orthodox theologians prioritize the church over Scripture, emphasizing that this priority occurs in history and in logic. By "history" I mean the fact that the church came into being first, and then centuries later defined its canon of Scripture. By "logic" I mean the idea that the text of Scripture only functions as Scripture when it is read and interpreted within the church. Orthodox theologian John Meyendorff argues that the late date for the establishment

---

45. Melanchthon, *De Ecclesia et de Autoritate Verbi Dei* (CR 23:603); *Melanchthon: Selected Writings*, 142, quoted in Thompson, "Sola Scriptura," 165.

46. Martin Luther, *Assertio omnium articulorum Lutheri per bullam Leonis X. novissimam damnatorum* (1520), WA 7:98.40–99.2, quoted in Thompson, "Sola Scriptura," 154.

of the Christian canon and the continued ambiguity regarding the deuterocanonical Old Testament books render the *sola Scriptura* claim untenable. His statement on how inspired Scripture speaks to Christians emphasizes what the living, sacramental tradition means in more down-to-earth ways.

> Tradition becomes the initial and fundamental source of Christian theology—not in competition with Scripture, but as Scripture's spiritual context. The ultimate truth was delivered to the saints when Jesus taught them and when the Spirit descended upon them as a community at Pentecost. The church, as eucharistic community, existed before the New Testament books were written, and these books were themselves composed in and for concrete local churches. Their written text is meant to be read and understood by baptized, committed people gathered in the name of the Lord. Theology, therefore, is not simply a science, using Scripture as initial data; it also presupposes living in communion with God and people, in Christ and the Spirit, within the community of the church. Biblical theology is, of course, the best theology, but being truly biblical implies living in communion in Christ, without which the Bible is a dead letter.[47]

The *Sola Scriptura* Principle in the Classroom

Whether you are Protestant, Catholic, or Orthodox, it is worth trying to understand how your theology professor relates Scripture, tradition, and authoritative teaching of your branch of the Christian family. The same goes for the textbooks you read and the sources you use when writing papers. Try to understand what sort of navigation system the author is using in his or her theological discourse: relying only on Scripture, claiming to rely only on Scripture while actually importing certain traditions or presuppositions, or relying on tradition and Scripture.

If you accept the principle of *sola Scriptura*, beware of those who use this principle simply to justify their own theology or ethical formulation. Prolific evangelical scholar F. F. Bruce (1910–1990) warned of this abuse when he described one of his predecessors in the particular denomination to which he belonged, the Plymouth Brethren. J. N. Darby (1800–1882), an early leader among the Plymouth Brethren, warned against reading biblical commentaries; he advocated simply reading the Bible itself. Bruce, an author of Bible commentaries, described Darby's approach as follows: "He only wanted men

---

47. Meyendorff, "Doing Theology," 82 (against *sola Scriptura*), 83 (quotation).

'to submit their understanding to God,' that is, to the Bible, that is, to his interpretation!"[48] So beware of anyone who cites *sola Scriptura* as a way to get you to follow their particular point of view.

THE *SOLA SCRIPTURA* PRINCIPLE IN MINISTRY

In whichever branch of the Christian family you minister, you will encounter people who take a different position from you on the *sola Scriptura* principle. Without consciously calling it the *sola Scriptura* principle, people often invoke it when rejecting others' interpretation of Scripture, whether in regard to a theoretical doctrine or a given behavior. For example, you may encourage someone to worship on Sundays at your church more often. If she or he does not appreciate this sort of encouragement, you may hear, "Well, I don't see anywhere in Scripture that says I have to attend every Sunday, so I don't need to come to church more often." You might direct them to Hebrews 10:23–25, but chances are their rejoinder will be, "It doesn't say that I have to go to church every week, so I don't have to!"

If someone tells you that they don't need to attend Bible studies or learn how Christian writers before them have interpreted Scripture, you might ask how that works out in real life. The following questions may be useful to bring your parishioner over to listen to tradition or others' interpretation of Scripture:

- If everyone can interpret Scripture for oneself, does that mean every interpretation of Scripture is equally legitimate?
- Are the Bible verses that are quoted on racists' websites legitimate readings of the Bible?
- What country allows each of its citizens to interpret its constitution and laws as he or she thinks best?

In general, it is useful to point out that every written text needs to be read within some sort of context and needs interpretation for it to function as a guide to any community.

If you are a Protestant whose community still invokes the *sola Scriptura* principle, you can follow Protestant theologian Alister McGrath in advocating a return at least to how Luther and other magisterial reformers advocated for

48. George, "Reading the Bible," 29.

some tradition to be used. Allowing each individual to interpret Scripture for himself or herself often results in a loss of church members as individuals seek other churches or establish their own churches that fit their particular interpretations.

If you are an Orthodox or Catholic in ministry, it is best, when dealing with people who seek to push the *sola Scriptura* principle, to point out that the church fathers were the ones who ruled on the canon of Scripture for Christians, and that they interpreted Scripture according to the rule of faith and tradition. It is also useful to walk through the Mass with your parishioners and show them how many of the prayers and responses are quotations from Scripture.

10

METANARRATIVES

If the real historical world described by the several biblical stories is a single world of one temporal sequence, there must in principle be one cumulative story to depict it. Consequently, the several biblical stories narrating sequential segments in time must fit together into one narrative. The interpretive means for joining them was to make earlier biblical stories figures or types of later stories and of their events and patterns of meaning.

—HANS FREI[1]

In March of 1525, peasants in Swabia followed up on the *sola Scriptura* approach to Scripture that had been invoked for the last seven years, beginning in Luther's Saxony, to draft a complaint to the nobility of Swabia. The peasants supported their *Twelve Articles* with references to texts from both the Old and the New Testament. These articles asked for access to the forests, fish, and game of the land. They asked for fair wages for their work and reasonable levels of rent and taxation. Luther was initially sympathetic to the peasants in his *Admonition to Peace.*[2] His second book to them, whose title was intensified by the publishers to *Against the Murderous, Thieving Hordes of Peasants*, was perceived as taking the side of the nobility.[3] While he later tried to explain his heated rhetoric with an "Open Letter on the Harsh Book against the Peasants," he continued to maintain that the peasants were wrong to rebel and wrong to align their cause of social justice with the gospel.[4]

From the vantage point of half a millennium later, it is clear that the peasants and Luther were reading Scripture with different metanarratives. The

---

1. Frei, *Eclipse of Biblical Narrative*, 2.
2. See the annotated translation of the *Twelve Articles* and Luther's *Admonition* in Null, "Admonition to Peace." For the primary text, see *WA* 18:291–334.
3. See the selection in Rupp and Drewery, *Martin Luther*, 121–26.
4. *LW* 46:68–80. For a wide-ranging presentation of primary sources related to the crisis described in this paragraph, see Scott and Scribner, *German Peasants' War*.

peasants were reading Scripture from a liberation metanarrative, perhaps combined with a creation metanarrative. This can be seen in the ways that their articles invoke Scripture against the oppression they experienced and to petition for free access to natural resources. In contrast, Luther was reading Scripture according to a redemption narrative that saw Scripture as the story of how individuals are freed from the guilt that the law brings by faith in Christ. There were also political reasons why Luther sided mostly with the nobility against the peasants. But in terms of how both sides were invoking Scripture, the peasants' articles and Luther's responses to them read Scripture with different metanarratives.

When we humans encounter anyone or any idea outside ourselves, we by necessity look for a story in which to understand that person or idea. No matter with which of the five models people read Scripture, many will use an overarching story that allows them to make sense of a particular Scripture passage by relating it to other Scriptures and to themselves as members of the community of faith and the human family. An overarching story for Scripture is what I am calling a metanarrative. It is a single, underlying narrative that can provide a context, a sense of belonging, for the passage of Scripture and its reader.

In this chapter we will survey basic categories of metanarratives with which Christians read Scripture. To facilitate this survey, we will cover the following categories of metanarratives: redemption, election, liberation, and creation. Many people combine aspects from two or more of these categories when describing what the Bible is all about, but we will examine them as pure types, the Platonic forms of metanarratives for reading Scripture, as it were.

The metanarrative one uses when trying to make sense of Scripture is closely linked to what one considers to be the essence or most significant characteristic of God's relationship with humanity. Since many Christians consider "salvation" to be central in this relationship, we will start with the category of redemption.

REDEMPTION

Those metanarratives that emphasize how humanity is guilty and then forgiven, or death-bound and then revived, can be placed in the redemption category. It is typically Western Christianity, whether in Catholic or Protestant branches, that views the human problem in terms of sin and guilt, from which Jesus provides redemption. Western Christians then see this narrative as worked out in Scripture, beginning with the oracle to the woman in Genesis 3:15, in which God predicts that the woman's descendant will bruise the head of the serpent.

Among the Western uses of this category, the Lutheran version is significant, since from the sixteenth century until now it has influenced how people read their Bibles. The Lutheran version of Scripture's story as redemption is primarily the story of Christ bringing grace to sinners after the sinners have become aware of their guilt by learning of God's law. Characteristics of the Lutheran metanarrative are that it hinges on the opposition of law and gospel and that all of Scripture, including the Old Testament, somehow points to Christ. Within a given paragraph of the New Testament, it is not uncommon for a Lutheran exegete to identify the evidence within the paragraph for law, framed as a demand from God that cannot be met by humans. Then the exegete will identify those parts of the paragraph that can be considered gospel. The narrative thus is primarily operative on an individual level: God's law presents a moral demand on a person, whether this was the Mosaic law given to Israel or a general moral law for all of humanity. The Lutheran approach then portrays this law as beyond the power of any person to keep, so that one is driven to seek grace from God. This function of the law, driving a person to seek grace, is called the Lutheran or second use of the law. The gospel—the good news of grace that God provides for the forgiveness of one's sins and the healing of sin-related dysfunctions and scars—then resolves the tension brought on by the human's encounter with divine law.

The law-gospel distinction that is central to the Lutheran metanarrative exists in the service of the christological focus of this metanarrative. For Luther, all of Scripture points to Christ. He criticized the great exegete Origen by saying, "In all of Origen, there is not one word of Christ." This accusation is surely an exaggeration; what Luther meant by it is that in certain Old Testament texts regarding which Origen did not mention Christ, Luther saw some typological or prophetic signal of Christ.

Melanchthon codified this metanarrative in his systematic theology, which he called the *Loci Communes*. He distinguishes between commandments and counsels that are in the Bible. The former are imperatives that must be obeyed. If they are violated or not kept, everlasting punishment is the result for those who are unregenerated. And since Melanchthon teaches that our human actions cannot merit remission of sin, even our keeping of the commandments is not enough to bring us eternal life. Counsels are teachings that do not require specific action.[5] At the end of his chapter on the gospel, Melanchthon distin-

---

5. Melanchthon, *Loci Communes*, chap. 8 (Manschreck, 130–31).

guishes between law and gospel by reiterating that the law section of Scripture requires full obedience and that this is impossible for people to achieve. In contrast, the gospel excludes human merit and insists that, on account of Christ, God can grant forgiveness of sins and eternal life.[6]

In chapter 16 of the *Loci Communes*, "Of the Difference between the Old and New Testaments," Melanchthon offers a Messiah-oriented portrait of Israel and of the Old Testament. Israel was divinely established as a nation in order that God's promises of the Messiah and of the church might have a place on earth. "God graciously led Abraham out of Chaldea and promised a Messiah to his children. God promised them land and a government that should last for two thousand years, until the Messiah appeared and preached and visibly accomplished his office."[7] Melanchthon goes on to say that the Old Testament prophets taught that humanity is saved through believing in the Messiah rather than by keeping the law. The New Testament then more fully describes the promise that comes through the Messiah.

Today, Lutheran theologian Ann Fritschel advocates returning to this reading of Scripture, for she finds Scripture's portraits of the cosmic Christ and the reign of God to be useful content for Christ-centered expressions of the gospel that can get past the spiritually malnourishing gospel expressions that see the gospel only as something that might help people feel better about themselves.[8] In Amos 9:7 the prophet communicates how God is at work with other people besides Israel. Fritschel analogously employs the term "cosmic Christ" to emphasize that Christ is working on the cosmic level, perhaps even through other religions. The "cosmic Christ" portrait also presents a Christ who is a creating and sustaining force behind more than the human race. To recognize Christ as "cosmic" includes the awareness of other aspects of the created world, such as water, earth, sky, and all the life forms that inhabit them.[9]

The focus on Christ that is part of the Lutheran metanarrative provides an opening for Fritschel to remind readers that the church is the body of Christ, and thus believers operating within the Lutheran metanarrative should rise above individualism and a human tendency to divide into factions. She advocates reading Scripture as a faith community, rather than reading and interpreting it as individuals.[10]

This Lutheran metanarrative, following Luther's account of his own spiritual journey in the years 1513–1517, while lecturing on the Psalms, Romans,

6. Melanchthon, *Loci Communes*, chap. 9 (Manschreck, 148–49).
7. Melanchthon, *Loci Communes*, chap. 16 (Manschreck, 192).
8. Fritschel, "Luther's Christological Hermeneutic."
9. Fritschel, "Luther's Christological Hermeneutic," 11–12.
10. Fritschel, "Luther's Christological Hermeneutic," 14.

and Galatians, has been one with which many can relate to their own experience. It prioritizes the letters of Galatians and Romans within the canon of Scripture. Luther actually called his wife "my letter to the Galatians" as a term of endearment for her! When the peasants wrote their *Twelve Articles* that were largely based on the Sermon on the Mount, Luther did not accept their pleas, partially because he did not start from the Sermon on the Mount in his understanding of the gospel.

Weaknesses of the law-gospel metanarrative include the following: (1) its intense focus on an initial encounter with the gospel as answer to the crisis prompted by law can contribute to an inattention on the part of some people to the healing and spiritual growth that God's grace can offer once one has tapped into the gospel; (2) it leads some to ignore the positive roles given to law within Scripture; and (3) it can lead some to ignore the way that the Old Testament and Romans 9–11 view Israel as chosen and valued by God for Israel's own sake, and instead consider Israel as only a means to the provision of a messiah for the world.

In the Eastern branches of the Christian family, among members in the Orthodox Church, there is little emphasis on original sin and less emphasis on sin as the problem from which Christ redeems humanity than we find in the West. Instead, Eastern Christians, beginning with the Greek fathers and continuing to this day, read the Bible as tracing the story of how Christ rescues humanity from death. Note how Orthodox theologian John Chryssavgis describes the fall of Adam and Eve: "For Orthodox theology and spirituality, the 'Fall' of humanity is the renunciation of the possibility of participating in true life, in personal relationship and in loving communion. The biblical account of the Fall refers to the initial choice of autonomy and self-sufficiency, as opposed to dependence upon and subsistence in God, the origin of life and love."[11]

Chryssavgis goes on to quote Gregory of Nyssa's exegesis of 1 Corinthians 15:22, an explanation that helps us see how the Orthodox metanarrative would characterize the general plot of Scripture:

> For as in Adam all people die, so also in Christ shall all be brought to life (I Cor. 15:22).
>
> The sin of Adam is clearly related to all people, just as salvation by Christ touches everyone. Surely, however, neither original sin nor salvation may be effected in one's life without personal and free responsibility. Now the

11. Chryssavgis, "Original Sin."

context of this passage is that of death in Adam and life in Christ, not of transgression and guilt. The distinction between the old and the new Adam is essentially one between death and life. The new Adam, Jesus Christ, is the model of existence, the source of life, the giver of salvation.[12]

Orthodox author Theodore Stylianopoulos reminds us that a well-known icon of Eastern Christianity is of the resurrected Christ breaking out of hell, holding the hands of Adam and Eve, with other representatives of Israel closely following them.[13] The life-giving person of Christ encapsulates the metanarrative of redemption that Orthodox authors employ when reading Scripture. As John Behr writes, "'Meaning' resides in the person of whom the text speaks, and our task is to come to know this person by understanding how the text speaks of him."[14]

Election

Those Christians who read Scripture as essentially a record of how God moved from choosing the nation of Israel as his special possession to choosing all who will follow Jesus have adopted the metanarrative of election. A key concept in this metanarrative is covenant. "Covenant" is the term for a set of promises that God makes with an individual or group of people, as narrated in the Bible. If someone's summary of the Bible emphasizes how one or more covenants or divine decrees drive the storyline, then the narrative form of election is definitely at work.

This metanarrative is a favorite of those Protestants who are influenced by Reformed theology, an approach to Christian theology that began with John Calvin. The Reformed metanarrative, partially as a response to the Lutheran metanarrative and the law-versus-gospel bifurcation with which Lutherans traditionally read Scripture, is to see the gospel throughout the canon of Scripture, emphasizing the unity of Scripture and the continuity of the plot of Scripture. The Reformed metanarrative of election moves in a linear direction through the following four parts: creation, fall, redemption, and restoration. These four parts of the metanarrative are not always explicitly labeled as Re-

---

12. Gregory of Nyssa, *De opificio hominis* 16 (PG 44:185B), quoted and translated by Chryssavgis, "Original Sin," 198–99.

13. Stylianopoulos, *New Testament*, 1:31.

14. Behr, *Mystery of Christ*, 50.

formed, but they are definitely the main movements of the metanarrative that Reformed theologians find in the Bible.[15] Creation, fall, redemption, and restoration are intuitively appealing to some Bible readers as emblematic of the Bible's overall narrative, for they resonate with a bird's-eye view of the canon from Genesis to Revelation.

As mentioned above, one way that some who have been influenced by Reformed theology find continuity in a biblical metanarrative is by emphasizing the covenants that God makes with humanity in the Scriptures. Henry Bullinger taught that there is a single covenant that God has made with humanity. But he is the exception; most theologians who emphasize the covenant idea find a series of covenants over which their metanarrative runs. A standard distinction among the covenants that Reformed theology makes is between a covenant of works and a covenant of grace. As earliest evidence for a covenant of works, Reformed theologian Louis Berkhof offers Hosea 6:7 and Augustine's description of a *testamentum* or *pactum* in which Adam lived in relation to God. (Most patristic authors are silent on the idea of covenant; it is not a metanarrative construct for their engagement with Scripture.) Berkhof cites Bullinger as an early proponent of what would become a covenant-driven metanarrative.[16] Protestant author Palmer Robertson traces these covenants in his book *The Christ of the Covenants*.

Catholic author Scott Hahn is also invested in the covenant-driven metanarrative of Scripture. His presentation is helpful in the way that it explains how covenants create and sustain kinship relationships. So in a way analogous to how God marked Israel as specially belonging to God in the Mosaic covenant, so in covenants extended to Christians God is designating them as belonging to God's family. The covenants especially significant in Hahn's study are the Abrahamic covenant, the Levitical covenant, and the Davidic covenant. Hahn notes how New Testament passages present the Abrahamic

---

15. For example, Ed Stetzer accepts these as "the big story of Scripture" ("Big Story of Scripture," citing Nelson, "Story of Mission"). Stetzer nowhere mentions how these four themes represent Reformed theology, and gives no argument for why he accepts these as Scripture's metanarrative.

16. Berkhof, *Systematic Theology*, 211. Hosea 6:7 is *wehemmah ke'adam 'aberu berit sam bagedu bi*. The phrase *ke'adam* is understood as "in/like Adam" by those who see a covenant of works in Gen 2–3. NABRE translates it as "at Adam" and suggests Josh 3:16 as a possible cross-refrence to a city known as Adam. Augustine refers to God's word to Adam, "In the day you shall eat of [the tree of the knowledge of good and evil], you will die," as a *testamentum* in *The City of God* 16.27. Henry Bullinger's *Compendium of the Christian Religion* is the work that helped bring federal theology to prominence, an outlook that views Scripture as fundamentally driven by the idea of covenant.

and Davidic covenants as fulfilled in Christ for those who believe in and follow Christ.[17] The Mosaic covenant does not receive extensive attention in Hahn's book. Paul in Galatians 3–4 treats the Mosaic covenant as a temporary covenant, offered to the Jewish people until the Messiah would come, and the author of Hebrews considers the Mosaic covenant a broken covenant. Hahn thus focuses more on the covenants of grant given to Abraham, the Levitical priests, and David.

The value of the covenant-driven metanarrative is that it highlights the biblical witness to a God who desires committed relationships with humanity. The covenant metanarrative also prompts Christian readers to engage with the Old Testament in ways that the Lutheran metanarrative seldom does. One difficulty of Christians' use of the covenant-driven metanarrative is that it can easily lead its proponents to say that God has withdrawn the covenants with Israel and now extended them instead to those who follow Jesus, the messiah of Israel. Thus, Hahn's heading for his exegesis of Galatians 4:21–31 is "God Disinherits the Circumcised Seed of Abraham."[18] While Paul's rhetoric in Galatians is focused on keeping his gentile church members from taking on the observance of Mosaic law, rigid readings of this letter might lead one to ignore Paul's clear statements in Romans that the covenants remain Israel's possession (Rom 9:4; 11:29).[19] Similar rhetoric of displacement occurs in another New Testament letter that seeks to keep its audience from returning to what its author views as an inappropriate dependence on Mosaic law—the Letter to the Hebrews. Because both Galatians and Hebrews employ the covenant category in their arguments, there can be a tendency to absolutize their statements on covenants, without factoring in the goal their authors had with their original audiences.

John Bergsma offers a popularized form of the covenant metanarrative. The chapter titles of his survey make this clear: "Setting the Son in the Garden: The Covenant with Adam," "Washing Up and Starting Over: The Covenant with Noah," "A New Hope: The Covenant with Abraham," "God's Laws, Israel's Flaws: The Covenant Through Moses," "Once and Future King: The Covenant of David," "Stormy Today, Sonny Tomorrow: The New Covenant in the Prophets," and "The Grand Finale: The Eucharistic Covenant."[20] The final chapter's

---

17. Hahn, *Kinship by Covenant*, 217–37, 256–77.

18. Hahn, *Kinship by Covenant*, 272–74, quotation from 272.

19. See also Kaminsky and Reasoner, "Israel's Election."

20. Bergsma, *Bible Basics for Catholics*, vii.

title illustrates how Bergsma's metanarrative has been cross-fertilized with a sacramental metanarrative.

A sacramental reading of Scripture can provide a secondary metanarrative, almost like a melodic theme that runs in harmony with the main melody, for those employing the covenantal metanarrative. In this reading of Scripture, human acts of worship are noted in the Old Testament, from the record of the early invocations of God (Gen 4:26), through the patriarchs' prayers at altars and sacred stones, through the use of the tabernacle and the temple cult. Then Christ's death is read as the ultimate fulfillment of Abraham's offering of Isaac and all animal sacrifices described in the Old Testament. Christ's institution of the Eucharist is read as a fulfillment of or later development in the human activity of sacrifice. As a re-presentation of Christ's death, the Eucharist becomes the primary sacrament through which humanity experiences the transcendent. A weakness of the sacramental metanarrative when exclusively used to understand Scripture is the possibility it opens for some to ignore their own growth in spiritual maturity by focusing only on a mechanical or formal participation in the sacraments.

The strength of the covenantal metanarrative for the Christian Scriptures is that it provides a unified model for helping Christians see how God works with Israel and ultimately all humanity through the canon of the Scriptures. Hahn sums up his covenantal narrative of Scripture as follows: "God takes Israel into filial-covenantal relationship as his firstborn son. While this involves a privilege for Israel, it is always ordered to the restoration of the familial solidarity of the covenant bond between God and all humanity, whose tribes and nations are God's other children and thus siblings of Israel."[21] Hahn sees Hebrews, Galatians, and Luke-Acts as teaching that gentile Christians are included under the Abrahamic and Davidic covenants, since these covenants even in their Old Testament contexts included the possibility for gentile participation. The covenant metanarrative therefore not only helps provide a holistic reading of the Scriptures; it also offers an identity to the church that is rooted in God's covenants with Israel.[22]

The election of Israel thus is the basis of this metanarrative, whose final emphasis is the election of those who are in Christ. As long as this metanarrative recognizes with Paul that Israel remains God's elect (Rom 9:4–5; 11:26–29), it can be a fruitful storyline for the Christian canon.

21. Hahn, *Kinship by Covenant*, 333.
22. Hahn, *Kinship by Covenant*, 337.

LIBERATION

Liberation theology provides a metanarrative that begins with the exodus of Israel from slavery in Egypt as the primary point of orientation for the human interaction with Scripture. Human experience is viewed through the lens of the oppression of the poor or otherwise marginalized by those with power. The gospel's primary point of relevance for humanity is then presented as its picture and promise of release from social oppression. Liberation theology understood itself in its beginnings as something very new, but a case can be made that it grew out of the student movements in secular society of the 1960s, as well as in some cases from changes within the church. For example, the bishops of Latin America met in Medellín, Colombia, in 1968 to discuss how to apply Vatican II to Latin America. One of their main points of emphasis in the meeting was "the option for the poor," or the prioritization of the poor in church policies. Around the same time, others in Latin America also realized that the Bible clearly speaks of God's favor toward the poor. Liberation theology was thus perceived as a way of getting back to a key, previously ignored narrative strand that runs through the whole Bible: God's attention to and mercy for the poor. University students, who by and large are from a socioeconomic level above the poor in many countries, also saw the poor in their societies in a new light, as those needing attention, whose plight could be addressed by changing society's structures. Since this was all happening in Latin America, it is easy to connect the metanarrative of liberation theology to Latin America.

A specific form of liberation theology, feminist liberation theology, was also beginning in the 1960s in Latin America, though it would not be until the 1980s that it gained attention.[23] In regard to how feminist liberation theology deals with Scripture, Ivone Gebara writes, "We have also reappropriated the Christian biblical tradition by trying not to look at many of the books as being sacred in themselves, but in relation to human life. In a similar way, we have tried to demonstrate the instrumentalization of the texts for imperialist interests of domination. We have pointed to the contradictions in the text and the significance of our contemporary contexts and the way in which we speak about how we live our lives in the future."[24]

This summary of how Latin American feminist liberation theology relates to Scripture illustrates how some metanarratives enforce a given construct on

23. Gebara, "Movement of May 1968," 265, 269–70.
24. Gebara, "Movement of May 1968," 270.

the whole canon of Scripture. For feminist liberation theologians, Scripture must be recognized as a product of patriarchal societies, and the past ways of reading Scripture that so often affect our expectations or interpretive process must be deconstructed to emasculate Scripture's metanarrative. There is certainly value in thinking through how Scripture marginalizes some peoples. I think especially of Hagar—who is the first person to name God in the Bible and whose son receives a covenant from God—and yet Paul allegorizes her negatively (Gen 16:13; 17:20; 21:13; Gal 4:21–31). I look forward to the day when Catholics and Orthodox will canonize Hagar and ask her to intercede on behalf of marginalized and silenced women. Still, the metanarratives for reading Scripture that have a chance for a long period of influence are those that continue to value the Bible as Scripture and that contain openings for multiple points of emphasis. The approach to Scripture by a feminist liberation theologian quoted above first of all contains within it the seeds of what will move the ideology to the sidelines of public attention, for as soon as Scripture ceases to be Scripture, it becomes one of a number of indistinguishable, earthbound texts. The potential for Scripture to speak to injustice on earth is tragically reduced when it is not regarded as Scripture. In addition, a one- or two-issue metanarrative—for example, "the Bible tells the story of how women and the poor have been oppressed through the ages"—can hinder people from seeing the positive regard for women and the poor that also can be found in the Bible, as well as a significant record of how the transcendent God encounters humanity.

Elsa Tamez is another Latin American theologian who could be said to read Scripture mostly in the category of liberation. Her book *Bible of the Oppressed* makes the case for finding a metanarrative in Scripture that is primarily oriented around the liberating work that God provides for the oppressed. The chapter "Justification by Faith in Romans" in her book *The Amnesty of Grace* attempts to shift readers from reading Paul's Letter to the Romans from within either an election or redemption metanarrative to a liberation metanarrative. After describing how this New Testament letter offers a different logic than the logic prevailing in first-century Roman society, Tamez writes, "Three words help to clarify this different logic that the apostle proposes: condemnation, liberation, and justice. In them can be seen the complete solidarity of the triune God with those condemned to death in human history."[25]

Oppression occurs around the whole globe, but people experience oppression in different ways, depending on the cultural, political, and socioeconomic

25. Tamez, *Amnesty of Grace*, 113.

circumstances. North American theologian James H. Cone gave voice to the liberation metanarrative as found in the African American experience, and this approach to reading Scripture is now also found in the United Kingdom and other parts of the world.[26] Articles in *Black Theology: An International Journal*, published in England, regularly intersect with questions of a liberation metanarrative of Scripture.[27]

In Asia, a significant source for the liberation metanarratives of Scripture is Minjung theology.[28] This is the form of liberation theology articulated by Korean theologians such as Ahn Byung-Mu (1922–1996), Suh Nam-Dong (1918–1984), Hyun Young-Hak (1921–2004), and others today such as Kim Yong-Bock and Chung Hyun-Kyung.[29]

The significant strength of the liberation metanarrative is that it gives full consideration to the biblical affirmation of God's identification with the oppressed and poor, an identification not always recognized in other metanarratives.[30] A second strength of this metanarrative is that it frequently enables the Scripture reader to identify and participate fully in the narrative of God's deliverance of the oppressed and poor. This metanarrative is especially effective in bridging the perceived gap between the world of the text and the reader's world.

A vulnerable area of the liberation metanarrative is that the close focus on the oppressed and identification with them can cause a confusion of subject and object in one's metaphysics and hermeneutics. Those immersed in the liberation metanarrative might be so invested in finding themselves within Scripture's narratives of oppressed peoples that they do not fully appreciate its visions of the transcendent God. According to the BPS grid in chapter 8, they would be so permanently attached to the "human subject" pole of the s axis that they miss how Scripture draws readers away from themselves and toward God. An example of this confusion can be seen in Joshua's encounter with the captain of the Lord's armies (Josh 5:13–15). Scripture readers employing other metanarratives are also vulnerable in this regard, but the personal investment that the liberation metanarrative elicits from the reader can especially threaten a divinely oriented construction of subject and object.[31]

---

26. Cone, *Black Theology of Liberation*; Reddie, *Black Theology in Transatlantic Dialogue*.

27. See, e.g., Dada, "Contextual Biblical Hermeneutics"; Charles, "Book of Revelation"; Kinyua, "Postcolonial Examination."

28. See Suh, *Korean Minjung in Christ*; Kwon, *Theology of Subjects*.

29. These liberation theologians are featured in Küster, *Protestant Theology of Passion*.

30. Deut 15:11; 24:12, 14–15; Ruth 2:1–4:12; Pss 10:12, 17; 14:6; 34:3, 7; 37:11; 69:34; 72:4, 12–13; 82:4; Isa 58:1–10; Amos 5:10–15; Luke 6:20–21; 16:19–31; Gal 2:10; Jas 2:1–7; 5:1–6.

31. See Gutiérrez González, *New Libertarian Gospel*.

CREATION

The ecological turn in public discourse and Christian theology has provided an impetus for reading the Christian Scriptures as a story of God's creation of the earth for human, animal, and plant life and the mixed record we humans have supplied as its stewards. As Richard Bauckham writes, "Reconciliation with God and reconciliation with the rest of God's creation are not alternatives but natural partners. In the end they are inseparable, as John's vision shows, and in the crises of our contemporary world both are urgent needs. The Church's 'ministry of reconciliation' today must surely embrace both. And finding our place in the biblical metanarrative—reconciled in Christ, on the way to the reconciliation of all things in Christ—will help to sustain hope in dark times."[32]

The ecological metanarrative is evident in the Earth Bible series, edited by Norman Habel. The authors who contribute to the studies in this series read the whole canon of Scripture through the lens of what is happening in the created world, using the phrase "earth story" in each of their books that reads the Bible within this metanarrative.[33] In the volume titled *The Earth Story in the New Testament*, Vicky Balabanski attempts to wrest the Gospel of John from a dualistic view of the cosmos below as evil and heaven above as good to one in which the cosmos is not necessarily evil. She does this by finding four uses of "cosmos" in John: (1) the place where light enters and lives, (2) the entirety of creation, (3) human life that does not recognize God, and (4) a realm at war with God's realm. Since the former two senses of the term are more positive, this strategy of finding multiple meanings of cosmos becomes a way to keep one from viewing the Gospel of John as being completely negative toward the cosmos, and consider that it "acknowledges our mutuality with Earth."[34]

David Horrell has single-handedly attempted an ecological metanarrative of the whole canon. On the Genesis texts, Horrell shows how the covenant with all of creation fits well with the ecological metanarrative, while the anthropocentrism of this part of Scripture actually detracts from the creation-based metanarrative that focuses on ecology.[35] He notes how the Psalms call all of

32. Bauckham, *Bible and Ecology*, 178.

33. Habel, *Readings from the Perspective of Earth*; Habel and Wurst, *Earth Story in Genesis*; Habel and Wurst, *Earth Story in Wisdom Traditions*; Habel, *Earth Story in the Psalms and the Prophets*; Habel and Balabanski, *Earth Story in the New Testament*.

34. Balabanski, "John 1," 91–94, quotation from 94.

35. Horrell, *Bible and the Environment*, 37–48, citing Gen 9:8–17 (covenant with all of

creation to praise God and how divine speech near the end of Job critiques an anthropocentric view of creation.[36] In turning to the New Testament, Horrell identifies the Gospels' portrait of Jesus as a "proto-environmentalist."[37] Paul's vision for a world redeemed and renewed by God and humanity reconciled by Christ also provides a significant segment of Horrell's metanarrative.[38] After considering the Gospels and Paul's letters, Horrell looks to the biblical vision of a created world that is renewed and at peace.[39] The metanarrative ends with an apocalyptic bang, focusing on catastrophes that Scripture pictures as coming on the earth.[40]

An ecological metanarrative is at work in chapter 2 of *Laudato Si'*, Pope Francis's encyclical on the environment. In this chapter he highlights how the creation story of Genesis 1 emphasizes the inherent goodness of all creation, and he reprises the Christian reading of creation texts that see God's love behind all of creation. The stewardship that humanity is given is not to be anthropocentric in a way that ignores the welfare of other species and elements of the natural world.[41] Without naming scholars, *Laudato Si'* directly responds to the claim that the Scriptures have facilitated humanity's exploitation of the environment.[42] This illustrates a key idea in our consideration of the metanarratives used to read Scripture: there are times when we must adopt a given metanarrative in order to respond to unhelpful emphases within a particular use of that metanarrative. In order to have meaningful dialogue about Scripture with another person, we often must adopt the other's metanarrative, just as we need to speak another's language in order to communicate. We enter into the other's metanarrative not as a permanent change in how we read Scripture but as a temporary means to facilitate communication.

---

creation); Gen 6:1–4 (angelic beings cohabiting with human women); and Gen 6:19; 7:16; 8:17; 9:16 (humans and animals are morally culpable).

36. Horrell, *Bible and the Environment*, 49–61, citing Ps 104 and Job 38–40.

37. Horrell, *Bible and the Environment*, 62–72, citing Matt 6:26; 10:29; Luke 12:6, 24 (God's care for birds); and Mark 1:13 (Jesus with the wild animals) among other texts.

38. Horrell, *Bible and the Environment*, 74–87, focusing on Rom 8:19–23 and Col 1:15–20. See also Horrell, Hunt, and Southgate, *Greening Paul*.

39. Horrell, *Bible and the Environment*, 90–103, citing Isa 11:1–9; 43:18–19; 65:17; 66:22; Joel 1:1–2:27; Rev 21:1–22:5.

40. Horrell, *Bible and the Environment*, 104–14, citing Joel 2:28–3:21; Mark 13; 2 Pet 3:10–13.

41. Francis, *Laudato Si'* §§65, 69 (inherent goodness of creation); §§65, 77 (God's love); §§67–69 (stewardship cannot be anthropocentric).

42. Francis, *Laudato Si'* §67. Cf. White, "Historical Roots."

After the Pentateuch, *Laudato Si'* turns to the Psalms in its ecological meta-narrative. Here the praise of God the creator and the invitations for other elements of creation to praise God are highlighted.[43] Next, *Laudato Si'* cites the prophets' unified characterization of the God of Israel, whose creation of the world and rescue of an enslaved or exiled people are indivisibly entwined.[44] *Laudato Si'* reads the wisdom literature of the Bible in order to show that creation occurs by means of God's love and that God's creation of all means that justice should be shown to all.[45] Within the New Testament, *Laudato Si'* highlights its presentation of the Son of God's role in creation (John 1:3; Col 1:16), his teaching on the Fatherhood of God (Matt 6:26; 11:25), his attention to and engagement with the natural world as incarnate man (Matt 13:31–32; Mark 6:3; John 1:14; 4:35), and his work of reconciling creation (Col 1:19–20), leading toward the end, when God's Son will hand everything over to God the Father (1 Cor 15:28).[46]

A key step in the ecological metanarrative is to note that the final book of the Bible, Revelation, includes three major players in its vision: God, humanity, and nonhuman elements of creation. Bauckham understands the ecological metanarrative as correcting Christianity's too-frequent neglect of the third partner in Scripture's overarching story.[47]

A strength of the ecological metanarrative is that it brings the Bible's witness, in both Old and New Testaments, into direct dialogue with secular voices that also seek to make sense of our ecological situation.[48]

One weakness of the ecological metanarrative is that it might lose sight of the transcendence of God in light of its concern with the natural world. In its focus on the immanent threats to our environment, those reading the Scriptures with this metanarrative in mind might lose sight of some dimensions of God's moral law that do not deal with the environment. But *Laudato Si'* explicitly argues that all relationships are intertwined, so this potential weakness does not necessarily occur in all ecological metanarratives offered for Scripture.[49]

---

43. Francis, *Laudato Si'* §§72, 77, citing Pss 33:6; 136:6; 148:3–5.

44. Francis, *Laudato Si'* §73, citing Isa 40:28b–29; Jer 32:17, 21; Rev 15:3, for an analogous emphasis on God as both creator and just ruler.

45. Francis, *Laudato Si'* §§77, 89, 94, citing Prov 22:2; Wis 6:7; 11:24, 26.

46. Francis, *Laudato Si'* §§96–100.

47. Bauckham, *Bible and Ecology*, 145.

48. Bauckham cites such texts as Lovelock, *Revenge of Gaia*; D. Noble, *Religion of Technology*.

49. Francis, *Laudato Si'* §70.

A second weakness of the ecological metanarrative is that it might lose sight of Israel as God's chosen people. In reading Old Testament narratives for their witness about ecology, there may be a tendency to read the narratives of Israel and its promised land as simply a cipher for humanity on the planet. While there is a sense in which Israel represents the world, its particularity must also be guarded in order to respect Scripture's presentation of Israel as God's chosen people.[50] The lack of any essays on the books of Exodus–Deuteronomy, the Deuteronomistic History, Ruth, or Chronicles in the Earth Bible series is one sign of its inattention to the particular focus that Scripture has on Israel.

CRITERIA FOR CONSTRUCTING A METANARRATIVE

Most Christians read Scripture with a metanarrative that combines the theme of redemption with one or more other categories. While there is a danger that *Sachkritik* can lead one to emphasize one idea in a way that ignores other key ideas in Scripture, Christians are free to construct a metanarrative—that is, tell the story of the Bible—in a variety of ways. Church history and tradition offer three criteria to keep in mind as we consider what storyline best summarizes all of Scripture. As long as the following three criteria are met, one can faithfully and fruitfully combine elements from two or more of the metanarrative categories when trying to describe the Bible's main narrative.

Does the Metanarrative Respect the Election of Israel as God's People?

In the last decades of the twentieth century, after the theological reverberations of the Shoah reached the ivory towers of theologians, Scripture scholars became more aware of the ways in which the New Testament is in continuity with the Old Testament. Israel and its story suddenly emerged as an essential context for understanding the New Testament. N. T. Wright is one scholar who attempts to situate the New Testament in the context of Israel's story.

Wright's metanarrative states that God chose Israel to do what humanity in general failed to do: represent God on earth. The purpose of Israel's call was to be a light to the nations, according to Wright, which presumably means to teach the nations about God's law. According to Wright, the New Testament author Paul views Israel to have failed in its calling to be a light to the nations,

50. On Israel representing the world, see Deut 32:8. On respecting Israel's particular status as the chosen people of God, see Exod 19:4–6; Rom 11:28–29.

and he views Messiah Jesus as completing what Israel failed to do. Wright views Paul's letters in the New Testament as redefining "Israel" in light of how the message of Jesus has come to the nations. While this may sound all right to some readers, this part of Wright's metanarrative can lead to the idea that ethnic Israel is no longer God's people.

But both Scripture and history warn us regarding narratives that marginalize ethnic Jews. Paul goes out of his way to tell gentile readers of his Letter to the Romans not to assume that they are better than Jews who are not yet following Jesus, and to inform his readers that these Jews still are God's people and beloved because of their ancestors (Rom 11:13–29). And when we consider church history, the second-century church rejected this idea when it was offered by Marcion. And since the extreme form of this idea contributed to the removal of Jews from the Protestant state church of Germany and ultimately to the execution of millions of Jews in the Holocaust, it is best to steer clear of any redefinition of Israel that rejects the claim found in the Old Testament and reaffirmed in Romans 9:4–5 and 11:13–29 that the Jews remain God's beloved people.

As you can see from the preceding paragraph, metanarratives must be tested against what Scripture says and must also be considered in relation to how they will influence people's lives on earth. Charles Cosgrove emphasizes that when reading the Bible, we should always consider how our interpretation will influence our actions, especially if it will lead to anti-Semitism.[51] This represents a particular application of Augustine's idea that the purpose of explaining the Bible should be to help people grow in love of God and love of neighbor, which is the second criterion for evaluating a metanarrative of Scripture.

Does the Metanarrative Encourage Me to Love God and Love My Neighbor?

Augustine's *On Christian Doctrine* is focused on how best to read Scripture. He makes the point that our interpretation of Scripture needs to promote love of God and love of neighbor, since God saves people in order that they may love in these ways.[52] This is definitely a reality check for those of us who engage in the academic study of Scripture. In the end, our goal in studying Scripture is not to solve puzzles or gain attention by publishing papers; it is rather to enable us and our readers to love as God commands. Thomas à

---

51. Cosgrove, "Rhetorical Suspense." See also Cosgrove, *Elusive Israel*.
52. Augustine, *On Christian Doctrine* 1.36.40.

Kempis sees through our academic pretensions as well. He writes that we do not receive credit in God's eyes for being great Scripture scholars, but rather for being "full of the love of God; . . . always seeking, purely and wholly, the honour of God."[53]

Does the Metanarrative Recognize the Incarnation, Death, and Resurrection of the Son of God as All-Significant for Humanity?

Todd Billings describes the church's rule of faith as summarizing what the church considers to be the foundational elements in the story of Christianity. He goes on to explain how the narrative form of the rule of faith provides a context for reading any part of the Bible.

> Since Christian readers read Scripture through a rule of faith . . . , which has a narrative shape, all genres of Scripture are taken up into this larger "story" of the biblical canon. A portion of the law, or an individual proverb, is seen in light of the canon's story of God's creating, judging, and redeeming work that *finds its fulfillment in Jesus Christ*. Whether or not narrative is a prominent feature in the biblical genre, the passage becomes a moment in the triune drama of salvation when read in light of the canonical story of Scripture, a story summarized in the rule of faith.[54]

Christ is the central figure of the metanarrative of Scripture, as can be seen in both Eastern and Western exegetes in the early centuries of church history.[55]

METANARRATIVES IN THE CLASSROOM

As already stated in this book, you will encounter the historical-critical method in your Scripture classes, whether in undergraduate, seminary, or graduate settings. You will find that some of the assigned readings approach Scripture only with the artifacts-of-the-past application of the documents model. These sorts of secondary texts are heavily weighted toward the historical-critical method

53. Thomas à Kempis, *Imitation of Christ* 3.7.6 (Knox and Oakley, 121).

54. Billings, *Word of God*, 17 (initial definition of rule of faith); 44–45 (quotation, my emphasis).

55. For Eastern exegetes, see Behr, *Mystery of Christ*, 33–40 (Gregory of Nyssa on the centrality of Jesus's death), 52–70 (Irenaeus on the centrality of Christ throughout the Scriptures). For Western exegetes, consider Augustine's exegesis as explained in Cameron, *Christ Meets Me Everywhere*.

and sometimes do not acknowledge the care that Jewish and Christian communities took in preserving, collecting, and canonizing the texts.

Sometimes you might be tempted not to read these historical-critical texts, whether because they take no account of the faith that Scripture readers in the congregation have, or because you do not wish to consider the historical problems these texts identify. But remember that Jesus also dealt with the equivalent of modernity's historical critics when he responded respectfully to the Sadducees who read the Torah in such a way as to deny the resurrection of the dead. And your long-term love affair with Scripture will be enhanced if you work through the historical problems that critics raise, rather than ignoring them. So keep reading the assigned texts, even the ones that operate with no metanarrative behind them. You will be a stronger witness for the truths of Scripture if you read and work through their claims rather than reflexively rejecting them before reading.

METANARRATIVES IN MINISTRY

You will encounter various metanarratives among your parishioners. Some will want you to present Scripture more in line with the metanarrative of liberation. Others will say you are not adequately glorifying God because you preach too little within the metanarrative of election. In general, it is best to listen and fully consider their perspective before offering any immediate responses.

Often the best response to feedback of this sort is to point out how throughout the year the homilies or sermons are based on a variety of biblical texts, and that the theme your parishioner considers shortchanged will be covered. If you are ministering in a community that uses a lectionary, you can inform the parishioner of the Sundays in which the texts will be especially representative of their favorite metanarrative. If you minister in a community that does not use a lectionary as the basis for the sermon or homily, you can use your parishioners' input for more attention on a given metanarrative when designing sermon series for the year.

Your job in ministry is to draw people in your congregation to Christ. It is therefore useful when preparing Bible studies or sermons not to limit yourself to sources that are invested only in the historical-critical method, but to read secondary literature such as commentaries or others' sermons that are clearly based on metanarratives that meet the three criteria covered above. The church fathers are especially helpful in providing metanarratives that meet the criterion of love of God and neighbor and the criterion of a Christocentric plotline.

As Jason Byassee writes in his book *Praise Seeking Understanding: Reading the Psalms with Augustine*, "As a preacher I spent a great deal of fruitless time seeking biblical commentaries to help me read Scripture well for the sake of the church. I have found modern commentaries helpful for certain things—in clarifying historical events or linguistic problems with greater confidence than ancient commentators could, for example. But I found ancient commentators more helpful in doing the most important thing that Christian preaching and teaching must do: drawing the church to Christ."[56]

56. Byassee, *Praise Seeking Understanding*, 1, quoted in Billings, *Word of God*, 188.

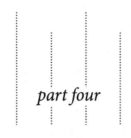

part four

SCRIPTURE
in REAL LIFE

SCRIPTURE IN WORSHIP

The Body of the Church . . . is constituted and continually nourished by the Body of Christ. Without that nourishment, the Word itself loses meaning because it is no longer actualized in the experience of the ecclesial community. The Bible then has no more interest and significance in the life of the believer than any other ancient historical document. Although the Word finds expression in the dogmatic and scriptural portions of the Liturgy, it can only become a "Word of life" insofar as it leads from repentance to participation, from conversion to communion.

—JOHN BRECK[1]

It would be a mistake to consider a faith community's use of Scripture without consideration of its worship. Scripture is embedded in some Christian groups' liturgies in ways that can go unnoticed. And beyond the direct connection of Scripture in the discourse of a worship service or Mass, there is also the relation between Scripture and the church that is shared by means of the Word who is Christ. In this regard, Orthodox theologian John Breck describes the necessity of regular communion in order to receive most benefit from Scripture in the quotation above.

Breck emphasizes the close relationship between proclamation of the word and the Eucharist because of a deeper truth, and that is the idea that Scripture's home is within the church. He recognizes that Protestants have much to teach the rest of Christianity in their care and emphasis regarding the sermon, which can include wonderful teaching from the Bible. But he thinks that both Protestants and Catholics need to realize that every aspect of how we deal with Scripture needs to be done in the context of all of church tradition. He argues that Catholics view Scripture and tradition too separately, that we have compartmentalized these. Instead, he advocates that Scripture be recognized as a core part of tradition, and thus insists that it be studied, interpreted, and

1. Breck, *Power of the Word*, 20.

proclaimed always in the context of the church, since "it is only in the Church that the Spirit actualizes the Word in the *liturgy*, in the *sacraments* and in the *preaching* of the Gospel."[2]

Protestant author Eugene Peterson echoes the emphasis on Scripture's home within the gathered assembly, though he does not mention Scripture's connection with the Eucharist: "The task of liturgy is to order the life of the holy community following the text of Holy Scripture."[3] In what follows, we will trace the ways in which Scripture informs Christians' corporate worship, whether in sacramentally oriented communions or in those communions where the main event each Sunday is the sermon. To trace all the ways that Scripture forms the basis for Christians' corporate worship would be impossible in a single chapter. But Peterson is onto something when he goes on to note how the church's liturgy offers us the Scriptures in a wide-ranging context that includes architecture, color, song, our ancestors in the faith, prayer, neighbors, and time.[4] The thick context in which Scripture comes to us helps us read its message in light of earlier generations' understanding and in connection to the church's worship patterns. The library housing a solitary scholar is not the ideal setting for reading Scripture. The ideal setting is corporate worship, with the lector and congregation engaged in the first and second readings, the cantor and assembly singing a psalm, and the celebrant proclaiming the gospel.

PRAYING THE SCRIPTURES

The Psalms constitute the prayer book of the Bible; their literary genre invites people to pray them. But it is also a useful practice to pray with the words of Scripture's narratives, thus placing and finding oneself within the ministry of Jesus or participating in God's work with others. Thus in the Mass, when we say, "Lord, I am not worthy that you should enter under my roof. But only say the word, and my soul shall be healed," we are entering into the biblical narrative, finding ourselves speaking the words of the faithful centurion (Matt 8:8). In night prayer of the daily office, we pray with Simeon, "Lord, now you may let your servant go in peace, for my eyes have seen . . ." Catholic prayers seem especially full of these Scripture-quoting prayers. For example, the Angelus repeats words from the narrator and Mary in the annunciation scene (Luke 1:26–38). The Hail Mary prayer employs Gabriel's and Elizabeth's greetings to Mary (Luke 1:28, 42).

---

2. Breck, *Power of the Word*, 45–46, quotation from 46.
3. Peterson, *Eat This Book*, 73.
4. Peterson, *Eat This Book*, 74.

One way that the Scriptures can be meaningfully prayed in public worship is to pray the blessings, or benedictions, over people. I know that in some Christian groups a worship service can simply end with "We love you guys. We'll see you next week." But such a final word misses an opportunity to speak God's word of blessing to the congregation. If your church's liturgy allows you to choose a final word, I encourage you to use a benediction from Scripture. These benedictions can speak God's blessings into people's lives or summon them into the worship taking place in heaven.

BENEDICTIONS IN SCRIPTURE

Reference	Opening Line
Num 6:24–26	"May the LORD bless you and may he keep you"
Rom 15:13	"May the God of hope supply you with all joy and peace in believing"
Eph 3:20–21	"Now to him who is able to accomplish far more than we ask or think"
Heb 13:20–21	"May the God of peace, who brought up from the dead the great shepherd of the sheep"
Jude 24–25	"To the one who is able to keep you from stumbling, and to present you without blemish in jubilation before his glory"
Rev 5:13	"To the one who sits on the throne and to the Lamb be blessing"
Rev 11:15	"The kingdom of the world has come to be the kingdom of our Lord and of his Anointed"

SCRIPTURAL CONTEXT OF THE SACRAMENTS

Jean Daniélou provides us with a marvelous account of the scriptural basis that the church fathers see behind the sacraments. I sample his account of the sacraments of initiation below.

Baptism

Early Christian iconography and patristic writings make a number of connections between Scripture and various instances and aspects of baptism. In early churches, baptisteries often had exquisite paintings of paradisiacal gardens, including deer. The garden theme was employed to communicate that the baptismal candidates were again entering Eden and God's presence. The deer were included to represent our longing for God, as found in the beginning of Psalm 42: "As a deer longs for streams of water, so my soul longs for you, O God."[5] Didymus of Alexandria sees a connection between the Holy Spirit coming down on the primeval waters and the Spirit's descent on Jesus when he was baptized in the Jordan.[6]

Confirmation

Tertullian connects the priestly anointing and the anointing of the Messiah with the anointing given to believers after their baptisms. Daniélou summarizes Tertullian's reasoning by making explicit the verbal links among the Greek words for chrism, anointed, and Christian (*chrisma, christos,* and *christianos*): "This [anointing] constitutes a new aspect of Confirmation: the oil is the chrism by which the baptized becomes a new *christos,* a *christianos.*"[7]

Eucharist

Because the "Holy, holy, holy" that is said in the preparation for the Eucharist comes from Isaiah's vision, John Chrysostom writes that communicants in the Eucharist are carried up into heaven and are saying the same words that the cherubim say in God's very presence.[8] Theodore of Mopsuestia and Pseudo-Dionysius both link the breaking of the bread as preparation for distributing the host with Christ's incarnation and the way that Jesus appeared to disparate individuals after his resurrection.[9] The connection between the elements of the Eucharist and Melchizedek's bread and wine is early and repeated.[10] The manna in the wilderness provides another type for the Eucharist. The typological signification between manna and the Christian's

---

5. Daniélou, *Bible and the Liturgy,* 36, citing Cyprian, *Letters* 73.10, 85.15.

6. Daniélou, *Bible and the Liturgy,* 73, citing Didymus of Alexandria (PG 39:692C).

7. Daniélou, *Bible and the Liturgy,* 115–16, quotation from 116, citing Tertullian, *On Baptism* 7. The texts in view are Lev 21:10–12 and Ps 2:2.

8. Daniélou, *Bible and the Liturgy,* 135, citing Chrysostom, *On the Incomprehensible* (PG 48:734C).

9. Daniélou, *Bible and the Liturgy,* 138–39, citing Pseudo-Dionysius, *On the Ecclesiastical Hierarchy* 3.13, ¶197 (PG 3:444C) and Theodore of Mopsuestia (PG 15:12; 16:18).

10. Daniélou, *Bible and the Liturgy,* 143–47, citing Heb 7:3; Clement of Alexandria, *Stromateis* 4.25; Cyprian, *Ep.* 63.4; Ambrose, *On Sacrifices* 4.10, 5.1.

sustenance is already made in John 6:32–35, 49–51; 1 Cor 10:3; Rev 2:7, 17. The church fathers take full advantage of Scripture when identifying scriptural types or precedents for the Eucharist.[11] They even quote the Song of Songs when describing the Eucharist as a marriage ceremony between Christ and the church.[12]

READING OF SCRIPTURE

In the weekday synagogue services from the Hellenistic period, the reading from the Torah for the upcoming Sabbath was read at the end of the service, after the blessing of Numbers 6:24–26 was pronounced over those gathered. It thus functioned as "an occasional appendix" to Jews' weekday worship.[13] In early Christian worship, selections from the Psalms may have been read when God's word was taught. Paul Bradshaw does not think that the Psalms were used as a basis for prayer in the public service.[14]

In his eminently readable volume *Eat This Book*, Peterson has a section called "Reading Scripture Liturgically" in which he writes of how all can read Scripture with Christians all around the world. He defines this liturgical reading as "a vast and dramatic 'story-ing,' making sure that we are taking our place in the story and letting everyone else have their parts in the story."[15] He does not specify the lectionary, but that is definitely a tool that keeps Christians reading through the whole Bible.

Those assigned with reading Scripture publicly need to prepare by practicing. Resources that help with pacing, pronunciation, and emphasis in the reading of the text are available and can be very helpful for readers.[16] Besides preparing in the basic ways of practicing the pacing, pronunciation of difficult words, and emphasis on key words in the day's reading, the reader should carefully consider the goal for her or his reading. The goal is to communicate God's word clearly. Like a referee or umpire at a sporting event, the Scripture reader should communicate clearly without trying to showboat or call attention to oneself.

---

11. Daniélou, *Bible and the Liturgy*, 148–51, citing Ambrose, *On Mysteries* 46; Cyprian, *Ep.* 68.14; Augustine, *Tractates on the Gospel of John* 26.6.12 (PL 35:1612).

12. Daniélou, *Bible and the Liturgy*, 203–7, citing Ambrose, *On Sacrifices* 4.16; 5.5–7, 14–15.

13. Bradshaw, *Daily Prayer*, 20.

14. Bradshaw, *Daily Prayer*, 43–44, citing 1 Cor 14:26.

15. Peterson, *Eat This Book*, 72–76, quotation from 76.

16. Park, Schaeffer, and Leal, *Workbook for Lectors*.

Scripture and the Homily

Christians regard the homily—the words that a pastor or celebrant speaks after the Scripture is read and before the celebration of the Eucharist—in different ways. In Protestant circles, the homily is often called the sermon and is regarded with almost sacramental value, especially if the speaker is highly regarded for his or her Christian character, biblical knowledge, or speaking ability. It is understandable why the sermon should be so highly regarded, at least in communities influenced by Reformed theology. For Reformed theology regards the preached word, the Scriptures proclaimed in God's name by someone God has commissioned, as a true means of grace, more significant than all other sacraments.[17]

The homily should seek to be relevant to the congregants' lives, but in a balanced way. If one seeks to be relevant only to a certain segment of the congregation, others may feel left out. In addition, what is relevant for one person may not be relevant for another. In any setting where Scriptures have been read from different parts of the Bible—for example, an Old Testament reading, a psalm that has been sung, a reading from a New Testament letter, and then a reading from a gospel—the homilist should try to make contact with at least two of the Scripture texts that the audience has heard.

Those who proclaim God's word in a sermon or homily must balance the innate drive for relevance with the purists' goal of simply letting the text speak for itself. There is a danger in trying to be too relevant and too specific in the homily. Karl Barth once wrote, "All honour to relevance, but preachers must aim their guns beyond the hills of relevance."[18] The great truths of the gospel will always speak to an audience, so there is real wisdom in focusing on these deep truths. Of course, there may be times when God moves you to preach about a specific situation. In the history of the United States, many pastors sought to apply Scripture directly to the assassination of Abraham Lincoln.[19] The nation's sense of loss was so raw and deep that really they had no choice. And yet those sermons are not very relevant for today.

In other cases, one needs to think twice about how relevant and specific one should be. Think of a weather forecast covering the next twenty-four hours. As soon as the twenty-four hours pass, the forecast is irrelevant and forgotten. The same might be the case for some topics that one might consider addressing in

17. Berkhof, *Systematic Theology*, 610.
18. Barth, *Homiletics*, 118–19.
19. See Chesebrough, *"No Sorrow Like Our Sorrow."*

a sermon or homily: a municipal, provincial, or national election; loss or other tragedies that people in a congregation may experience; and anniversaries of community or national calamities. It is therefore best in most cases to address local, national, or global situations at the level of general principles and not with laser-specific references. In this way, your homily will reach more people and will have a longer shelf life in your congregation's minds.

The sermon has been described as truth through personality. But anyone giving a homily should take care that his or her personality, possibly including desires to appear funny or intelligent, does not obstruct Christ as the focus of the gospel, or other truths from the Scriptures of the day. Someone has also stated that it is impossible to prove that one is intelligent and that Christ is wonderful at the same time. It is thus best to follow Paul's example and focus on proclaiming Christ crucified, without trying to impress an audience with one's rhetorical ability (1 Cor 1:17; 2:1–5).

The prioritization of the church over Scripture seen in Orthodox theologian Breck in the section above can also be seen in Stylianopoulos's insistence that the church is one of the living sources for Christian proclamation, while Scripture constitutes only a resource.[20] The evangelical who responded to Stylianopoulos expressed surprise that Scripture was not regarded as a primary source for preaching, citing the high view of Scripture held by Jesus and the apostles as evidence that Scripture should be accorded higher value.[21] Part of the disconnect here in the relative value assigned to Scripture for preaching might arise from the evangelical's unfamiliarity with the extent to which Scripture is used in the whole liturgy of the Orthodox Church. Since the liturgy is filled with Scripture, an Orthodox person might not consider it a first-order source specifically for preaching. Also at work in the evangelical's response is the influence of a move of Protestant orthodoxy, after the first generation of reformers, to equate the word of God with written Scripture. This move can cause some to lose sight of the fact that in Christian theology the Word of God is first of all the risen Christ, and secondly it is God's message when proclaimed by the power of the Spirit in the Church.

Preparation for the Homily/Sermon

Since exegesis is part of the process of revelation, and since we seek to allow Scripture to speak to our own communities, the preparation for the sermon

---

20. Stylianopoulos, "Christ, Church and Preacher," 75–76, 79–86.
21. Spires, "Response," 94.

is not simply an academic exercise that can be practiced mechanistically. The goal is to receive *theōria*, a vision of spiritual truth. Thus, exegesis must be contemplative, prayerful, and in receptive conversation with others who have encountered Christ the Word through Scripture. Its goal is not finally more data to be learned about the text; its goal is rather to give praise to God and to lead others to a closer relationship with the Lord Jesus.[22]

My homiletics teacher in seminary used to say that one should have decided on what Scripture text one will preach on by at least a week before the sermon is scheduled. Yes, there are those who "intentionally" do not prepare their sermons, sometimes citing Jesus's words to "take no thought beforehand for what you will say" (Matt 10:19 // Mark 13:11 // Luke 12:11). But Jesus's words are spoken in the context of how to respond to arrest and trial before authorities. They are not spoken about how one is to prepare for all settings of communal worship. And in the one detailed account of Jesus's participation in corporate, organized worship, his visit to his home synagogue, we read that Jesus "found the place in the scroll where it was written" (Luke 4:17). That is, Jesus had decided beforehand what he would read and say; he did not open the scroll randomly. Those pastors whose congregations use a lectionary may think they are automatically keeping my teacher's charge to decide on one's sermon text at least one week before the service. But even with a lectionary there are choices to make. By one week before the worship service, the pastor who uses the lectionary should decide on which of the day's texts she or he will focus.

When ministering in a faith community that uses the lectionary, you may consider it a no-brainer to go with the gospel reading as your main focus whenever possible. This is commendable in light of the precedence that most Christians give to the Gospels.[23] However, one must also keep in mind that the Scripture of the apostles was our Old Testament. They preached from it often, as we can see in the sermons of Acts. Robert Jenson's observation that "the habit of preaching almost always on a Gospel reading, is not faithful to the apostles" is not quite the whole story, because we rightfully use the Gospels in place of the eyewitness testimony that the apostles gave to Christ in their preaching. [24] Still, Jenson's observation is worth considering. There are certainly riches in our Old Testament that are not fully utilized in many pulpits today. We should keep our Old Testament readings as live options for our main focus on some Sundays.

22. Breck, *Power of the Word*, 111–13.
23. *Dei Verbum* §18.
24. Jenson, *Lutheran Slogans*, 64n95.

The Goal of the Homily/Sermon

The goal of the one giving the homily or sermon is never to make oneself appear eloquent, funny, or intelligent. The goal is rather to move people toward faith, praise of God, and action on behalf of the world. Breck helpfully notes how the dictum *lex orandi lex credendi* (the law/pattern of praying is the law/pattern of believing) is incomplete. These must be linked to *lex agendi* (the law/pattern of acting), the principle of action. He notes how Chrysostom called service to others "the sacrament of our brother" and concludes that all creedal affirmations and liturgies are empty if they do not lead to our participation with divine grace in serving the church and the world.[25]

Delivery of the Homily/Sermon

As part of the preacher's call to prioritize God's word over oneself, special care needs to be given to how one begins the homily. Those who always begin a homily with a story or anecdote from their own lives not only risk overloading their audience with personal references; they also are sending a message that the truths of God's word are not demanding in their own right. It is best, when in doubt regarding how to begin, to start the homily with the central truth of one or more of the Scripture's texts for the day. This coheres with Scripture's assertion that God's ways are higher than our human ways, and it models for the congregation an accurate regard for God's word as more life-giving and attention-worthy than our human need for entertainment.

God's word as we encounter it in Scripture is more significant than any human project in which we are engaged, so this means, for example, that even guest speakers who are giving a "missions appeal" during the homily/sermon segment of a worship service should still seek first to explain and proclaim God's word as found in the Scriptures. To speak first of one's own missions project is to prioritize one's own work or agenda over God's word and to shortchange the congregation, who deserve first to hear and ponder God's word proclaimed to them in the Mass or church service. There are a number of ways that a guest speaker or one giving a missions appeal can integrate the appeal with the primary role of proclaiming God's word within the Mass: one could describe how people in one's place of ministry—that is, people in another cultural setting—would hear one or more of the Scripture texts for the day; one could explain how a Scripture text for the day relates to the calling or

25. Breck, *Power of the Word*, 184.

vision of those who started the mission or ministry in which one is engaged; one could explain how a Scripture text for the day gives those doing ministry the encouragement or focus they need to continue through difficult times in their mission work; and finally one could explain how a Scripture text for the day includes a call for those in the audience to contribute to or join in the mission work.

God's word is also more profound and has more lasting appeal than any of our thematic rubrics for sermons. It is better to preach on the Scripture texts for the day (if one is using the lectionary) or to preach through a book of the Bible (if one does not use the lectionary) than to preach on topics or themes. For those who do not use the lectionary or wish to preach through a book of the Bible, the topic-oriented sermon series can be useful, but pastors should allow plenty of input from others when crafting any such series, in order not to repeat their favorite emphases. If one is in a setting where one is expected to present a weekly sermon as part of a multi-Sunday series, one does well to vary the approach. When one is not in the seasons of Advent or Lent, it would be good to offer a topically oriented series, followed by a more explicitly biblically based series that goes through a given book of Scripture. At some point within Advent and Lent, sermons should develop the spiritual significance found in Christmas and Easter.

The believer's understanding of the purpose of Scripture and his or her relationship with Jesus are at stake in the design of a sermon series and selection of sermon topics. If all the congregation hears are sermon series that address attention-getting topics of interest to the general public, they may get the impression that Scripture is only a treasure house of useful examples and teachings that can help us meet our own goals of reaching wholeness. This would contribute to a misunderstanding of what it means to be "in Christ." The congregation might be led to believe that the primary reason for following Christ is to have a comfortable and peaceful life, a misconception of the New Testament's teaching.[26] This would amount to malnutrition over time, for Scripture guides us through God's own purposes for humanity, which are far above our own conceptions of success, and then Scripture leads us into God's own presence, a place far better than our own idea of wholeness (Isa 6:1–8; 55:6–13).

26. Cf. Matt 6:10; 10:34; Luke 22:42; Phil 1:20.

The Homily/Sermon and Politics

There are times when the homily must address what is on people's minds. In times of war or other crises, it is incumbent on the person preaching the homily to bring God's word to bear on the situation. In the same month in which Lincoln was first elected president, Henry Ward Beecher preached a Thanksgiving Day sermon on Luke 4:17-19, Jesus's public reading of the liberating words in Isaiah 61:1-2. Note how Beecher's sermon calls people to rise above a focus on their country to what God is doing within the whole world.

> These words are remarkable, to-day, for their meaning and for their historical position. The first sermon which Christ made, upon entering his public ministry, was this one at Nazareth. . . . That he chose these words in entering upon his mission—these words, of all the Law, of all the Psalms, and of all the Prophets—gives them peculiar significancy. . . . Christ came to save the world,—not laws, not governments, not institutions, not dynasties, but the *people*. . . .
>
> We are, then, to study the advance of Christ's kingdom in the whole aspect of the world. The Church is of the people. God's Church includes the whole human race. Our separate churches are but doors to the grand spiritual interior. The good men who love God and man with overruling affection, of all nations, and of every tongue, are the true Church.[27]

And we must always remember that the kingdom of God can never be equated with a nation-state here on earth. German theologian Emanuel Hirsch found it very difficult to separate the kingdom of God from his beloved Germany. In 1914, when Germany was entering World War I, he preached on Jacob wrestling with the man at Peniel (Gen 32:24-30): "All sacrifices of possessions and blood are nothing but the attempt to force from God a decision in our favor: we do not leave him alone, then he will bless us." The war was not going well for Germany in the spring of 1918, when Hirsch—still unable to separate God's will from the success of his country—preached, "Despite our timidity and indecision, despite our innumerable follies, we are standing now within sight of a brilliant victory. But God has not yet given us the decisive answer to our bold venture." Then on October 21, three weeks before Germany sur-

---

27. Henry Ward Beecher, "Against a Compromise of Principle," Thanksgiving Day, November 29, 1860, quoted in Chesebrough, *"God Ordained This War,"* 65-66.

rendered, he was still calling for a great effort for Kaiser Wilhelm.[28] When Germany was defeated and when its political system fell apart in the years that followed, Hirsch was very disappointed. This disappointment perhaps was partially accountable for his decision years later to support Hitler: "No other Volk in the world has a leading statesman such as ours, who takes Christianity so seriously. On 1 May when Adolf Hitler closed his great speech with a prayer, the whole world could sense the wonderful sincerity in that."[29]

In rehearing these politically oriented sermons, we can see how both Beecher and Hirsch found their respective nations' situations in Scripture. The former called his congregation to rise above their own government and see what God was doing. The latter could not get past the "kingdom of God = Germany" equation, an equation that proved to be an ill-fated and tragic gamble. A few questions emerge as good tests for the manner in which one brings Scripture to bear in politically charged moments: Does my homily respect the difference between the kingdom of God and my own nation? Will my words about my nation's current political situation stand the test of time? How will my sermon sound in heaven today or here on earth ten years from now?

The Homily and the Human Predicament

A little volume called *God's Living Word* contains essays on how Scripture should be used in preaching and sample sermons of Orthodox and evangelical Christians.[30] The conclusion of one Orthodox sermon includes the following lines that represent an Orthodox view of the gospel; note how Christ's victory over death is emphasized, which fits with the Orthodox focus on death as humanity's ultimate problem: "And our Church's singular annunciation of glad tidings to an always moribund and lost world is none other than *Christos aneste!* Christ is risen! For in the mystery of Christ's victory over death, we find an abiding new hope, we are assured that we are deeply loved by God's incarnate love."[31]

The sample sermon of an evangelical illustrates the Western preoccupation with sin and the guilt it brings; this captures the Western church's focus on guilt

---

28. Ericksen, *Theologians under Hitler*, 125. Ericksen has taken the quotations from Schjørring, *Theologische Gewissensethik*, 58 (quotation from September 13, 1914), 64 (quotation from spring 1918 and description of October 21, 1918, sermon).

29. Ericksen, *Theologians under Hitler*, 148, citing Emanuel Hirsch, *Das kirchliche Wollen*, 24.

30. Stylianopoulos, *God's Living Word*.

31. Calivas, "Man as Icon of God," 140.

as humanity's ultimate problem: "Mercy is offered freely to all. It is not our sin which condemns us at the last but our refusal to acknowledge it. Misdeeds will not doom us unless we have scorned the mercy that could blot them out. Our hope is simply and only this, to embrace the gospel made plain, to be among the sinners whom Jesus saves. All our life and service, worship and witness, strength and comfort, begin with this: 'Jesus, remember me!'"[32]

Both these sermons are exemplary in connecting Scripture with a deep-seated problem facing humanity. They are not primarily driven by desires to entertain or impress. Instead, they offer models in helping humanity stand directly before God's offer to deliver us through Christ, an offer that is at the heart of the Christian canon.

SCRIPTURE COMMUNICATED BY ICONOGRAPHY

The icon both expresses teachings of the church and unites the one in worship by faith with the subject portrayed in the icon.[33] If you display a cross in your worship space, or like to set up a manger scene in your church or home, you accept the conclusion of the Second Council of Nicaea regarding visual imagery. This council directed that Christians use visual imagery for Jesus, saints, and angels to help in their prayer lives. It is not that the visual images are worshiped. It is rather that one can pray "through" the images by using the images to help one focus on God, seeking God as the saint or angel pictured in an image sought God. It is worthwhile for all Christians to consider how their homes, study spaces, worship spaces, and websites employ visual imagery to communicate the truths of Scripture and call viewers into communion with Christ the Word.

We need to consider how our iconography can be inclusive or exclusive in its appeal to others. For example, in a panel discussion on Mel Gibson's *Passion of the Christ*, an African American minister at a predominantly white Methodist church commented that while his parishioners found the movie to be devotionally helpful and meaningful, he himself had difficulty fully appreciating the movie, because it was "too white." Two other African Americans have asked me on separate occasions why it is that Jesus is predominantly pictured as a white male in church iconography that they see. Since Jesus became human for all humanity, our depictions of him should not leave people feeling like they are not part of Jesus's audience on earth. We should intentionally use

32. Brownson, "Meaning of the Gospel," 145.
33. Breck, *Power of the Word*, 215.

iconography and depict scriptural narratives in ways that call all peoples of the earth into worship of God the Father, Son, and Spirit.

Scripture as Filter: The Regulative Principle in Worship

Imagine that you are on a basketball team that plays in a league observing the basketball rulebook according to the following train of thought:

1. The basketball rulebook alone is our authority in determining how we may play basketball.
2. The basketball rulebook prohibits excessive physical contact or running with the ball when not dribbling.
3. We should only play basketball as the rulebook stipulates.
4. If a given behavior is not in the basketball rulebook, it must not be allowed in basketball today.
5. Since the rulebook does not mention the jump shot, jab step, head fake, double-pump layup, full-court press, huddle before free throws, and hand clasps after the first of multiple free throws, these behaviors cannot be allowed in basketball games.

This may sound extreme to some readers, but in the strictest application of the regulative principle in worship, arising out of the *sola Scriptura* principle, a similar logic is at work, seen in the five assertions below.

1. Scripture alone is our authority in determining God's will.
2. In Scripture, God commanded his people not to make any graven images when worshiping him.
3. We should only worship God as God has commanded.
4. If a given behavior is not commanded or specifically allowed in Scripture as an act of corporate worship, we must not include it in our worship today.[34]
5. Since the Bible does not mention praise bands with electric guitars during worship or the celebration of the Christmas holiday, these behaviors should not be allowed in our worship today.

34. This seems to fit with the sense of the Heidelberg Catechism Q & A 96: "What does God require in the second commandment? We are not to make an image of God in any way [Deut 4:15–19; Isa 40:18–25; Acts 17:29; Rom 1:23], nor to worship him in any other manner than he has commanded in his Word [Lev 10:1–7; Deut 12:30; 1 Sam 15:22, 23; Matt 15:9; John 4:23, 24]."

In order to prepare you for encounters in ministry in which people tell you that, according to Scripture, your church's worship patterns must change, we will consider some key moments and texts from church history that help us understand the regulative principle in worship. After that, we will consider biblical ambiguities that allow for our differences in worship today.

The Regulative Principle of Worship in Church History

The Reformed tradition values the regulative principle when prescribing how its members should worship. This principle is a specific application of the *sola Scriptura* idea to public worship practices. The more famous example of this principle in popular memory may be the Puritans, but their practice is thoroughly rooted in Calvin's teaching.[35]

So how would you structure Sunday worship if handed a blank slate and asked to be as faithful to Scripture as possible? The following outline shows how John Calvin met that challenge:[36]

Liturgy of the Word
Call to worship: Psalm 124:8
Confession of sins
Prayer for pardon
Singing of a psalm
Prayer for illumination
Scripture reading
Sermon

Liturgy of the Upper Room
Collection of offerings
Prayers of intercession and a long paraphrase of the Lord's Prayer
Singing of the Apostles' Creed (while elements of the Lord's Supper
    are prepared)
Words of institution
Instruction and exhortation

---

35. Barrett, "Crux of Genuine Reform," 59–60, citing Calvin, "On the Necessity of Reforming the Church," in *Selected Works of John Calvin*, 1:128–29.

36. Barrett, "Crux of Genuine Reform," 58–59, quoting Maxwell, *Outline of Christian Worship*, 114.

Communion (while a psalm is sung or Scripture is read)
Prayer of thanksgiving
Benediction: Numbers 6:24–26

Even before Calvin died, John Knox (1514–1572) began applying the regulative principle in his own efforts at reforming Scotland. For Knox, visual
iconography and liturgical practices not found in Scripture amounted to idolatry. Knox even considered kneeling during the rite of Communion to be
idolatry. The Presbyterian Church he founded in Scotland would go on to
oppose the *Book of Common Prayer* from the Church of England as a breach
of the regulative principle.[37]

As one can infer from the reference to the *Book of Common Prayer*, the
Church of England did not follow the regulative principle. Article 20 of the
original Forty-Two Articles of Religion drafted by Thomas Cranmer (1489–
1556), the first non-Catholic archbishop of Canterbury, reads as follows: "The
Church hath power to decree Rites or Ceremonies, and aucthoritie in con-
trouersies of fayth: And yet it is not lawfull for the Church to ordayne any
thyng that is contrarie to Gods worde written. . . . Wherefore, although the
Churche be a witnesse and a keper of holy writ: yet, as it ought not to decree any thing against the same, so besides the same, ought it not to enforce
any thing to be beleued for necessitie of saluation."[38] This article prioritizes
church over Scripture, since it insists that the church can institute practices
in worship not found in Scripture, so long as the practices do not conflict
with Scripture.

Of course, in the next century England experienced a stronger threat to its
newly formed state church than the Presbyterians in Scotland. The regulative
principle of worship experienced significant attention and development in the
Puritans' reaction against the Church of England. The Puritans considered
the Church of England to have remained too Catholic in its worship by keeping practices not found in Scripture. So the Puritans and those influenced by
them, in the window of time in which Puritans were in political ascendency
in England, sought to articulate just what Christian worship should be.

The Puritan-influenced Parliament of England requested during the period
of the English Civil War (1642–1651) that theologians come up with directives
for worship. An early result of this request was the Directory of Publick Worship of God, promulgated in 1645. R. J. Gore Jr. describes this document as

37. Trueman and Kim, "Reformers and Their Reformations," 135.
38. Schaff, *Creeds of Christendom*, 3:500, quoted in Thompson, "*Sola Scriptura*," 180.

a compromise document. As such, it did not mention certain controversial practices about which Protestants disagreed: the exchange of rings in a wedding, kneeling when receiving Communion, the sacrament of confirmation, and the designation of godparents. The only sort of music that it directed for use in worship was the singing of Scripture's Psalms. It specifically called for the observance of a weekly Sabbath, while prohibiting all other church holidays or feasts.[39] This time period is instructive for us, because it illustrates how assertions of the regulative principle can be significantly motivated by one group's perceived need to distinguish itself from another group. In these cases, ambiguous texts in Scripture are read according to what will facilitate separation from other branches of the Christian family, and not always according to a fully considered exegesis.

Biblical Ambiguities regarding Worship and the Regulative Principle

Our New Testament offers different portraits of the Jerusalem temple. The Gospel of John portrays Jesus as the complete replacement of the temple. The Jerusalem temple in John is therefore portrayed as a place where Jesus is met with fiercest opposition.[40] In contrast, the Gospel of Luke has a more positive view of the temple. It is where Zechariah receives the annunciation regarding John the Baptist, and after Jesus's ascension it is the place to which the rejoicing disciples return. In Acts, the apostles and believers meet there, and even the apostle to the nations goes there to fulfill a vow.[41] This ambiguity can contribute, along with differences in our understanding of Jesus's real presence in the Eucharist, to differences in regard for the place of our worship. Do we regard our church in its physical dimension as a sacred space, following Luke-Acts, or do we regard it—along the lines of a popular summary of Calvinistic ecclesiology—simply as "four bare walls and a sermon"?[42]

The phrases "as often as you drink" and "as often as you eat" in Paul's directions for the Eucharist are also ambiguous (1 Cor 11:25–26). Jesus and his apostles were eating an annual meal, the Passover seder. But Paul arguably applies Passover imagery to the Lord's Supper or Eucharist in 1 Corinthians 5:7–8. So should we partake of the Eucharist once a year, along the lines of the Passover seder, or should we partake of it daily as might be indicated by the

---

39. Gore, "Regulative Principle," 35, 37.

40. John 1:14; 2:18–21; 8:2–59; see also Rev 21:22.

41. Luke 1:5–22; 24:52–53; Acts 2:46–47; 3:1–26; 5:12–16; 6:7; 21:23–26.

42. The basis for this "four bare walls and a sermon" summary can be found in Calvin, *Inst.* 1.11.12–14, 4.1.5, 4.2.3, 4.10.29.

early believers' practice in Acts 2:46, or perhaps weekly as indicated by "first day of every week" or "the Lord's day" (1 Cor 16:2; Rev 1:10)? I hope you see that someone could claim to have scriptural support for receiving Jesus in the Eucharist on an annual, weekly, or daily basis.

What about head coverings for women? On the basis of 1 Corinthians 11:2–16, Calvin taught that all women should have their heads covered when meeting in public worship. This practice is continued by some within Reformed, Anabaptist, and Catholic communities today.[43] Yet when one reads this paragraph in Paul's letter, it is clear that Paul is operating within a cultural milieu that considers it natural for men to have short hair and women to have long hair, and in which married women should have their heads covered. But not all cultures operate with these assumptions about hair. Paul says that nature teaches that it is shameful for men to have long hair, but this is clearly culturally conditioned. Medieval Europe, indigenous tribal areas, and sumo wrestling through the millennia are all examples of cultural milieus in which men's long hair is honorable and natural. Some traditions continue to follow Calvin's lead in a straightforward reading of Paul's culturally specific command for women to have their heads covered. But other traditions justifiably observe that the foundational principle of 1 Corinthians 11:2–16 is to maintain a distinction between men and women when the community gathers for worship. Such a distinction can be upheld in other culturally specific ways than the Jewish-influenced guidelines Paul gave to his church in first-century Corinth.

A False Dilemma behind the Regulative Principle of Worship

Let's return to the two trains of thought we considered at the beginning of this section regarding how a basketball league might observe the rulebook and how Christian worship might conform to the Bible. In both cases, the logic seems to predicate comprehensive and only positive stipulation (identifying what should be done) on an authority that never claims to be comprehensive in its description of allowable behaviors and is significantly negative in directives (identifying what is not allowed). Both arguments, first for playing basketball only according to the rulebook and then the regulative principle in worship, partake of the fallacy of the false dilemma, also called the false alternative, in the progression from step three to step four. It is a false dilemma to say that either something is directed by God (whether by positive command or prohibition) or it is not allowed.

43. Petrovich, "First Corinthians 11:2–16," 130–31, citing Calvin, *Inst.* 4.10.29, p. 1207.

CONCLUSION

In this chapter we have considered a number of specific questions related to how Scripture is used in worship settings. Lest we lose the forest for the trees, here are the main points to remember.

We need to include Scripture in our worship services, not simply during the homily or sermon, but in other parts of the service as well. Scripture can be incorporated into the congregation's liturgical responses and into congregational singing.

We need to beware of trying to be too relevant or too specific in how we apply Scripture. This is because the specificity of our application of Scripture is in inverse relationship with the length of time that the homily or sermon will remain relevant and the number of people directly addressed by the sermon. The more specific we are, the shorter the sermon's relevance and the smaller the sermon's implied audience.

At the times when a pastor feels compelled to bring Scripture to bear on a current event, the pastor must avoid equating the kingdom of God with his or her own nation. It would be wise to ask how the sermon will sound in heaven, how Christians in other parts of the world would understand it, and how it will sound ten years after its day of delivery.

In keeping with the Second Council of Nicaea, we should use visual imagery to communicate the truths of Scripture and imagery of Jesus, the saints, and angels to help our people in their prayer lives. This visual imagery should intentionally communicate how Christ came as a human for all the peoples of the world.

DEVOTIONAL, ACADEMIC, *and*

PROFESSIONAL USES *of* SCRIPTURE

People say to me, "How can philosophical knowledge contribute [to the understanding of Holy Scripture]?"
My answer is, "How does ignorance contribute to it?"

—DESIDERIUS ERASMUS[1]

Those of us who study the Bible in the classroom while engaging in ministry within the church are constantly faced with the question of how we are to treat the Bible. Is it merely a textbook, providing data that we use to interpret Christianity, or is it a road map for the heart, providing guidance for one's inner pilgrimage? Three scenes from my seminary days continue to spur my thinking on this question.

In my second quarter of seminary, I was required to interview a pastor. During the interaction he stated that he always tried to keep his devotional reading in biblical texts other than those from which he was preparing sermons. He said that he did this so the Word would not become "dry" for him.

Later on in seminary, one of my favorite teachers told me that he did not observe the practice of personal devotions. He stated that he was called to study God's word, and since this was what he did all the time, he did not keep a special "quiet time" or time for reading Scripture and prayer on a daily basis.

Finally, in a meeting of my advisee group in seminary, we were celebrating the upcoming graduation of one of our group. When asked to share a few words, he frankly stated that he had lost the spiritual edge with which he entered seminary. Now that his master of divinity degree was to be awarded and he had completed his formal training for ministry, he was no longer drawn to Bible study; it had become a chore for him. I heard something similar decades later when asking some students at a Catholic seminary about their Scripture classes.

1. Erasmus and Luther, *Discourse on Free Will*, 17.

This chapter examines the relationship between devotional and academic study of Scripture. It also raises the possibility, for those who minister in the church, of a professional use of Scripture. The thesis of this chapter is that we who study Scripture in the classroom or quote Scripture to our congregations must consume, digest, and meditate on Scripture. The academic and professional uses of Scripture must never supplant its devotional use.

THE RELATIONSHIP BETWEEN DEVOTIONAL AND ACADEMIC USES OF SCRIPTURE

The separation between devotional and academic uses of Scripture has only become possible since the rise of a discipline called "biblical studies." Michael Legaspi chronicles how this discipline arose. He describes how Johann Michaelis, Old Testament professor at the University of Göttingen, reconceived the Old Testament as an anthology of documents from the ancient Near East. By his refusal to rely on the idea of God as the author of all Scripture, and his focus instead on the cultural continuities between the ancient Near East and parts of the Old Testament, Michaelis paved the way for the new discipline of biblical studies.[2]

I agree with what Legaspi is saying between the lines, which is that the displacement of Scripture for the academic Bible is a tragedy. The whole reason why the separate books of our Bibles were copied and included in the canon of Scripture is that they spoke to people's hearts and minds. It is therefore a breach from the Scriptures' foundational identity to treat them only as documentary artifacts of some cultures of the ancient Near East.

Now that we can recognize a difference between devotional and academic uses of Scripture, there are at least two ways of negotiating how we as believers relate to Scripture.

First, like the pastor mentioned above who took his devotional reading from portions of Scripture outside his sermon texts, one can view the two ways of reading Scripture as separate. This perspective can be seen when comparing the works of some who have filled dual roles of scholar and pastor. For example, in Anglican scholar J. B. Lightfoot's essay "St. Paul's Preparation for the Ministry," there is not a hint of how Paul's life can serve as spiritual motivation for people today. The author's interest is on understanding Paul in his historical context. But Lightfoot, while canon of St. Paul's Cathedral, preached there on the Feast of the Conversion of St. Paul in 1874, and one may note in his sermon

2. Legaspi, *Death of Scripture*, 79–153.

an entirely different use of Scripture: "S. Paul's life was the great example to all time of union with God in Christ. Such is his appeal to us to-day: 'I have striven to grow into Christ, to put on Christ, to live with Christ, to die with Christ. This was the one guiding principle of my life. Be ye followers of me.'"[3] It is not that Bishop Lightfoot saw an absolute disjunction between the use of the Bible in the two activities of lecturing to educate and preaching to edify. Indeed, his sermon shows the fruit of his careful academic study. But the texts of the two addresses show that he was not disposed to moralize while lecturing on Paul's relation to Roman society. Nor was he disposed to quote Cicero while preaching on Paul the example. Lightfoot maintained a distinction between the academic and devotional uses of Scripture.

A second approach is one that recognizes little or no difference between the academic and devotional uses of Scripture. Like my seminary professor described in the second scene above, this approach expects devotional warmth directly from cold, academic study. It would seem that nothing could be further from religious sentiment than the compilation of a dictionary. But at the end of his preface to a dictionary of Talmudic vocabulary, Marcus Jastrow writes, "The religious sentiments inspiring the author at the completion of his labors of five and twenty years are too sacred to be sent abroad beyond the sanctuary of heart and home."[4] So neither my seminary teacher nor Jastrow would want to draw a line between what is devotional and what is academic. For them, all study of Scripture can build up one's spiritual life.

This approach seems to have been the predominant way of viewing Scripture before changes in Scripture reading, related to church realignments in the sixteenth century, became permanently fixed in some sectors of the Christian family. Before the sixteenth century, no one seems to have distinguished between academic and devotional uses of Scripture. For example, after a philosophically profound exploration of the nature of time and detailed exegesis of Genesis 1, Augustine prays,

> But the seventh day has no evening and sinks toward no sunset, for you sanctified it that it might abide for ever. After completing your exceedingly good works you rested on the seventh day, though you achieved them in repose; and you willed your book to tell us this as a promise that when our works are finished (works exceedingly good inasmuch as they are your gift to us) we too may rest in you, in the Sabbath of eternal life.

3. Lightfoot, "S. Paul Our Example," 228.
4. Jastrow, *Dictionary of the Targumim*, xiii.

And then you will rest in us, as now you work in us, and your rest will be rest through us as now those works of yours are wrought through us. But you yourself, Lord, are ever working, ever resting. You neither see for a time nor change for a time nor enjoy repose for a time, yet you create our temporal seeing and time itself and our repose after time.[5]

At the end of a semester-long class on 1 Corinthians for undergraduates, one student wrote the following in a course evaluation: "As a biblical studies class, the course was great. However, in my personal journey interacting with the bible in such a systematic 'cut and dry' manner has killed my faith. It has turned the bible and God into a subject matter to be critiqued, at the expense of passion and vision. That is not this course's fault, but rather it is the idea of biblical studies in general that I am disenfranchised from."[6] Legaspi would knowingly nod in agreement with this student's comment. Biblical studies has a way of distancing the reader from the text. For those of us teaching the Bible as Scripture, we must find ways of allowing students to continue to engage with the text as Scripture. I now try to include opportunities for engaging with Scripture on different levels in my classes. Instead of offering only academically oriented assignments in class, I have also tried to offer such opportunities as hand writing and illustrating a chapter of a biblical book, so that the class as a whole produces its own manuscript of that book; writing on a favorite book in the Bible; and playing the "Reacting Game" in regard to a narrative in the Bible.

Our attitudes toward Scripture and even toward God can change when the academic study of Scripture includes elements of biblical criticism. Novels such as *In the Beginning* or *The Flight of Peter Fromm* explore the changes that academic study brings for an Orthodox Jew and a Pentecostal Christian, respectively.[7] We must always guard our hearts when studying Scripture, in order that we may closely follow the one who gives us the reason to study it.

Is there a priority between feeding the head and the heart? Which is more important? First Corinthians 8:2–3 and 13:2 rank love over knowledge. Romans 15:4 states in regard to Scripture, "Whatever was written in former days was written for our instruction, that by the steadfastness and encouragement of the writings we might have hope." It seems that if one must choose between the two, heart nourishment is the final goal of our biblical studies. In this regard,

---

5. Augustine, *Confessions* 13.36.51–13.37.52 (Boulding, 379).

6. Anonymous student evaluation of BIB375 First Corinthians at Bethel University, St. Paul, MN, spring 2010.

7. Potok, *In the Beginning*; Gardner, *Flight of Peter Fromm*.

Jonathan Edwards writes, "I should think myself in the way of my duty, to raise the affections of my hearers as high as I possibly can, provided they are affected with nothing but truth, and with affections that are not disagreeable to the nature of what they are affected with."[8]

So if we regard the Bible as Scripture for Christians, as inspired by God for the church to use, then how it speaks to the heart, leading to trust in God and growth in the virtues, is the most significant outcome for our Scripture-based discourse.

THE PROFESSIONAL USE OF SCRIPTURE

For those going into the priesthood or ministry, Scripture-based discourse becomes a professional obligation. You will probably identify key texts of Scripture to use when engaged in ministry—for example, in the sacrament of reconciliation, when giving a sermon on giving, or when visiting the sick. After several years of preparing and delivering homilies/sermons, you may have exegesis outlines of Scripture texts that worked especially well.

It can be very easy to shift into a professional gear when reading Scripture, then. You may be praying the daily office only because you are expected to do so. Instead, pray it as someone starving for food, or as a tired spelunker, desperate to see light.

You may be preparing for a sermon and realize that you can simply use an outline from two years ago. There is nothing wrong with doing so, but if such a sermon is primarily a recitation, you shortchange your flock. Scripture gives us the model of singing a new song to the Lord.[9] It is most honoring to God and most nourishing to our own souls if we can find something new and fresh to add when returning to a previously used outline.

The professional use of Scripture can become a trek through the desert if all we are doing is repeating the Scriptures that we are supposed to use in specific situations. We need to refill our water bottles at the oases of our own times of reading, praying, and meditating on Scripture.

HOW TO GAIN NOURISHMENT FROM SCRIPTURE

All the branches of the Christian family provide resources for the devotional use of Scripture. In what follows, I mention several.

8. Edwards, *Jonathan Edwards*, xxiii, quoted in Piper, "Biblical Exegesis," 2.
9. Jdt 16:1, 13; Pss 33:3; 40:3; 96:1; 98:1; 144:9; 149:1; Isa 42:10; Rev 5:9.

Read through the Bible

Luther used to read through the whole Bible on an annual basis. There are a number of plans for reading through the whole Bible in a year that allow one to read from different sections of it so as not to get bogged down in what might seem a strange and repetitive book of the Bible. A reading program, whether it extends through the whole Bible in a year or longer, is a good way to draw nourishment from Scripture.

Lectionary Readings

Those branches of the Christian family that use a lectionary have a built-in reading plan. It can be very helpful to read the Scripture readings for each day, or to spend the week reading and rereading the Scriptures for the upcoming Sunday.

Lectio Divina

A time-tested approach to Scripture that allows one to live it, enter into it, and be formed by it is called *lectio divina*. The value of *lectio divina* is that it helps us overcome the many strategies we have for avoiding Scripture's call to enter into God's world.[10]

Lectio divina involves slow, repeated readings of a text that are interspersed with time for meditation on what stands out in the text. It is often done with others. Someone reads the text aloud and then pauses to allow the text to sink in or let people voice words or phrases from the text that speak to them. Then the process is repeated. The process of *lectio divina* should include four components: *lectio* (reading), *meditatio* (meditation), *oratio* (prayer), and *contemplatio* (thoughtful enacting of the text). These four components do not need to be practiced in a set order. In fact, it is probably most helpful to loop back and return to one or another component while one is practicing all four.[11]

Meditatio is the component of *lectio divina* that draws us from merely looking at the words on the page to enter into the world of the text. The danger of reading is that the reader becomes too passive before a fixed and silent text. Peterson illustrates this well with the story of the god Thoth and the Egyptian king Thamus, found in Plato's *Phaedrus*. Thoth is proud of having invented a

---

10. Peterson, *Eat This Book*, 116–17.
11. Peterson, *Eat This Book*, 91.

script that now enabled people to write. King Thamus is not impressed, saying that it will cause people's memories to atrophy, and yield only the form of words without their full substance, which is actualized in spoken conversation.[12]

Meditatio also helps to keep us from compartmentalizing individual texts of Scripture. *Meditatio* helps us engage with Scripture in light of its whole context. Scripture interprets Scripture. For Christians, Scripture taken as a whole points to Jesus.[13] Luther helpfully states that the Bible "is the swaddling clothes and the manger in which Christ lies."[14]

Oratio is the component of *lectio divina* that happens when one recognizes that God is speaking and then responds prayerfully to God. The Psalms are the best part of the Bible for providing examples of hearing God speak and then responding back to God. The range of content and emotion in the Psalms, contained in a variety of genres (lament, thanksgiving, praise, enthronement, royal, and wisdom psalms), is an eloquent witness to the open protocol for prayer. We can pray back to God all our emotions and all thoughts, whether faith-filled or doubtful.[15]

Contemplatio is the component of *lectio divina* that means to live out the Scriptures in one's daily life. It is not limited only to those who have the time and social setting to live relatively quiet lives. It is an activity of *lectio divina* that all of us, even those who make the rush-hour commute into cities, can enact. Essentially, contemplation means that one practices behaviors that arise out of reading the Bible. Peterson distinguishes *contemplatio* from the other components, *lectio, meditatio,* and *oratio,* by describing *contemplatio* as the one component that simply happens without our intentionally practicing it or recognizing it as happening. He says that when we enter into the reading, meditation, and prayer, then the *contemplatio*—the lived contemplation—can happen.[16]

The Rosary

The Rosary is another form of prayer that can feed us from Scripture, since it is thoroughly grounded in the Gospels. One can pray the given mysteries for the day and then contemplate how to live them out, how to follow Jesus's example in them, for the rest of the day. The structure of the Rosary encourages me to

12. Peterson, *Eat This Book,* 98–99.
13. Peterson, *Eat This Book,* 100–102.
14. LW 35:236.
15. Peterson, *Eat This Book,* 103–5.
16. Peterson, *Eat This Book,* 109–16.

keep praying and not to worry about my mind wandering. It is structured in a way that is perfect for our distracted and multitasking age. One can pray it while thinking of Mary, of Jesus, of others who appear in each mystery, or of the people in our own lives for whom we are praying. And all the time we are following Scripture's record of key events in the lives of Jesus and Mary.

The Liturgy of the Hours

The speaker in Psalm 119 says he will praise God seven times in a day for God's law and describes meditating on God's law throughout the day, in the middle of the night, and very early in the morning.[17] Christian monasticism developed the Liturgy of the Hours as a way of following this pattern. Today, one can pray this liturgy, also called the Divine Office, with thousands around the world. It involves extensive prayer from the Psalms and can ground a person as one goes through the day.

COMPLEMENTARITY OF THE ACADEMIC AND DEVOTIONAL USES OF SCRIPTURE

The complementary nature of the academic and devotional approaches to Scripture can be seen in the narrative of the disciples on the road to Emmaus (Luke 24:13–35). Jesus first criticizes the depressed disciples he has joined by calling them "foolish." He addresses their foolishness by teaching information, modeling how to read their Scriptures in a Christocentric way. At the end of the episode, the disciples say that their hearts were burning while Jesus opened the Scriptures to them. This story illustrates how the academic or data-oriented approach to Scripture can complement the devotional appreciation of Scripture. Jesus was teaching them how to read Scripture Christocentrically, a somewhat academic, data-heavy approach. But at the end of the encounter that day, the disciples exclaimed how their hearts were burning during Jesus's presentation. In somewhat analogous ways, academic questions about Scripture that might initially seem boring, trivial, or dangerously skeptical can contribute to one's devotional appreciation of a text or one's spiritual growth. I'll give an example from both Old and New Testaments to illustrate.

Imagine that you are in a class on the Pentateuch. Your instructor is discussing the source criticism of the Pentateuch and considering the repeated stories of the matriarchs taken into a foreign king's harem (Gen 12:10–20;

17. Ps 119:62, 97, 147–48, 164.

20:1–18; 26:1–11). Your instructor, whether favorable or critical of the Documentary Hypothesis, notes that this hypothesis labels the accounts in chapters 12 and 26 as coming from the J source, and the account in chapter 20, with its vivid depiction of Abimelech's dream, as coming from the E source. You think about whether or not the narratives come from different sources, and this seems totally useless for your spiritual life or what you could use in a homily or sermon. But actually, discussion of the sources behind these three accounts at least shows that the author of Genesis was inspired to include all three narratives that have the same plot. The plot shows God caring for his chosen people when they are living outside the land or among foreigners within the land. In that sense the repeated plot is emphasizing how God defends his chosen people. Or perhaps you will even come to appreciate the depth of Scripture more when you understand the evidence for multiple human authors of the Pentateuch. As one book that advocates for the Documentary Hypothesis of the Pentateuch concludes, "For those who hold the Bible as sacred, it can mean new possibilities of interpretation; and it can mean a new awe before the great chain of events, persons, and centuries that came together so intricately to produce an incomparable book of teachings."[18]

Suppose you are in an Introduction to the New Testament class, or a class on the Gospels. Your instructor is talking about redaction criticism and points out how the arrest scene in John's Gospel depicts Jesus as orchestrating his own arrest and follows a narrative in which Jesus does not pray to escape from the cup (of death) awaiting him (John 18:1–11; cf. Matt 26:36–56; Mark 14:32–50; Luke 22:39–54). The difference between John and the Synoptic Gospels here makes you uneasy. You wonder if your instructor is trying to discredit the truth of Scripture, and this is yet one more complaint you plan to add to your assessment of the instructor and the class. But actually, the difference between John and the Synoptic Gospels here points to the challenge of writing about Jesus's human life on earth. The Synoptic Gospels are depicting how any mortal would respond when confronted with an impending death. The Gospel of John emphasizes Jesus's divine, all-knowing character (John 18:4). As you think about Jesus's human and divine natures and the difference between the Gethsemane scenes in the four Gospels, you realize that a similar divergence in description could characterize your life as a believer. You are afraid of setbacks in your life and of death itself. Yet as a disciple of Jesus, you also know that God is with you and that God's Spirit empowers you. You begin to pray that your fear and requests to escape setbacks in life would decrease and that your trust and reliance on God's Spirit to fill you would increase. You look forward

18. Friedman, *Who Wrote the Bible?*, 245.

to times when you can share with others how God's knowledge of the future, emphasized in the way John depicts Jesus, is a real source of peace and strength for our lives (John 6:6; 13:1, 3; 18:4).

People in the natural sciences speak of doing "pure research," research into an area in which they see absolutely no application to real life. Yet often such "pure research" will turn out later to be very applicable to people's daily lives. For example, breakthroughs in pure mathematics turn out to be very useful for physics and end up in seemingly miraculous ways to corroborate exactly what later research will inductively demonstrate.[19] While G. H. Hardy labeled pure math as useless and applied math as boring, times have changed, and the number theory resulting from what Hardy considered to be pure math has been proven useful in encoding and thus protecting transmitted data.[20]

In an analogous way, the academic study of Scripture can lead to insights that strengthen one's spiritual life. Once I was looking up a verb I had encountered while reading Genesis 18 in Hebrew, as I prepared for a Hebrew proficiency test. The entry for עָמַד (*amad*) in the Brown-Driver-Briggs lexicon notes that the verb, "stand," implies persistence. Since I was looking up this verb while reading Genesis 18:22, the account of Abraham's plea for God not to destroy Sodom, the lexicon's entry helped me see how the text was emphasizing Abraham's persistence in prayer. The lexicon's definition helped me understand prayer in a new way, since it showed me how the text portrays Abraham as refusing to leave and instead continuing to stand in God's presence.

One value of learning the languages from the Bible's world is that we realize how ordinary the Bible's language is. Eugene Peterson makes this point when he says that the discoveries of the letters at Ugarit showed us how enmeshed the Israelites were in a common Semitic culture, while their faith was radically different. And the discoveries of Greek papyri in Egypt show us that the New Testament was written in the very ordinary language of daily life in the Hellenistic world. The incarnation, God's entrance into the human world, echoes even in the language of the New Testament.[21]

Learning how to recognize aorist verbs in the Greek New Testament seems boringly and quintessentially academic. But the day will come when you will realize that a verb is aorist and not imperfect, and in its context, that will be spiritually significant—for example, "the kingdom of God has come upon you" (Luke 11:20).

---

19. Wigner, "Unreasonable Effectiveness."
20. Hardy, *Mathematician's Apology*, 32–33; Dudek, "Your Number's Up."
21. Peterson, *Eat This Book*, 151–56.

Feed Yourself First

God sent Elijah to a widow in Sidon—that is, Phoenicia. When he got to the widow's home, he learned that her resources were almost completely depleted and found her in the process of preparing a last meal for herself and her son. Elijah then directed the widow in what might seem a very selfish way. He told her to make for him a cake from the last flour she had, and then to prepare something for herself and her son (1 Kgs 17:8–16).

We may draw an allegorical lesson from this: the prophet needs to be fed first. Before we can minister to others, we need to be fed. Before speaking God's word to others, we need to feed on God's word for ourselves. A metaphor from our own day may also be useful here. Think of an airplane that has lost cabin pressure in midflight. One needs first to place the oxygen mask over one's own mouth and nose before helping others access the oxygen.

Yes, it can be easy to get turned off to the Bible during seminary because of the dry way it can be treated—as a textbook to be analyzed. But the Bible does feed the heart. It speaks to humanity's questions regarding ultimate meaning, the nature of human companionship, and humanity's relationship with the transcendent. Whatever you need to do to remember that the Bible does speak to these heart questions of humanity is worth doing. Ask yourself how Scripture responds to questions regarding the brevity and meaning of our lives on earth. Read and reread those sections of Scripture that point your attention toward a holy and transcendent God.

I cannot give an exact formula of how to balance the academic and professional uses of Scripture with the devotional use. There is no single blend of cognitive facts and heartwarming truths that will fit every believer. Since each person's spirituality is different, people will be edified in different ways. People have different saturation points for knowledge qua knowledge and exhortation of a devotional sort. Because of this difference among people, we must beware of imposing our own balance of devotional and academic readings of Scripture on others.

Scripture might begin to dry up for us while in school or in ministry if all we do is use it to fulfill class requirements or our obligations to parishioners. We must draw from Scripture our own spiritual nourishment if we are to continue to fulfill our calling of bringing God's word to others.

CONCLUSION

I will spread out before you the meadows of Holy Scripture, so that, your heart no more a prisoner, you may begin to run along the road of my commandments. Then you will say, I do not count these present sufferings as the measure of that glory which is to be revealed in us.

—THOMAS À KEMPIS[1]

Of the five models presented in this book, the prayers model is the one model necessary for believers who regard the Christian canon as their Scripture. If you began studying Scripture or theology because you wanted to learn more of Scripture, or learn more about God through Scripture, the prayers model is the one model you cannot abandon. Even in the middle of a busy semester, when you are working on papers that treat biblical texts as documents or narratives, pray at least one psalm a day and try to pray through even the texts on which you are writing academic papers or preparing homilies. But even the person who reads Scripture mostly as prayers will need the stories model, whether applied when identifying discrete stories within Scripture or to construct a metanarrative that encompasses Old and New Testaments, to provide orientation and significance for the use of Scripture as a thesaurus of prayer. The oracles and laws models will also frequently accompany the prayers model. For the person praying with Scripture will look at some texts within Scripture as oracular words that speak into her or his own situation, and adopt some of its ethical messages for her or his own life.

So no single model of those surveyed here—documents, stories, prayers, laws, oracles—is sufficient by itself to bring the riches of Scripture to a believer. To relish the feast that is Scripture, we need to use multiple models.

There are academics who attempt to treat Scripture only as documents. They recognize that parts of Scripture functioned and continue to function as stories, prayers, laws, and oracles for others, but they study these only as artifacts of others' lives. This is a dry enterprise driven by assump-

1. *Imitation of Christ* 3.51.2, citing Rom 8:18 (Knox and Oakley, 197).

tions about Scripture that sabotage its significance. Not all of the individual language games and constructs offered by various academic approaches to Scripture enable people's engagement with the transcendent when reading the Bible.

The historical-critical method is a necessary approach to Scripture. It is most readily applied within the documents, laws, and stories models. The method is necessary to satisfy questions that modernity has planted within us, such as "Did this really happen?" or "How does the archaeological record compare with the story of Jericho's fall?" It is also useful in helping us understand that the text of Scripture was not written in the first place for us. This deepens our engagement with Scripture, for it helps us see that our questions are not the only questions that the text raises. The authors and first audiences of our Scriptures in many cases had questions that drove their participation in the text that are much different from our questions. For example, you may read the Gospel of John with the question "How can I be a Christian?" or "How can I be a good disciple of Jesus?" in mind. But the author and early readers of John might well have been asking questions like "What does it mean to believe Jesus?" or "Why isn't it enough for me to fulfill Mosaic law?" The historical-critical method can help us get past our own questions and recognize others' questions. The more questions that we see are related to the text, the deeper our engagement with the text. But as a method, it is insufficient by itself to satisfy any reader who understands the biblical canon to be authoritative Scripture.

How to Navigate Differences in Understanding Scripture

My Jewish friend is not bothered when he reads Paul's quotations of the Old Testament within his argument that Christ is the foundation stone (Rom 9:33) or that the church experienced the same divine food and drink as the Israelites in the exodus generation received (1 Cor 10:1–4). What bothers him is when people write about these texts as though they represent the only way to read the Old Testament text. He has helped me realize that if I want others to respect how I read Scripture, I need to respect how they read Scripture. So even though I am more ready to accept a messianic reading of Isaiah 8:14 and 28:16, the texts Paul combines in Romans 9:33, I need to fully respect my friend's reading of these texts in Isaiah as referring only to God's plans for postexilic Judah.

This has helped me think about how to navigate other differences that we readily encounter when reading Scripture with others. In all these areas, exegetical argument will rarely persuade someone to change their mind. What matters is listening for understanding and then presenting one's own position as clearly as possible.

I hope that this book will help you do that. I have no doubt disappointed some of my readers by not presenting their positions as fully as they would like. But I hope you come away from this book with a deepened understanding that Christians who read Scripture differently than you do have definite precedents and reasons for why they read Scripture as they do. In most cases, they also regard Scripture as seriously as you do.

Yes, it can be a pleasurable experience to hit someone over the head with Scripture texts, to prove they are wrong. But this is not the best way to build up the body of Christ. When discussing Scripture with someone who has a different theological framework, it is best to listen and seek to understand how that person's framework makes sense of their lives and of Scripture. After you have heard the person out, you might try to summarize their view while asking if your summary is fair to their theological framework. Only after receiving their approval that you have summarized their view correctly would it be useful to ask about inconsistencies or missteps you see in their exegesis or theological framework.

A Mansion and a Feast

At the beginning of this book, I mentioned how the church fathers can picture Scripture as a many-roomed mansion or as an abundant feast. There is more to Origen's picture of Scripture as a many-roomed mansion. The doors of its many rooms were closed, with keys in all the locks. But in Origen's description, the keys had been moved from the doors to which they originally belonged.[2] So the exegete has to find the right key for a given door, before that door can be opened. The metaphor is significant for the way it communicates that Scripture has much to offer, with many rooms. This plenitude is accompanied by variety, for the doors have different locks, requiring different keys. In this metaphor, a sense of mystery is communicated as well. Some meanings require keys to unlock. This idea that Scripture has mysterious or hidden meanings is different from what some sixteenth-century interpreters taught about the clarity or perspicuity of Scripture.

The metaphor of the feast similarly emphasizes the idea of abundance, that Scripture has much to offer. Because a feast is an abundance of food, this metaphor includes the idea of sustenance, that Scripture provides what people need

2. Origen, *Philocalia* 2.3 (Lewis, 32).

to live.[3] This reminds us of the text Jesus quotes when tempted, "One does not live by bread alone, but by every word that comes out of God's mouth" (Matt 4:4, quoting Deut 8:3). A feast also includes the idea of pleasure; people get delight from eating from a lavish spread of food. This communicates the idea that hearing or reading Scripture brings delight, a common expression in some of the psalms (19:9b–10; 119:16, 103) and in Jeremiah 15:16. A feast is usually also a community affair. The master of the great banquet in Jesus's parable, for example, wants the banquet hall filled with people (Matt 22:9–10, intensified in Luke 14:21–23). This points to the truth that hearing and reading Scripture is a community matter. Scripture has been read in community for centuries. I hope that this book can contribute to motivating people to read Scripture more communally with others. Dangerous things happen when a person is allowed to read and interpret Scripture all by himself.[4] Paul says that within a church service, a prophet needs to give way if someone else has a revelation (1 Cor 14:29–30).

Both of these metaphors are open-ended. The mansion with many rooms cannot be explored in several visits; it must be repeatedly visited or lived in, in order to find entry into all the rooms. The feast cannot be fully enjoyed at one meal. As one can enjoy and benefit from meals each day, so each interaction with Scripture can bring delightful, new sustenance. Scripture cannot be fully experienced or mastered with limited exposure to it. You have not mastered or fully tapped into Scripture by completing the required Scripture classes that cover the Old and New Testaments. Nor will you master or fully understand Scripture after preaching through every cycle of the lectionary. There will always be more truths to discover and more ways to savor and take nourishment from Scripture.

---

3. For Scripture as food, see Origen, *Philocalia* 12.2; 15.9–10 (Lewis, 56, 69–70). For Scripture as a feast or banquet, see Gregory the Great, *Moralia in Job* 1.21.29 (Bliss and Marriott, 47).

4. Consider John of Leiden (Münster, 1534–1536), Jim Jones (Jonestown, 1974–1978), and David Koresh (Waco, 1983–1993).

BIBLIOGRAPHY

Catholic Documents

Constitutions and Declaration of Church Councils

Dei Filius (1870). Excerpts in Béchard, *Scripture Documents*, 14–18.
Dei Verbum (1965). In Béchard, *Scripture Documents*, 19–31.
Nostra Aetate (1965). In *The Documents of Vatican II*, edited by Walter M. Abbott, SJ, 660–68. New York: Guild Press, 1966.

Papal Encyclicals, Apostolic Exhortations, and Addresses

Benedict XVI. *Verbum Domini* (2010). http://www.vatican.va/content/benedict
-xvi/enapost_exhortations/documents/hf_ben-xvi_exh_20100930_verbum
-domini.html.
Francis. *Laudato Si'* (2015). http://www.vatican.va/content/francesco/en/encyclicals
/documents/papa-francesco_20150524_enciclica-laudato-si.html.
John Paul II. "Address on *The Interpretation of the Bible in the Church*" (1993). In Béchard, *Scripture Documents*, 170–80.
———. *Evangelium vitae* (1995). http://www.vatican.va/content/john-paul-ii/en
/encyclicals/documents/hf_jp-ii_enc_25031995_evangelium-vitae.html.
Leo XIII. *Providentissimus Deus* (1893). In Béchard, *Scripture Documents*, 37–61.
Pius XII. *Divino afflante Spiritu* (1943). In Béchard, *Scripture Documents*, 115–39.

Statements of the Pontifical Biblical Commission

Instruction on the Historical Truth of the Gospels (1964; also called *Sancta Mater Ecclesia*). In Béchard, *Scripture Documents*, 227–35.
The Interpretation of the Bible in the Church (1993). In Béchard, *Scripture Documents*, 244–317.
The Jewish People and Their Sacred Scriptures in the Christian Bible (2002). https://
www.vatican.va/roman_curia/congregations/cfaith/pcb_documents/rc
_con_cfaith_doc_20020212_popolo-ebraico_en.html.

Miscellaneous Catholic Documents

Augustine, Saint. *The Rule of Saint Augustine*. Edited by Tarsicius J. Van Bavel, OSA. Translated by Raymond Canning, OSA. Garden City, NY: Image, 1986.

Benedict, Saint. *The Rule of Saint Benedict*. Edited by Timothy Fry, OSB. Vintage Spiritual Classics. New York: Vintage, 1998.

Catechism of the Catholic Church. New York: Doubleday, 1995.

General Instruction of the Roman Missal. Washington, DC: United States Conference of Catholic Bishops, 2011.

Towards a Common Understanding of the Church: Reformed/Roman Catholic International Dialogue: Second Phase (1984–1990). http://www.vatican.va/roman_curia/pontifical_councils/chrstuni/alliance-reform-docs/rc_pc_chrstuni_doc_19900101_second-phase-dialogue_en.html.

PROTESTANT CREEDS AND STATEMENT

Schaff, Philip, ed. *The Creeds of Christendom: With a History and Critical Notes*. Vol. 3, *The Evangelical Protestant Creeds*. Revised by David S. Schaff. 1877. Reprint, Grand Rapids: Baker, 2007.

Chicago Statement on Biblical Inerrancy. October 1978. https://library.dts.edu/Pages/TL/Special/ICBI_1.pdf.

JEWISH PRAYERBOOK

Davis, Avrohom, ed. *The Metsudah Siddur*. Brooklyn, NY: Metsudah, 1982.

ANCIENT, PATRISTIC, AND LATE ANTIQUE AUTHORS

Athanasius. "From Letter XXXIX." In *Athanasius: Select Works and Letters*, edited by Archibald Robertson, vol. 4 of *The Nicene and Post-Nicene Fathers*, Series 2, 551–52. 1892. Reprint, Peabody, MA: Hendrickson, 1994.

———. *The Life of Antony and the Letter to Marcellinus*. Translated by R. C. Gregg. New York: Paulist, 1980.

Augustine. *Confessions*. Translated by Henry Chadwick. New York: Oxford University Press, 1991.

———. *The Confessions*. Translated by Maria Boulding, OSB. WSA I/1. Hyde Park, NY: New City, 1997.

———. *On Christian Teaching*. Translated by R. P. H. Green. New York: Oxford University Press, 1999.

————. *Questions on the Gospels.* In *New Testament I and II*, edited by Boniface Ramsey, translated by Kim Paffenroth. WSA I/15–16. New York: New City, 2014.

————. *Rule.* https://opeast.org/about/our-order/rule-st-augustine/. Adapted from George Lawless, *Augustine of Hippo and His Monastic Rule.* Oxford: Clarendon Press, 1987.

Eusebius. *Ecclesiastical History*, vol. 1. Translated by Kirsopp Lake. Loeb Classical Library. Cambridge, MA: Harvard University Press, 1926.

Gregory the Great. *Moralia in Job.* Translated by James Bliss and Charles Marriott. Library of the Fathers of the Holy Catholic Church Anterior to the Division of the East and West. Oxford: John Henry Parker, 1844.

Holmes, Michael W., ed. and trans. *The Apostolic Fathers: Greek Texts and English Translations.* 3rd ed. Grand Rapids: Baker Academic, 2007.

Origen. *Commentary on the Gospel of John, Books 1–10.* Translated by Ronald E. Heine. FC. Washington, DC: Catholic University of America Press, 1989.

————. *Commentary on the Gospel of John, Books 13–32.* Translated by Ronald E. Heine. FC. Washington, DC: Catholic University of America Press, 1993.

————. *On First Principles.* Translated by G. W. Butterworth. 1936. Reprint, Notre Dame, IN: Christian Classics, 2013.

————. *Origenes Werke VII: Homiliae zum Hexateuch in Rufins Übersetzung.* Edited by W. A. Baehrens. Greichischen Christliche Schriftsteller 30. Leipzig: Hinrichs, 1921.

————. *The Philocalia of Origen: A Compilation of Selected Passages from Origen's Works Made by St. Gregory of Nazianzus and St. Basil of Caesarea.* Translated by George Lewis. Edinburgh: T. & T. Clark, 1911.

Tyconius. *The Book of Rules.* Translated by William S. Babcock. Society of Biblical Literature Texts and Translations 31. Atlanta: Scholars, 1989.

Ward, Benedicta, trans. *The Sayings of the Desert Fathers: The Alphabetical Collection.* Rev. ed. Cistercian Studies 59. Kalamazoo, MI: Cistercian Publications, 1984.

GENERAL BIBLIOGRAPHY

Books

Alter, Robert. *The Art of Biblical Narrative.* New York: Basic Books, 1981.

————. *The Book of Psalms: A Translation with Commentary.* New York: Norton, 2007.

————. *Genesis: Translation and Commentary.* New York: Norton, 1996.

Aquinas, Thomas. *Summa Theologiae: Latin Text and English Translation, Introductions, Notes, Appendices, and Glossaries*. 61 vols. Cambridge: Blackfriars; New York: McGraw-Hill, 1964–1981.

Bainton, Roland H. *Here I Stand: A Life of Martin Luther*. New York: Mentor Books, 1950.

Balthasar, Hans Urs von. *Cosmic Liturgy: The Universe According to Maximus the Confessor*. Translated by Brian E. Daley, SJ. San Francisco: Ignatius, 2003.

Barrett, Matthew, ed. *Reformation Theology: A Systematic Summary*. Wheaton: Crossway, 2017.

Barth, Karl. *Homiletics*. Translated by G. W. Bromiley and D. E. Daniels. Louisville: Westminster John Knox, 1991.

———. *The Word of God and the Word of Man*. Translated and edited by Douglas Horton. Gloucester, MA: Peter Smith, 1978.

Bauckham, Richard. *The Bible and Ecology: Rediscovering the Community of Creation*. Waco: Baylor University Press, 2010.

———. *Jesus and the Eyewitnesses: The Gospels as Eyewitness Testimony*. Grand Rapids: Eerdmans, 2006.

Béchard, Dean P., SJ, ed. and trans. *The Scripture Documents: An Anthology of Official Catholic Teachings*. Collegeville, MN: Liturgical Press, 2002.

Behr, John. *John the Theologian and His Paschal Gospel: A Prologue to Theology*. Oxford: Oxford University Press, 2019.

———. *The Mystery of Christ: Life in Death*. Crestwood, NY: St. Vladimir's Seminary Press, 2006.

Bergsma, John. *Bible Basics for Catholics: A New Picture of Salvation History*. Notre Dame, IN: Ave Maria, 2012.

Berkhof, Louis. *Systematic Theology*. Grand Rapids: Eerdmans, 1941.

Berrin, Shani L. *The Pesher Nahum Scroll from Qumran: An Exegetical Study of 4Q169*. Boston: Brill, 2004.

Billings, J. Todd. *The Word of God for the People of God: An Entryway to the Theological Interpretation of Scripture*. Grand Rapids: Eerdmans, 2010.

Bobertz, Charles A. *The Gospel of Mark: A Liturgical Commentary*. Grand Rapids: Baker Academic, 2016.

Bonz, Marianne Palmer. *The Past as Legacy: Luke-Acts and Ancient Epic*. Minneapolis: Fortress, 2000.

Boulnois, Olivier. *Être et representation: Une généalogie de la métaphysique moderne à l'époque de Duns Scot (XIIIe–XIVe siècle)*. Paris: Presses Universitaires de France, 1999.

Bradshaw, Paul F. *Daily Prayer in the Early Church: A Study of the Origin and Early Development of the Divine Office*. 1981. Reprint, Eugene: Wipf & Stock, 2008.

Breck, John. *The Power of the Word in the Worshiping Church*. Crestwood, NY: St. Vladimir's Seminary Press, 1986.

———. *Scripture in Tradition: The Bible and Its Interpretation in the Orthodox Church*. Crestwood, NY: St. Vladimir's Seminary Press, 2001.

Brown, Peter. *Augustine of Hippo*. Berkeley: University of California Press, 2000.

Brown, Raymond E., S. S. *The Birth of the Messiah: A Commentary on the Infancy Narratives in the Gospels of Matthew and Luke*. New York: Doubleday, 1993.

———. *The Community of the Beloved Disciple: The Life, Loves, and Hates of an Individual Church in New Testament Times*. New York: Paulist, 1979.

Brown, Robert McAfee. *Unexpected News: Reading the Bible with Third World Eyes*. Philadelphia: Westminster, 1984.

Bruce, F. F. *The New Testament Documents: Are They Reliable?* 6th ed. Grand Rapids: Eerdmans, 1981.

Brueggemann, Walter. *The Message of the Psalms: A Theological Commentary*. Augsburg Old Testament Studies. Minneapolis: Augsburg, 1984.

Bullinger, E. W. *The Companion Bible*. 1922. Reprint, Grand Rapids: Kregel, 1999.

Bullinger, Henry. *The Decades of Henry Bullinger, Minister of the Church of Zurich*. Edited by Thomas Harding. Translated by H. I. Parker Society for the Publication of the Works of the Fathers and Early Writers of the Reformed English Church. 1587. Reprint, Cambridge: Cambridge University Press, 1849.

———. *Sermonum Decades quinque, de potissimis Christianae religionis capitibus*. Zurich: Froschoveri, 1557.

Bultmann, Rudolf. *Jesus and the Word*. Translated by Louise Pettibone Smith and Erminie Huntress Lantero. New York: Scribner, 1958.

Byassee, Jason. *Praise Seeking Understanding: Reading the Psalms with Augustine*. Grand Rapids: Eerdmans, 2007.

Callahan, Allen Dwight. *Embassy of Onesimus: The Letter of Paul to Philemon*. New Testament in Context. Harrisburg, PA: Trinity Press International, 1997.

Calvin, John. *Commentary on the Book of Psalms*. 5 vols. Translated by James Anderson. Edinburgh: Calvin Translation Society, 1845–49.

———. *Institutes of the Christian Religion*. 2 vols. Edited by John T. McNeill. Translated by Ford Lewis Battles. LCC 20–21. Philadelphia: Westminster, 1960.

———. *Selected Works of John Calvin*. 7 vols. Edited by Henry Beveridge and Jules Bonnet. Grand Rapids: Baker, 1983.

Cameron, Michael. *Christ Meets Me Everywhere: Augustine's Early Figurative Exegesis*. OSHTh. New York: Oxford University Press, 2012.

Carter, Thomas. *Shakespeare and Holy Scripture, with the Version He Used*. London, 1905.

Casey, Michael. *Sacred Reading: The Ancient Art of Lectio Divina*. Liguori, MO: Triumph, 1995.

Chesebrough, David B., ed. *"God Ordained This War": Sermons on the Sectional Crisis, 1830–1865*. Columbia: University of South Carolina Press, 1991.

———, ed. *"No Sorrow like Our Sorrow": Northern Protestant Ministers and the Assassination of Lincoln*. Kent, OH: Kent State University Press, 1994.

Childs, Brevard S. *Myth and Reality in the Old Testament*. Studies in Biblical Theology 27. London: SCM, 1960.

Clendenin, Daniel B., ed. *Eastern Orthodox Theology: A Contemporary Reader*. 2nd ed. Grand Rapids: Baker Academic, 2003.

Coleman, Lyman, ed. *The Serendipity Bible*. Grand Rapids: Zondervan, 1988.

Collins, John J. *A Short Introduction to the Hebrew Bible and Deuterocanonical Books*. 2nd ed. Minneapolis: Fortress, 2014.

Cone, James H. *A Black Theology of Liberation*. 1970. Reprint, Maryknoll, NY: Orbis, 2010.

Copeland, Kenneth. *The Blessing of the Lord Makes Rich and He Adds No Sorrow with It*. Fort Worth: Kenneth Copeland, 2011.

Cosgrove, Charles H. *Elusive Israel: The Puzzle of Election in Romans*. Louisville: Westminster John Knox, 1997.

Crouzel, Henri, SJ. *Origen*. Translated by A. S. Worrall. San Francisco: Harper & Row, 1989.

Daniélou, Jean, SJ. *The Bible and the Liturgy*. 1956. Reprint, Notre Dame, IN: University of Notre Dame Press, 2014.

———. *From Shadows to Reality: Studies in the Biblical Typology of the Fathers*. Translated by Walston Hibberd. Westminster, MD: Newman Press, 1960.

Dodd, C. H. *The Bible Today*. Cambridge: Cambridge University Press, 1962.

Dunn, J. D. G. *Christianity in the Making*. Vol. 1, *Jesus Remembered*. Grand Rapids: Eerdmans, 2003.

———. *Romans 1–8*. Word Biblical Commentary 38A. Dallas: Word, 1988.

Edwards, Jonathan. *Jonathan Edwards: Representative Selections, with Introduction, Bibliography, and Notes*. Edited by C. H. Faust and T. H. Johnson. New York: Hill and Wang, 1962.

Ehrman, Bart D. *The New Testament: A Historical Introduction to the Early Christian Writings*. 4th ed. New York: Oxford University Press, 2008.

Enns, Peter. *The Bible Tells Me So: Why Defending Scripture Has Made Us Unable to Read It*. San Francisco: HarperOne, 2014.

———. *Inspiration and Incarnation: Evangelicals and the Problem of the Old Testament*. 2nd ed. Grand Rapids: Baker Academic, 2015.

Erasmus, Desiderius, and Martin Luther. *Discourse on Free Will*. Translated by Ernst Winter. New York: Ungar, 1961.

Ericksen, Robert P. *Theologians under Hitler: Gerhard Kittel, Paul Althaus, and Emanuel Hirsch*. New Haven: Yale University Press, 1985.

Farkasfalvy, Denis, O. Cist. *A Theology of the Christian Bible: Revelation, Inspiration, Canon*. Washington, DC: Catholic University of America Press, 2018.

Fitzmyer, Joseph A., SJ. *The Gospel According to Luke I–IX*. AB 28. Garden City, NY: Doubleday, 1981.

———. *The Gospel According to Luke X–XXIV*. AB 28A. Garden City, NY: Doubleday, 1985.

Florovsky, Georges. *The Eastern Fathers of the Fourth Century*. Translated by Catherine Edmunds. Vaduz: Büchervertriebsanstalt, 1987.

Fox, Everett. *The Five Books of Moses: A New Translation with Introductions, Commentary, and Notes*. New York: Schocken Books, 1995.

Frei, Hans W. *The Eclipse of Biblical Narrative: A Study in Eighteenth and Nineteenth Century Hermeneutics*. New Haven: Yale University Press, 1974.

Friedman, Richard Elliott. *Who Wrote the Bible?* San Francisco: HarperSanFrancisco, 1997.

Frye, Northrup. *The Great Code: The Bible and Literature*. New York: Harcourt Brace Jovanovich, 1982.

Gager, John G., ed. *Curse Tablets and Binding Spells from the Ancient World*. New York: Oxford University Press, 1992.

Gardner, Martin. *The Flight of Peter Fromm*. Los Altos, CA: Kaufmann, 1973.

Goldingay, John. *Models for Interpretation of Scripture*. Grand Rapids: Eerdmans, 1995.

———. *Models for Scripture*. Grand Rapids: Eerdmans, 1994.

Grant, Robert M., and David Tracy. *A Short History of the Interpretation of the Bible*. Philadelphia: Fortress, 1984.

Greenberg, Moshe. *Biblical Prose Prayer as a Window to the Popular Religion of Ancient Israel*. Berkeley: University of California Press, 1980.

Grudem, Wayne A. *Systematic Theology: An Introduction to Biblical Doctrine*. Grand Rapids: Zondervan, 1994.

Guilding, Aileen. *The Fourth Gospel and Jewish Worship: A Study of the Relation of St. John's Gospel to the Ancient Jewish Lectionary System*. Oxford: Clarendon, 1960.

Gundry, Robert H. *Matthew: A Commentary on His Literary and Theological Art*. Grand Rapids: Eerdmans, 1982.

Gutiérrez González, Juan. *The New Libertarian Gospel: Pitfalls of the Theology of Liberation*. Translated by Paul Burns. Chicago: Franciscan Herald Press, 1977.

Habel, Norman C., ed. *The Earth Story in the Psalms and the Prophets*. EB 4. Sheffield: Sheffield Academic, 2001.

———, ed. *Readings from the Perspective of Earth*. EB 1. Sheffield: Sheffield Academic, 2000.

Habel, Norman C., and Vicky Balabanski, eds. *The Earth Story in the New Testament*. EB 5. Sheffield: Sheffield Academic, 2002.

Habel, Norman C., and Shirley Wurst, eds. *The Earth Story in Genesis*. EB 2. Sheffield: Sheffield Academic, 2000.

———, eds. *The Earth Story in Wisdom Traditions*. EB 3. Sheffield: Sheffield Academic, 2001.

Hahn, Scott W. *Kinship by Covenant: A Canonical Approach to the Fulfillment of God's Saving Promises*. Anchor Yale Bible Reference Library. New Haven: Yale University Press, 2009.

Hardy, G. H. *A Mathematician's Apology*. Cambridge: Cambridge University Press, 1940.

Hatch, Nathan O., and Mark A. Noll, eds. *The Bible in America: Essays in Cultural History*. New York: Oxford University Press, 1982.

Hays, Richard B. *The Faith of Jesus Christ: The Narrative Substructure of Galatians 3:1–4:11*. 2nd ed. Grand Rapids: Eerdmans, 2002.

Hirsch, E. D., Jr. *Validity in Interpretation*. New Haven: Yale University Press, 1967.

Hirsch, Emanuel. *Das kirchliche Wollen der Deutschen Christen*. Berlin-Charlottenburg: Grevenmeyer, 1933.

Horrell, David G. *The Bible and the Environment: Towards a Critical Ecological Biblical Theology*. Durham: Acumen, 2010.

Horrell, David G., Cherryl Hunt, and Christopher Southgate. *Greening Paul: Rereading the Apostle in a Time of Ecological Crisis*. Waco: Baylor University Press, 2010.

Ingham, Mary Beth, and Mechthild Dreyer. *The Philosophical Vision of John Duns Scotus*. Washington, DC: Catholic University of America Press, 2004.

Jacobs, A. J. *The Year of Living Biblically: One Man's Humble Quest to Follow the Bible as Literally as Possible*. New York: Simon & Schuster, 2008.

Janzen, J. Gerald. *At the Scent of Water: The Ground of Hope in the Book of Job*. Grand Rapids: Eerdmans, 2009.

———. *When Prayer Takes Place: Forays into a Biblical World*. Eugene: Cascade, 2012.

Jastrow, Marcus. *A Dictionary of the Targumim, the Talmud Babli and Yerushalmi, and the Midrashic Literature*. New York: Judaica, 1982.

Jenson, Robert W. *Lutheran Slogans: Use and Abuse*. Delphi, NY: American Lutheran Publicity Bureau Books, 2011.

———. *Systematic Theology*. Vol. 2, *The Works of God*. New York: Oxford University Press, 1999.

Kaminsky, Joel S. *Yet I Loved Jacob: Reclaiming the Biblical Concept of Election*. 2007. Reprint, Eugene: Wipf & Stock, 2016.

Kelhoffer, James A. *Miracle and Mission: The Authentication of Missionaries and Their Message in the Longer Ending of Mark*. Wissenschaftliche Untersuchungen zum Neuen Testament 2.112. Tübingen: Mohr Siebeck, 2000.

Kenyon, Frederic. *The Bible and Archaeology*. New York: Harper & Brothers, 1940.

Kingdon, Robert M., Thomas A. Lambert, and Isabella M. Watt, eds. *The Registers of the Consistory of Geneva at the Time of Calvin*. Vol. 1, *1542–1544*. Translated by M. Wallace McDonald. Grand Rapids: Eerdmans, 2000.

Kittelson, James M. *Luther the Reformer: The Story of the Man and His Career*. Minneapolis: Fortress, 2003.

Knox, John. *Chapters in a Life of Paul*. Rev. ed. Macon, GA: Mercer University Press, 1987.

———. *Philemon among the Letters of Paul: A New View of Its Place and Importance*. Chicago: University of Chicago Press, 1935.

Küster, Volker. *A Protestant Theology of Passion: Korean Minjung Theology Revisited*. Studies in Systematic Theology 4. Boston: Brill, 2010.

Kugel, James. *The God of Old: Inside the Lost World of the Bible*. New York: Free Press, 2003.

———. *In Potiphar's House: The Interpretive Life of Biblical Texts*. Cambridge, MA: Harvard University Press, 1994.

Kuula, Kari. *The Law, the Covenant and God's Plan*. Vol. 2, *Paul's Treatment of the Law and Israel in Romans*. Publications of the Finnish Exegetical Society 85. Helsinki: Finnish Exegetical Society; Göttingen: Vandenhoeck & Ruprecht, 2003.

Kwon, Jin-Kwan. *Theology of Subjects: Towards a New Minjung Theology*. Tainan: PTCA, 2011.

Legaspi, Michael C. *The Death of Scripture and the Rise of Biblical Studies*. OSHTh. New York: Oxford University Press, 2010.

L'Engle, Madeleine. *A Stone for a Pillow: Journeys with Jacob*. Carmel, NY: Guideposts, 1986.

Lessing, Gotthold. *Lessing's Theological Writings*. Edited and translated by Henry Chadwick. Stanford, CA: Stanford University Press, 1956.

Levenson, Jon D. *Creation and the Persistence of Evil: The Jewish Drama of Divine Omnipotence*. 1988. Reprint, Princeton: Princeton University Press, 1994.

———. *The Hebrew Bible, the Old Testament, and Historical Criticism: Jews and Christians in Biblical Studies.* Louisville: Westminster John Knox, 1993.

———. *Sinai and Zion: An Entry into the Jewish Bible.* San Francisco: HarperSanFrancisco, 1987.

Levering, Matthew. *Participatory Biblical Exegesis: A Theology of Biblical Interpretation.* Notre Dame, IN: University of Notre Dame Press, 2008.

Lindsell, Harold. *The Battle for the Bible.* Grand Rapids: Zondervan, 1976.

Linebaugh, Jonathan A. *God, Grace, and Righteousness in Wisdom of Solomon and Paul's Letter to the Romans: Texts in Conversation.* Supplements to Novum Testamentum 152. Boston: Brill, 2013.

Lovelock, James. *The Revenge of Gaia: Why the Earth Is Fighting Back—and How We Can Still Save Humanity.* London: Allen Lane, 2006.

Lubac, Henri de, SJ. *Medieval Exegesis: The Four Senses of Scripture.* Vol. 1. Translated by Mark Sebanc. Grand Rapids: Eerdmans, 1998.

Luijendijk, AnneMarie, and William E. Klingshirn, eds. *My Lots Are in Thy Hands: Sortilege and Its Practitioners in Late Antiquity.* Boston: Brill, 2019.

Luther, Martin. *The Christian in Society I.* Edited by James Atkinson. LW 44. Philadelphia: Fortress, 1966.

———. *The Christian in Society III.* Edited by Robert Charles Schultz. LW 46. Philadelphia: Fortress, 1967.

———. *Word and Sacrament I.* Edited by E. Theodore Bachmann. LW 35. Philadelphia: Fortress, 1960.

MacDonald, Dennis Ronald. *Does the New Testament Imitate Homer? Four Cases from the Acts of the Apostles.* New Haven: Yale University Press, 2003.

———. *The Homeric Epics and the Gospel of Mark.* New Haven: Yale University Press, 2000.

MacDonald, Nathan. *Deuteronomy and the Meaning of "Monotheism."* Forschungen zum Alten Testament 2.1. Tübingen: Mohr Siebeck, 2003.

Mannheim, Karl. *Ideology and Utopia: An Introduction to the Sociology of Knowledge.* Translated by Louis Wirth and Edward Shils. 1936. Reprint, New York: Harcourt Brace Jovanovich, 1985.

Martin, James, SJ. *The Jesuit Guide to (Almost) Everything: A Spirituality for Real Life.* New York: HarperCollins, 2010.

Mathison, Keith A. *The Shape of Sola Scriptura.* Moscow, ID: Canon, 2001.

Maxwell, William D. *An Outline of Christian Worship.* London: Oxford University Press, 1958.

McGrath, Alister. *In the Beginning: The Story of the King James Bible and How It Changed a Nation, a Language, and a Culture.* New York: Random House, 2001.

———. *Reformation Thought: An Introduction.* 2nd ed. Oxford: Blackwell, 1993.

McKim, Donald K., ed. *Dictionary of Major Biblical Interpreters.* Downers Grove, IL: IVP Academic, 2007.

McMillen, S. I., and David E. Stern. *None of These Diseases: The Bible's Health Secrets for the 21st Century.* Rev. ed. Grand Rapids: Revell, 2000.

Melanchthon, Philipp. *Melanchthon on Christian Doctrine, Loci Communes, 1555.* Edited and translated by Clyde L. Manschreck. New York: Oxford University Press, 1965.

———. *Melanchthon: Selected Writings.* Edited by Elmer W. Flack and Lowell J. Satre. Translated by Charles L. Hill. Minneapolis: Augsburg, 1962.

Metzger, Bruce M. *An Introduction to the Apocrypha.* New York: Oxford University Press, 1957.

Mickelsen, A. Berkeley. *Interpreting the Bible.* Grand Rapids: Eerdmans, 1963.

Murphy, Roland E., O. Carm. *Experiencing Our Biblical Heritage.* Peabody, MA: Hendrickson, 2001.

———. *The Song of Songs: A Commentary on the Book of Canticles or the Song of Songs.* Hermeneia. Minneapolis: Fortress, 1990.

Nevin, John W. *Catholic and Reformed: Selected Theological Writings of John Williamson Nevin.* Edited by Charles Yrigoyen Jr. and George H. Bricker. Pittsburgh: Pickwick, 1978.

Newman, John Henry. *An Essay on the Development of Christian Doctrine.* 1878. Reprint, Notre Dame, IN: University of Notre Dame Press, 1993.

Noble, David E. *The Religion of Technology: The Divinity of Man and the Spirit of Invention.* New York: Penguin, 1999.

Noble, Richmond. *Shakespeare's Biblical Knowledge and Use of the Book of Common Prayer.* London, 1935.

O'Keefe, John J., and R. R. Reno. *Sanctified Vision: An Introduction to Early Christian Interpretation of the Bible.* Baltimore: Johns Hopkins University Press, 2005.

Park, Elaine, Konrad Schaeffer, and Douglas Leal, eds. *Workbook for Lectors, Gospel Readers, and Proclaimers of the Word 2019.* Chicago: Liturgy Training Publications, 2018.

Pelikan, Jaroslav. *Luther the Expositor: Introduction to the Reformer's Exegetical Writings.* St. Louis: Concordia, 1959.

Pentiuc, Eugen J. *The Old Testament in Eastern Orthodox Tradition.* Oxford: Oxford University Press, 2014.

Pervo, Richard I. *Dating Acts: Between the Evangelists and the Apologists.* Santa Rosa, CA: Polebridge, 2006.

Peterson, Eugene. *Eat This Book: A Conversation in the Art of Spiritual Reading.* Grand Rapids: Eerdmans, 2006.

Popkin, Richard H. *The History of Scepticism: From Savonarola to Bayle.* Rev. ed. Oxford: Oxford University Press, 2003.

Potok, Chaim. *In the Beginning.* Greenwich, CT: Fawcett, 1975.

Preus, James Samuel. *From Shadow to Promise: Old Testament Interpretation from Augustine to the Young Luther.* Cambridge, MA: Belknap, 1969.

Rad, Gerhard von. *The Message of the Prophets.* New York: Harper & Row, 1965.

Ratzinger, Joseph (Pope Benedict XVI). *Jesus of Nazareth: From the Baptism in the Jordan to the Transfiguration.* Translated by Adrian J. Walker. San Francisco: Ignatius, 2007.

———. *Jesus of Nazareth: Holy Week; From the Entrance into Jerusalem to the Resurrection.* Translated by Philip J. Whitmore. San Francisco: Ignatius, 2011.

———. *Jesus of Nazareth: The Infancy Narratives.* Translated by Philip J. Whitmore. New York: Image, 2012.

———, ed. *Schriftauslegung im Widerstreit.* Quaestiones Disputatae 117. Freiburg: Herder, 1989.

Reddie, Anthony G. *Black Theology in Transatlantic Dialogue.* New York: Palgrave Macmillan, 2006.

Robertson, O. Palmer. *The Christ of the Covenants.* Phillipsburg, NJ: Presbyterian and Reformed, 1980.

Rupp, E. G., and Benjamin Drewery, eds. *Martin Luther.* Documents of Modern History. London: Edward Arnold, 1970.

Ryken, Leland. *How to Read the Bible as Literature.* Grand Rapids: Zondervan, 1984.

Sailhamer, John H. *The Pentateuch as Narrative.* Grand Rapids: Zondervan, 1992.

Sanders, E. P. *Paul and Palestinian Judaism: A Comparison of Patterns of Religion.* Philadelphia: Fortress, 1977.

Scarisbrick, J. J. *Henry VIII.* New Haven: Yale University Press, 1997.

Schjørring, Jens Holger. *Theologische Gewissensethik und politische Wirklichkeit: Das Beispiel Eduard Geismars und Emanuel Hirschs.* Göttingen: Vandenhoeck & Ruprecht, 1979.

Schuller, Eileen. *Post-exilic Prophets.* Message of Biblical Spirituality 4. Wilmington, DE: Glazier, 1988.

Scott, Tom, and Robert W. Scribner, eds. *The German Peasants' War: A History in Documents.* Atlantic Highlands, NJ: Humanities Press International, 1991.

Seiss, Joseph A. *The Assassinated President.* Philadelphia, 1865.

Seitz, Christopher, and Kathryn Greene-McCreight, eds. *Theological Exegesis: Essays in Honor of Brevard S. Childs.* Grand Rapids: Eerdmans, 1999.

Sim, David C. *The Gospel of Matthew and Christian Judaism: The History and Social Setting of the Matthean Community*. Studies of the New Testament and Its World. Edinburgh: T&T Clark, 1998.

Smith, Elias. *The Life, Conversion, Preaching, Travels and Sufferings of Elias Smith*. Boston: True, 1840.

Sommer, Benjamin D. *A Prophet Reads Scripture: Allusion in Isaiah 40–66*. Stanford, CA: Stanford University Press, 1998.

———. *Revelation and Authority: Sinai in Jewish Scripture and Tradition*. New Haven: Yale University Press, 2015.

Sparks, Kenton L. *God's Word in Human Words: An Evangelical Appropriation of Critical Biblical Scholarship*. Grand Rapids: Baker Academic, 2008.

Stein, Robert H. *A Basic Guide to Interpreting the Bible: Playing by the Rules*. 2nd ed. Grand Rapids: Baker Academic, 2011.

Streeter, B. H. *The Four Gospels: A Study of the Origins, Treating of the Manuscript Tradition, Sources, Authorship, and Dates*. 1924. Reprint, London: Macmillan, 1953.

Stylianopoulos, Theodore G., ed. *God's Living Word: Orthodox and Evangelical Essays on Preaching*. Brookline, MA: Holy Cross Orthodox Press, 1983.

———. *The New Testament: An Orthodox Perspective*. Vol. 1, *Scripture, Tradition, Hermeneutics*. Brookline, MA: Holy Cross Orthodox Press, 1997.

Suh, David Kwang-Sun. *The Korean Minjung in Christ*. 1991. Reprint, Eugene: Wipf & Stock, 2001.

Tamez, Elsa. *The Amnesty of Grace: Justification by Faith from a Latin American Perspective*. Translated by Sharon H. Ringe. Nashville: Abingdon, 1993.

———. *Bible of the Oppressed*. Translated by Matthew J. O'Connell. Maryknoll, NY: Orbis, 1982.

Thomas à Kempis. *The Imitation of Christ*. Translated by Ronald Knox and Michael Oakley. 1959. Reprint, San Francisco: Ignatius, 2005.

Vesco, Jean-Luc. *Le psautier de David traduit et commenté*. Lectio Divina 210. Paris: Cerf, 2006.

Watson, Francis. *Paul and the Hermeneutics of Faith*. New York: T&T Clark International, 2004.

Wellhausen, Julius. *Die Composition des Hexateuchs und der historischen Bücher des Alten Testaments*. 2nd ed. Berlin: Reimer, 1889.

Wenham, Gordon J. *Psalms as Torah: Reading Biblical Song Ethically*. Grand Rapids: Baker Academic, 2012.

———. *Story as Torah: Reading Old Testament Narrative Ethically*. Grand Rapids: Baker Academic, 2000.

White, Thomas Joseph, OP. *The Light of Christ: An Introduction to Catholicism.* Washington, DC: Catholic University of America Press, 2017.

Wilkinson, Bruce H. *The Prayer of Jabez: Breaking Through to the Blessed Life.* Multnomah, OR: Multnomah, 2000.

Winter, Bruce W. *After Paul Left Corinth: The Influence of Secular Ethics and Social Change.* Grand Rapids: Eerdmans, 2001.

Witherup, Ronald D., SS. *Scripture: Dei Verbum.* New York: Paulist, 2006.

Wright, N. T. *Paul and the Faithfulness of God.* 2 vols. Christian Origins and the Question of God 4. Minneapolis: Fortress, 2013.

Young, Frances M. *Biblical Exegesis and the Formation of Christian Culture.* Cambridge: Cambridge University Press, 1997.

Zwingli, Ulrich. *Huldreich Zwinglis sämtliche Werke.* Vol. 1. Edited by Emil Egli. Berlin: Schwetschke and Son, 1905.

Articles and Chapters

Alter, Robert. "Psalms." In *The Literary Guide to the Bible*, edited by Robert Alter and Frank Kermode, 244–62. Cambridge, MA: Belknap, 1987.

Auerbach, Erich. "Odysseus' Scar." In *Mimesis: The Representation of Reality in Western Literature*, 3–23. Princeton Classics 78. Princeton: Princeton University Press, 2013.

Balabanski, Vicky. "John 1—the Earth Bible Challenge: An Intra-textual Approach to Reading John 1." In Habel and Balabanski, *Earth Story in the New Testament*, 91–94.

Barr, James. "'Abbā Isn't 'Daddy.'" *JTS* 39 (1988): 28–47.

Barrett, Matthew. "The Crux of Genuine Reform." In Barrett, *Reformation Theology*, 43–65.

Barron, Robert. "Bridging a False Divide: Systematic Theology and Scriptural Exegesis Belong Together." *First Things*, April 2014. http://www.firstthings.com/article/2014/04/bridging-a-false-divide.

Bloesch, Donald G. "The Sword of the Spirit: The Meaning of Inspiration." *Themelios* 5 (1980): 14–19.

Bokser, Ben Zion. "Justin Martyr and the Jews: II." *Jewish Quarterly Review* 64 (1974): 204–11.

Boulnois, Olivier. "Reading Duns Scotus: From History to Philosophy." *Modern Theology* 21 (2005): 603–7.

Brownson, William C., Jr. "The Meaning of the Gospel: An Evangelical Homily on Luke 23.32–43." In Stylianopoulos, *God's Living Word*, 141–45.

Byrne, Brendan, SJ. "The Faith of the Beloved Disciple and the Community in John 20." *Journal for the Study of the New Testament* 7 (1985): 83–97.

Calivas, Alkiviadis. "Man as Icon of God: An Orthodox Homily." In Stylianopoulos, *God's Living Word*, 135–40.

Capetz, Paul E. "Reformation Heritage and the Question of *Sachkritik*: Theological Criticism of the Bible." *CurTM* 45 (2018): 41–62.

Charles, Ronald. "Interpreting the Book of Revelation in the Haitian Context." *BT* 9 (2011): 177–98.

Childers, Jeff W. "Hermeneutics and Divination: A Unique Syriac Biblical Manuscript as an Oracle of Interpretation." In Luijendijk and Klingshirn, *My Lots Are in Thy Hands*, 124–37.

Chryssavgis, John. "Original Sin—an Orthodox Perspective." In *Grace and Disgrace: A Theology of Self-Esteem, Society and History*, edited by Neil Ormerod, 197–206. Newtown, NSW: Dwyer, 1992.

Congar, Yves. "Reflections on the Schism of Israel in the Perspective of Christian Divisions." In *Dialogue between Christians: Catholic Contributions to Ecumenism*, 160–83. London: Chapman, 1966.

Cosgrove, Charles H. "Rhetorical Suspense in Romans 9–11: A Study in Polyvalence and Hermeneutical Election." *Journal of Biblical Literature* 115 (1996): 271–87.

Dada, Adekunle Oyinloye. "Repositioning Contextual Biblical Hermeneutics in Africa towards Holistic Empowerment." *BT* 8 (2010): 160–74.

Deems, Mervin Monroe. "Augustine's Use of Scripture." *Church History* 14 (1945): 188–200.

Dudek, Adrian. "Your Number's Up—a Case for the Usefulness of Useless Maths." The Conversation, April 7, 2013. http://theconversation.com/your-numbers -up-a-case-for-the-usefulness-of-useless-maths-11799.

Ebeling, Gerhard. "Church History Is the History of the Exposition of Scripture." In *Word of God and Tradition: Historical Studies Interpreting the Divisions of Christianity*, 11–31. Philadelphia: Fortress, 1968.

Florovsky, Georges. "The Function of Tradition in the Ancient Church." In Clendenin, *Eastern Orthodox Theology*, 97–114.

Fritschel, Ann. "Re-envisioning Luther's Christological Hermeneutic." *CurTM* 45 (2018): 11–15.

Gebara, Ivone. "The Movement of May 1968 and Theology in Latin America: The Third World in the Theology of Liberation." *Ecumenical Review* 70 (2018): 264–71.

George, Timothy. "Reading the Bible with the Reformers." *First Things* 211 (March 2011): 27–33.

Gore, R. J., Jr. "Reviewing the Puritan Regulative Principle of Worship." *Presbyterion* 21 (1995): 29–47.

Hatch, Nathan O. "*Sola Scriptura* and *Novus Ordo Seclorum.*" In Hatch and Noll, *Bible in America*, 59–78.

Hays, Richard B. "Christ Prays the Psalms: Paul's Use of an Early Christian Convention." In *The Future of Christology: Essays in Honor of Leander E. Keck*, edited by Abraham J. Malherbe and Wayne A. Meeks, 122–36. Minneapolis: Fortress, 1993.

Huizenga, Leroy A. "The Tradition of Christian Allegory Yesterday and Today." *Letter and Spirit* 8 (2013): 77–99.

Jenson, Robert. "The Praying Animal." In *Essays in Theology of Culture*, 117–31. Grand Rapids: Eerdmans, 1995.

Johns, Loren L. "Reading the Maccabean Literature by the Light of the Stake: Anabaptist Appropriations in the Reformation." *Mennonite Quarterly Review* 86 (2012): 151–73.

Kaminsky, Joel S., and Mark Reasoner. "The Meaning and Telos of Israel's Election: An Interfaith Response to N. T. Wright's Reading of Paul." *Harvard Theological Review* 112 (2019): 421–46.

Kelhoffer, James. "The Witness of Eusebius' *ad Marinum* and Other Christian Writings to Text-Critical Debates concerning the Original Conclusion to Mark's Gospel." *Zeitschrift für die neutestamentliche Wissenschaft* 92 (2001): 78–112.

Kermode, Frank. "Matthew." In *The Literary Guide to the Bible*, edited by Robert Alter and Frank Kermode, 387–401. Cambridge, MA: Belknap, 1987.

Keylock, Leslie R. "Evangelical Scholars Remove Robert Gundry for His Views on Matthew." *Christianity Today*, February 3, 1984, 36–38.

Kinyua, Johnson. "A Postcolonial Examination of Matthew 16:13–23 and Related Issues in Biblical Hermeneutics." *BT* 13 (2015): 4–28.

Kinzig, Wolfram. "Καινὴ διαθήκη: The Title of the New Testament in the Second and Third Centuries." *JTS* 45 (1994): 519–44.

Kolbet, Paul R. "Torture and Origen's Hermeneutics of Nonviolence." *Journal of the American Academy of Religion* 76 (2008): 545–72.

Lightfoot, J. B. "S. Paul Our Example." In *Sermons Preached in St. Paul's Cathedral*, 218–29. 1891. Reprint, London: Macmillan, 1893.

———. "St. Paul's Preparation for the Ministry." In *Biblical Essays*, 2nd ed., 199–211. London: Macmillan, 1904.

Louth, Andrew. "Return to Allegory." In *Discerning the Mystery: An Essay on the Nature of Theology*, 96–131. Oxford: Oxford University Press, 1989.

Luijendijk, AnneMarie, and William E. Klingshirn. "The Literature of Lot Divination." In Luijendijk and Klingshirn, *My Lots Are in Thy Hands*, 19–59.

Luther, Martin. "Assertio omnium articulorum Lutheri per bullam Leonis X. novisssimam damnatorum (1520)." *WA* 79:98–99.

———. "Vorwort zu den *Annotationes Philippi Melanchthonis in epistolas Pauli ad Romanos et Corinthios* (1522)." *WA* 10.2:310.

Melanchthon, Philipp. "Defensio contra Johannem Eckium (1519)." In *Melanchthons Werke in Auswahl*, edited by Robert Stupperich, 1:13–22. Gütersloh: Bertelsmann, 1951.

Metzger, Bruce M. "Introduction to the Apocrypha." In *The Apocrypha of the Old Testament, Revised Standard Version*, edited by Bruce M. Metzger. New York: Oxford University Press, 1977.

Meyendorff, John. "Doing Theology in an Eastern Orthodox Perspective." In Clendenin, *Eastern Orthodox Theology*, 79–96.

Nelson, David. "The Story of Mission: The Grand Biblical Narrative." In *Theology and Practice of Mission: God, the Church, and the Nations*, edited by Bruce Riley Ashford, 6–17. Nashville: B&H Academic, 2011.

Newman, John Henry. "Self-Contemplation." In *Parochial and Plain Sermons*, 331–37. London: Longmans, Green, 1891. Reprint, San Francisco: Ignatius, 1997.

Nissiotis, Nikos A. "The Unity of Scripture and Tradition: An Eastern Orthodox Contribution to the Prolegomena of Hermeneutics." *Greek Orthodox Theological Review* 11 (1966): 183–208.

Noll, Mark A. "The Image of the United States as a Biblical Nation, 1776–1865." In Hatch and Noll, *Bible in America*, 39–58.

Null, Ashley. "Admonition to Peace: A Reply to the Twelve Articles of the Peasants in Swabia, 1525." In *The Annotated Luther*, vol. 5, *Christian Life in the World*, edited by Hans J. Hillerbrand, 281–333. Minneapolis: Fortress, 2017.

Patton, Corrine. "Canon and Tradition: Limits of the Old Testament in Scholastic Discussion." In Seitz and Greene-McCreight, *Theological Exegesis*, 75–95.

Petrovich, Christopher G. "First Corinthians 11:2–16, Calvin, and Reformed Praxis." *Westminster Theological Journal* 77 (2015): 111–33.

Piper, John. "Biblical Exegesis: Goals and Procedures." Unpublished paper, Bethel College, ca. 1976.

Radner, Ephraim. "The Absence of the Comforter: Scripture and the Divided Church." In Seitz and Greene-McCreight, *Theological Exegesis*, 355–94.

Reasoner, Mark. "*Dei Verbum* and the Twentieth-Century Drama of Scripture's Literal Sense." *Nova et Vetera* 15 (2017): 219–54.

———. "Paul's Use of Lament Psalms in Romans." *Word and World* 39 (2019): 208–16.

Roberts, J. J. M. "Isaiah and His Children." In *Biblical and Related Studies Presented to Samuel Iwry*, edited by Ann Kort and Scott Morschauser, 193–203. Winona Lake, IN: Eisenbrauns, 1985.

Spires, Grady. "A Response to Theodore Stylianopoulos' 'Sources for Preaching.'" In Stylianopoulos, *God's Living Word*, 93–96.

Steinmetz, David C. "The Superiority of Pre-critical Exegesis." *Theology Today* 37 (1980): 27–38.

Stetzer, Ed. "The Big Story of Scripture (Creation, Fall, Redemption, Restoration) in Pictures: Your Input Required." *Christianity Today*, November 28, 2012. https://www.christianitytoday.com/edstetzer/2012/november/big-story-of-scripture-creation-fall-redemption.html.

Stout, Harry S. "Word and Order in Colonial New England." In Hatch and Noll, *Bible in America*, 19–38.

Stylianopoulos, Theodore G. "Christ, Church and Preacher: The Living Sources for Preaching." In Stylianopoulos, *God's Living Word*, 75–92.

Thacher, Peter. "A Sermon Preached before the Artillery Company." In *Political Sermons of the American Founding Era, 1730–1805*, 2nd ed., edited by Ellis Sandoz, 2:1133–47. Indianapolis: Liberty Fund, 1998.

Thompson, Mark D. "*Sola Scriptura*." In Barrett, *Reformation Theology*, 145–87.

Trueman, Carl R., and Eunjin Kim. "The Reformers and Their Reformations." In Barrett, *Reformation Theology*, 111–43.

Vledder, Evan-Jan, and Andries G. van Aarde. "The Social Stratification of the Matthean Community." *Neotestamentica* 28 (1994): 511–22.

Wacker, Grant. "The Demise of Biblical Civilization." In Hatch and Noll, *Bible in America*, 121–38.

White, Lyn, Jr. "The Historical Roots of Our Ecologic Crisis." *Science* 155, no. 3767 (March 10, 1967): 1203–7.

Wigner, Eugene. "The Unreasonable Effectiveness of Mathematics in the Natural Sciences." *Communications in Pure and Applied Mathematics* 13, no. 1 (February 1960): 1–14.

Wilkinson, Kevin. "*Hermēneiai* in Manuscripts of John's Gospel: An Aid to Bibliomancy." In Luijendijk and Klingshirn, *My Lots Are in Thy Hands*, 101–23.

Wimsatt, W. K., Jr., and M. C. Beardsley. "The Intentional Fallacy." *Sewanee Review* 54 (1946): 468–88.

Zwingli, Ulrich. "Of the Clarity and Certainty of the Word of God." 1522. In *Zwingli and Bullinger: Selected Translations with Introductions and Notes*, edited by G. W. Bromiley, 49–95. LCC 24. Philadelphia: Westminster, 1953.

INDEX OF NAMES AND SUBJECTS

INDEX OF SCRIPTURE AND OTHER ANCIENT WORKS